Thrive!

Bassim Hamadeh, CEO and Publisher
Mieka Portier, Field Acquisitions Editor
Tony Paese, Project Editor
Abbey Hastings, Associate Production Editor
Jess Estrella, Senior Graphic Designer
Don Kesner, Interior Designer
Natalie Piccotti, Senior Marketing Manager
Kassie Graves, Vice President of Editorial
Jamie Giganti, Director of Academic Publishing

Cover image copyright © 2014 Depositphotos/ksushsh.

Printed in the United States of America.

ISBN: 978-1-5165-2260-6 (pbk) / 978-1-5165-2261-3 (br) / 978-1-5165-9346-0 (al)

Thrive!

THE CREATIVE'S GUIDEBOOK TO PROFESSIONAL TENACITY

Cyndi Coon

DEDICATION

This book is dedicated to LRC for your unique teaching style.

JB—thank you for helping me through the last 7%.

Olive and Hattie Rose—thank you for waiting for me to finish just one more sentence.

Mama Rose—thank you—without you I wouldn't be.

Sarah Spencer—thank you for being the rescue, release, and relief.

Suzanne Blanck—thank you for the galactic energy.

My Truth Tribe, Collective Gesture Core (Hon Jaddock) and the magical creative community of Phoenix, Arizona—thank you.

A special thank you Kjellgren Alkire for entrusting me with twelve students in a Friday afternoon class, that opportunity became this book.

A cosmic scale thank you to my editor Susana Christie. This manuscript became a book because of your passionate support, incredible patience and your ability to know just what I needed.

To all creatives who pick up this book—thank you for your work towards a better creative community.

Brief Contents

SECTION I: TELL YOUR STORY 1

Chapter 1 Your Story: It's Worth It.. 3

Chapter 2 Creative Personal Branding: The Essential Skills............................. 9

Chapter 3 Tell Your Story: Fire Up Your Bravery... 19

SECTION II: SPREAD THE WORD 27

Chapter 4 Business Cards and Letterhead: Your Unique Identity..................... 29

Chapter 5 Resume and CV: It's Just the Appetizer... 43

Chapter 6 Biographies, Statements, and Philosophies:
Use Words That Matter 51

SECTION III: ASSERT YOUR VALUE 61

Chapter 7 Portfolios and Presentations: Style Rules the Room....................... 63

Chapter 8 Pricing and Sales: Crunch the Numbers 71

Chapter 9 Contracts and Coverage: A Handshake Isn't Enough...................... 81

Chapter 10 Nonprofit vs. For Profit, Plus Grants:
The Mission is the Difference... 89

SECTION IV: READY YOUR TOOLS 97

Chapter 11 Creative Tools: Keeping Your Practice Alive................................. 99

Chapter 12 Pitching Products, Projects, and Plans: Sharing Your Passion 107

Chapter 13 Organize Your Business: This Will Change Your Life!..................... 117

Chapter 14 Social Networking: The Human Connection.................................. 127

SECTION V: GO THE DISTANCE 139

Chapter 15 Identifying Your Strengths: Exercise Devices 141

Chapter 16 Dreaming Big and Setting Goals: It's a Destination *and* a Journey .. 147

Chapter 17 The Job Hunt: Hot Careers and Temporary Gigs........................... 157

SECTION VI: PROCLAIM YOUR PRESENCE 173

Chapter 18 Press Push: Tell the Whole Story... 175

Chapter 19 Knowing Where to Show, Sell, Produce, and Perform:
Know Your Audience 185

Chapter 20 Thinking Differently: Blaze Your Own Trail........................... 195

Chapter 21 Have a Plan: Follow Your Map but Consider the Detours.......... 203

CONCLUSION: A PROFESSION OF REFLECTION 213

Index 219

Detailed Contents

SECTION I TELL YOUR STORY 1

Chapter 1 Your Story: It's Worth It 3

Introduction 3
Terms the Creative Needs 3
What the Creative Needs to Know 3
What the Creative Will Learn in This Chapter 4
Are There Any Prerequisites Before Reading This Book? 5
Quotes 6
Reflection 6
Examples 6
    How will the creative use this information going forward? 6
    Building your creative network 6
Author Story 7

Chapter 2 Creative Personal Branding: The Essential Skills 9

Introduction 9
Terms The Creative Needs 9
What the Creative Needs to Know 9
What the Creative Will Learn in This Chapter 10
Standing Out From the Crowd 10
Focus on Your Why 10
You Are Branding You! 11
Watered-Down Brands 11
The Dependency of the Starving Artist 12
Clear Values 12
How It Works 12
Brand Engagement 14
Target Audience 15
Designed Client 15
Reading the Room 16
Multiple Brands 16
Words Matter 17
Reflection 17
    How will the creative use this information going forward? 18
    Brand statement 18
    Building your creative network 18

Chapter 3 Tell Your Story: Fire Up Your Bravery 19

Introduction 19
Terms The Creative Needs 19

What the Creative Needs to Know **19**

What the Creative Will Learn in This Chapter **20**

Tell Your Story...**20**

How Much to Share..**20**

Character Development **21**

Setting **21**

Plot...**21**

Conflict...**22**

Resolution...**22**

Styles of Storytelling **22**

Live Storytelling...**23**

Written Storytelling..**23**

Visual Storytelling..**23**

Mashup Storytelling...**23**

Serve Up Sample Sizes..**24**

Build a Truth Tribe...**24**

Take a Breath **25**

Process Over Product **25**

Reflection...**25**

     How will the creative use this information going forward? **26**

     Building your creative network **26**

SECTION II SPREAD THE WORD **27**

Chapter 4 Business Cards and Letterhead: Your Unique Identity............................ **29**

Introduction..**29**

Terms The Creative Needs...**29**

What the Creative Needs to Know **29**

What the Creative Will Learn in This Chapter **30**

Color Your Identity **30**

Your Identity Type **30**

Clean, Clear Connections **31**

Identity Your Way **31**

Rectangle, Circles, Squares—Oh My! **32**

Card-Carrying Member **33**

Handmade Identity **33**

Metal Business Cards...**33**

What Goes Down on Paper? **34**

Print Quality **34**

One Hundred at a Time **35**

Letterhead Logistics **35**

E-mail Signature **35**

Letter Writing **36**

Steps...**38**

Just Like Dating..**39**

Bonus Round **41**

Sending It Off **41**

Reflection **41**

    How will the creative use this information going forward? **41**

    Building your creative network **42**

Chapter 5 Resume and CV: It's Just the Appetizer **43**

Introduction **43**

Terms The Creative Needs **43**

What the Creative Needs to Know **43**

What the Creative Will Learn in This Chapter **44**

Resumes and Curriculum Vitae **44**

Building Your Resume **44**

Maintaining Your CV **45**

Dates **45**

Tough Love **45**

Landing a Gig Is Like Dating **46**

Don't Fill Up Space **46**

The Big List **47**

Volunteer **48**

Build Your Categories **48**

Commissions **48**

Name and Location **48**

Awards **48**

Memberships **49**

Include Links **49**

References **49**

Apply Some Design **49**

Reflection **50**

    How will the creative use this information going forward? **50**

    Building your creative network **50**

Chapter 6 Biographies, Statements, and Philosophies: Use Words That Matter **51**

Introduction **51**

Terms The Creative Needs **51**

What the Creative Needs to Know **51**

What the Creative Will Learn in This Chapter **52**

Share, Don't Tell **52**

Building Your Bio **53**

Build Your Nugget **53**

Don't Date Yourself **54**

Highlights and Hits Are the Rule **54**

The Short and Long **54**

Longer Bio Format **54**

Closing **55**

Who Is Your Audience? 55

Look for Examples 55

Several Bios Needed 55

Statements 56

Be Generous 56

Your Statement Stands Alone 57

Building Your Statement 57

Steps to Writing a Statement 58

    Paragraph One 58

    Paragraph Two 58

    Third Paragraph 59

Philosophy Statement 59

Reflection 60

    How will the creative use this information going forward? 60

    Building your creative network 60

SECTION III ASSERT YOUR VALUE 61

Chapter 7 Portfolios and Presentations:Style Rules the Room 63

Introduction 63

Terms The Creative Needs 63

What the Creative Needs to Know 63

What the Creative Will Learn in This Chapter 64

Pulling Together Your Portfolio 64

Review Panels: Weighing the Odds 65

Your Portfolio: Twenty Images Strong 65

What Should Your Portfolio Include? 65

Look Good Sound Good 65

The Look of Your Portfolio 66

Companion List 67

Demo Reels 67

Call for Artists/Creatives 67

How Review Panels Work 68

Becoming Feedback Friendly 69

Presentations 69

Reflection 70

    How will the creative use this information going forward ? 70

    Building your creative network 70

Chapter 8 Pricing and Sales: Crunch the Numbers 71

Introduction 71

Terms The Creative Needs 71

What the Creative Needs to Know 72

What the Creative Will Learn in This Chapter 72

Start With Your Homework 72

Wholesale vs. Retail Costs—Explained 73

The Basic Pricing Formula **74**

Steps for Selling Objects... **74**

Example **74**

But Wait; There's More **74**

Basic Pricing Formula for Services **74**

Steps for Pricing Services **75**

The Math on Shipping **75**

Discount Requests.. **76**

Invoices.. **76**

Steps to Creating An Invoice... **77**

Payment Types **78**

Minimums **78**

What if They Don't Pay You? **79**

Representation **79**

Reflection... **79**

How will the creative use this information going forward? **79**

Building your creative network **80**

Chapter 9 Contracts and Coverage: A Handshake Isn't Enough............................. **81**

Introduction... **81**

Terms The Creative Needs... **81**

What the Creative Needs to Know **81**

What the Creative Will Learn in This Chapter **82**

Before You Begin **82**

Commissions.. **82**

Deposits **82**

Agreements **83**

Electronic Agreements **83**

When to Hire a Lawyer... **84**

Incorporating... **84**

Business Insurance **85**

Brokers... **85**

Health Insurance... **85**

Other Insurance Types to Consider.. **86**

Reflection... **87**

How will the creative use this information going forward? **87**

Building your creative network **87**

Chapter 10 Nonprofit vs. For Profit, Plus Grants: The Mission is the Difference .. **89**

Introduction... **89**

Terms The Creative Needs... **89**

What the Creative Needs to Know **90**

What the Creative Will Learn in This Chapter **90**

For-Profit vs. Not-For-Profit **90**

Finding Funding... **91**

Completing the Application **92**

Pixie Dust **93**

Panelists And Timelines **94**

Final Reports **94**

Feedback **95**

Cost **95**

Reflection **96**

    How will the creative use this information going forward? **96**

    Building your creative network **96**

SECTION IV READY YOUR TOOLS **97**

Chapter 11 Creative Tools: Keeping Your Practice Alive...**99**

Introduction.. **99**

Terms The Creative Needs... **99**

What the Creative Needs to Know **99**

What the Creative Will Learn in This Chapter **100**

Time Check.. **100**

Steal Time... **101**

Go Ahead and Procrastinate.. **102**

Make Kits.. **102**

Create Micro Moments **103**

Have a Plan... **104**

Stress-Relief Tactics... **104**

Schedule Creative Playdates.. **105**

Reflection **106**

    How will the creative use this information going forward? **106**

    Building your creative network **106**

Chapter 12 Pitching Products, Projects, and Plans: Sharing Your Passion...........**107**

Introduction.. **107**

Terms The Creative Needs... **107**

What the Creative Needs to Know **108**

What the Creative Will Learn in This Chapter **108**

Elevator Pitch... **108**

    Step One... **108**

    Step Two... **108**

    Step Three... **108**

    Step Four... **108**

An Ever-Changing Pitch **110**

The Business Pitch **111**

    Steps... **111**

        Step 1: The Problem, Also Known As the Pain Point... **111**

        Step 2: The Solution... **112**

        Step 3: Target Market... **112**

        Step 4: The Competition **112**

Step 5: Make Them Believe 113

Step 6: The Ask 113

Follow Up 114

Reflection 115

How will the creative use this information going forward? 115

Building your creative network 115

Chapter 13 Organize Your Business: This Will Change Your Life! 117

Introduction 117

Terms The Creative Needs 117

What the Creative Needs to Know 118

What the Creative Will Learn in This Chapter 118

Ask 118

The Pareto Principle 118

Hire Help 119

Assistants 119

Virtual Assistants 120

Barter and Trade 120

App Support 121

Legal 122

Sole Proprietor 122

Types of Corporations 122

File An LLC 122

Taxes 123

Bookkeeping 123

Payroll 124

Don't Buy Retail 124

Grammar Check 124

Storing Documents 125

Ethical Check-Up 125

Reflection 126

How will the creative use this information going forward? 126

Building your creative network 126

Chapter 14 Social Networking: The Human Connection 127

Introduction 127

Terms The Creative Needs 127

What the Creative Needs to Know 128

What the Creative Will Learn in This Chapter 128

Multiple Accounts 128

Elements of Post 129

It's a Party 129

Show Up Authentically 130

Going Viral 130

Handles and Hashtags 131

Followers 131

Another Dating Analogy 132
Be Generous 132
Embarrass Yourself 133
Ideas for Social Media Posts 133
Where to Post 134
Schedule Posts 134
Matchy Matchy 135
Negativity Online 135
Trolls 135
Seven Connection 135
Stay in Touch 136
Offer Your Special 136
Testimonials 136
Headshots 136
Networking 137
Handshakes and Name Tags 137
Start Networking Before You Get There 137
Reflection 138
    How will the creative use this information going forward? 138
    Building your creative network 138

SECTION V GO THE DISTANCE 139

Chapter 15 Identifying Your Strengths: Exercise Devices 141
Introduction 141
Terms The Creative Needs 141
What the Creative Needs to Know 141
What the Creative Will Learn in This Chapter 142
Measuring Your Strengths 142
Other Ways to Discover Your Strengths 144
Who Do You Admire? 145
Reflection 145
    How will the creative use this information going forward? 146
    Building your creative network 146

Chapter 16 Dreaming Big and Setting Goals: It's a Destination *and* a Journey 147
Introduction 147
Terms The Creative Needs 147
What the Creative Needs to Know 147
What the Creative Will Learn in This Chapter 148
Write It Down 148
What If I Achieve All My Goals? 148
Steps to Goal Setting 150
    Steps 151
Goals on the Go 152

Distractions and Derailments 152

Bucket-List Goals 152

Stay Awake 152

Types of Goals 153

Be Accountable 154

Reflection 155

    How will the creative use this information going forward? 155

    Building your creative network 156

Chapter 17 The Job Hunt: Hot Careers and Temporary Gigs **157**

Introduction 157

Terms The Creative Needs 157

What the Creative Needs to Know 157

What the Creative Will Learn in This Chapter 158

The Hunt 158

Stay in Job-Ready Shape 158

Job Board 159

The Interview 159

Do Your Homework 159

Practice, Practice, Practice 160

Show Up Early 160

Go Solo 160

What to Bring 160

Dress the Part 161

A Great Handshake 161

Smile and Make Eye Contact 161

Listen and Answer 162

Stay Positive 162

Ask Questions 162

Talk Up Your Skills 163

Follow Up 163

Thank You 163

Thank-You Note Magic 164

Negotiation 165

Take Your Time 165

Get It in Writing 166

References 166

Internship 167

List of Creative Careers 168

Reflection 172

    How will the Creative use this information going forward? 172

    Building your creative network 172

SECTION VI PROCLAIM YOUR PRESENCE 173

Chapter 18 Press Push: Tell the Whole Story 175

Introduction 175
Terms The Creative Needs 175
What the Creative Needs to Know 175
What the Creative Will Learn in This Chapter 176
Telling Your Story 176
Press Kit 176
    1. Cover letter 176
    2. Company profile 176
    3. Product/Service sheet 177
    4. Other coverage 177
    5. Press release 177
    6. Testimonials and reviews 177
    7. FAQs 177
    8. Audio/Video/Still 177
Get Creative 177
Press Release 178
Layout Logistics 178
Order of Press Release 178
    For Immediate Release 178
    Date 178
    Media Contact 178
    Title 178
    The Body 179
        Who 179
        What 179
        Where 179
        When 179
        How much 179
        Public Contact 180
        Closing 180
Who's Invited? 180
Sending Your Press Release 180
Editorial Meetings 181
Editorial Calendars 181
Appearance Pitch 182
It Takes Time 182
Carry Reminder Notes 183
Reflection 183
    How will the creative use this information going forward? 184
    Building your creative network 184

Chapter 19 Knowing Where to Show, Sell, Produce, and Perform: Know Your Audience 185

Introduction...185
Terms The Creative Needs..185
What the Creative Needs to Know 186
What the Creative Will Learn in This Chapter 186
Places to Show, Sell, Produce, and Perform 186
Residencies..186
Galleries...187
Pop-Ups and Trunk Shows 187
Open Studios and Backstage Experiences 188
Fairs 188
Festivals...188
Local Facilities 189
Trade Shows 189
People Who Can Help You Show, Sell, Produce, and Perform...................189
Brokers and Designers..189
Agents and Reps...190
Stagers...190
Ideas That Can Help You Show, Sell, Produce, and Perform 191
Getting Things Produced 191
    Manufactured...191
Produced 191
Outdoors Opportunities 192
Collaborations..192
Reflection 193
    How will the creative use this information going forward? 193
    Building your creative network 193
    Fresh ideas 194

Chapter 20 Thinking Differently: Blaze Your Own Trail..........................195

Introduction...195
Terms The Creative Needs..195
What the Creative Needs to Know 195
What the Creative Will Learn in This Chapter 196
Why Your Creativity Matters...196
Thinking Differently 196
Creative Commonalities 196
Ask Your Way In...197
Speak Up..198
Show Them 198
Champions 198
Scale 199
Stay Open 199
See What Others Miss 200

Reflection 200

    How will the creative use this information going forward? 201

    Building your creative network 201

Chapter 21 Have a Plan: Follow Your Map but Consider the Detours 203

Introduction 203

Terms The Creative Needs 203

What the Creative Needs to Know 203

What the Creative Will Learn in This Chapter 204

Stand Up/Speak Up 205

Embrace Failure 205

Healing the Creative Wounds 205

Practice Being an Optimist 205

Don't Take Things Personally 206

Manage Your Expectations 206

Creative Happiness 206

Comparison Is not a Motivator 207

Your Plan—Comparison Page 207

Confidence Is a Motivator 207

Your Plan—Unshakable Confidence Page 207

Always Behave Like Someone Is Watching 208

Venting the Right Way 208

Slow Down. Pause. Take Care of Yourself. 208

Your Me Time Plan 209

Inspiration 209

Knock the Creative Block 209

The Gift 209

Your Gift 209

Don't Be a Seagull 210

Show Up Curious 210

Use Your Curiosity 210

Build Your Rolodex 210

Your Plan—Rolodex Page 211

Have an Amazing Network 211

Your Plan—Networking Page 211

Staying on Top of Professional Documents 211

Your Plan—Docs Page 211

Use a Calendar 211

Your Plan—Calendar Page 212

Reflection 212

    How will the creative use this information going forward? 212

    Building your creative network 212

CONCLUSION: A PROFESSION OF REFLECTION 213

Honor Your Creativity 213

Lead With Bravery 213

Carry Yourself in Confidence **214**

Practice Generosity..**215**

Always Have Fun **215**

Allow for Procrastination...**215**

Fail Often **216**

Comparison is a Waste...**216**

Give Credit **217**

Stay Passionate **217**

It's All in Who You Know **217**

Always Carry a Business Card...**217**

Build Tribes and Champions **218**

Always Say Thank You...**218**

Tell Your Awesome Story...**218**

Index **219**

SECTION I

TELL YOUR STORY

CHAPTER ONE

Your Story

IT'S WORTH IT

INTRODUCTION

This book was written to shed light on what it looks like to be a professional in creative fields and how to do it bravely. There is a lot that goes into being a professional creative; some elements are unique to our industry. Of the things shared in this book, some you may have heard before, but reminders lead to confirmation of things you know you should be doing. You will discover other things you may not have heard of because they are business tools and, as creatives, traditional business tools often don't fit with how we think. Creatives like to do things their way, and at the heart of it, that is what this book offers: permission to explore the tools, capture the tips, and experience stories about creative professions. You are worth it, and your creativity is worth it.

TERMS THE CREATIVE NEEDS

You will find a list of terms at the beginning of each chapter. If you are familiar with the terms, skim them and move into the section. If the terms are new to you, take advantage of the opportunity, read through them, and look them up further as they may be of great assistance.

WHAT THE CREATIVE NEEDS TO KNOW

You chose to enter into the creative fields. You already know that there is work involved. You are already signed up to do things that are on a different path than everyone else that you know. If you are uncomfortable promoting yourself, you'll likely find this book distressing at first. I am confident, however, that you will learn some things of value from this book. It is the only way to get on the other side of the feelings. Use this book to find the tools that help you become confident in your talent.

Being honest with yourself is frequently addressed throughout this book. Reading this book allows you to get to know

FIG 1-1

As a creative, carry confidence, bravery, and honesty with you always.

who you are as a human. Many creatives have no idea of who they are, who they want to be, or what they want to offer to the world. It feels scary to imagine, "Who do I dare to be?" That is important to get a handle on, though, because who you want to be and what you want to produce into the world matters and people are waiting for it, waiting for you. As a creative professional in the workplace, you have to be a leader, and that means bringing a "Here's who I am, this is how I'm showing up" attitude. The only way that you can do that is if you are confident and you are comfortable with who you are in the world. Being honest with yourself becomes crucial as you move forward in your career. Your intuition and listening to what your gut is telling you is a skill you want to grow.

WHAT THE CREATIVE WILL LEARN IN THIS CHAPTER

Throughout this book, we'll talk about what it means to be a creative professional. Your journey to becoming a creative professional begins with being able to tell your story. You have to get to the point where you can articulate what it is you do, why you do it, and why people should care. That is your work. We'll look at why it is hard for creatives to tell a compelling story about the work they do. As a creative, you should be proud of what you do and not be interested in hiding. Through storytelling, you will learn how to share, with pride, the work you put forth into the world.

FIG 1-2

The point of this book is for you to learn the business of being a creative professional. You are going to learn the hard part, the scary part, the parts that require you to be a risk taker, a hustler, and a doer. I say hustler with positive energy. If you have skills to hustle, you are going to be successful. After reading this book cover to cover, you will be more equipped for a career in creative fields. You will have the knowledge and skills that will give you a toolbox for your practice. The dossier that you create is your toolkit. Preparedness offers an automatic confidence boost. Take action throughout this book: Complete the exercises so that you have templates for everything when you are ready.

Value is another reoccurring theme throughout this book. If you are still suffering from when your families told you that you were crazy for going after your dream of being an artist, this book will give you all the ammunition you need to prove them wrong. The first thing to know is that creatives are the problem solvers of tomorrow. To learn all about that, you must remain open and step boldly in with all your courage and bravery. You will gain skills while reading this book, you'll create professional documents, but the most important thing that I can give you is an understanding of your value. That means being brave, being honest with yourself, and being confident. You chose this dream; it is time to put in the effort. To be a professional creative and be known in your field, step into a space that is uncomfortable, every day, and get ready for a challenging journey; the rewards are many.

ARE THERE ANY PREREQUISITES BEFORE READING THIS BOOK?

The only thing you need to get the most out of this book is a 1.) a readiness to be a creative professional 2.) a willingness to be dangerous and 3.) cause a ruckus. If someone asks you a question, do they get an answer more significant than they ever expected? When someone gives you a project, do they get a return more significant than they had ever hoped would be possible? When you take on a challenge, do you finish it with pride? If this is your reputation, you may not always fit in, but you will be the one people seek out. That should be a goal of yours. If this is not you or anywhere near you, doesn't sound like you, or you don't want this to be you, then don't bother reading this book—it's not for you.

FIG 1-3

Prerequisites: Have a willingness to (a) be a creative professional, (b) be slightly dangerous, and (c) cause a ruckus.

If you are comfortable and want to spend your life in the invisible middle, then put this book down. If you want more out of your life, then push yourself and challenge yourself to see what happens when you are brave. If you are fearful, gift yourself some time to think about why it is hard for you, why you are living afraid; this book will give you some strategies on how to make it better and take some of the fear away. Your goal in reading this book should be to become brave. If you are not feeling it today or tomorrow, don't discount yourself because there are strategies for you. Use this time; make it about you. If you aren't happy about something, if you don't like something, do something about it: Use your voice, talk it out, tell somebody, contribute in a meaningful fashion. You will learn methods for that throughout this book.

This book will remind you that you have to speak up, you have to talk, you have to be brave, you have to share your stories. Be willing to do that and to work hard, and you are well on your way to finding your place in the creative fields. Sometimes things are meant to remain a hobby, but if you are going to make creativity your profession, then do this with full confidence.

take action

My best piece of advice for reading this book is to treat it as if it is your job. The first step is to show up, crack open the book, take notes, and get committed to the career you want to have. Keep a journal and a favorite pen nearby as you read because each chapter holds a TAKE ACTION activity, and you will want to take notes, write things down, and complete TAKE ACTION assignments.

Throughout this book, you will find tips offered in each chapter. Tips are ideas to consider that are insider tips, things to boost your opportunities or ideas for going deeper. Take note of tips that resonate with you, and write them down in your journal.

QUOTES

"Quotation, n: The act of repeating erroneously the words of another."

—*Ambrose Bierce*

FIG 1-4

Shop for a pen and journal.

Throughout this book, you will find many great quotes. I like to sprinkle them in to confirm that a lot of minds do think alike. Plus, they are inspirational and aspirational.

REFLECTION

The end of each chapter will conclude with a reflection. These are recaps of highlights from the section, reminders and additional ideas to inspire and motivate. You are encouraged to take time to reflect on the information in the chapter before moving on to the next.

The chapters will close with fill-in-the-blank questions that are focused on how the creative will use the information from the chapter going forward. Write the answers in this book or use your journal to take notes and answer questions.

EXAMPLES

HOW WILL THE CREATIVE USE THIS INFORMATION GOING FORWARD?
Directions: Take a few minutes to think about how, specifically, you will apply the information from this chapter in your professional life. Write down three ideas in the space below.

BUILDING YOUR CREATIVE NETWORK
Directions: Think of people, organizations, or other resources that can help you act on the information from this chapter. Write down these creative network connections in the space provided. Write a specific goal for contacting or making use of one of them.

AUTHOR STORY

I am a storyteller, and I teach through telling my own stories, including successes, failures, and things that I have learned about being a professional. I founded a company called Laboratory 5 Inc. in 2001. I have done many different things over the years that have led to my own personal discoveries and what I am capable of offering. I am not a full-time faculty at the university; I run in from my work day to teach a class because I am deeply passionate about our creative community, locally, nationally, and internationally. I am excited about working with creatives at all levels, from students just beginning to explore the field to lifelong artists looking to learn new things. I am passionate about making sure that you have all the tools you need when you enter this wonderful, opportunity-filled profession. It is complicated out there, and there's a lot you are going to have to know to best navigate the many incredible opportunities and the pitfalls. However, I am only one voice, and that is important to remember. I may say some things that you disagree with, or that you heard completely different from someone else. That is a good thing; take it all in and decide what works for you and what's appropriate. It can't be all one story, one experience, one way to do this. I am but one voice, and through reading this book, you will learn to include your voice in your story, too.

My degrees are in fine art. At any given time, I am up to all sorts of creative projects. Mostly, I use my degrees for my trained creative brain. People hire me to think creatively, to solved big problems and small simple ones in a way that non-creatives are just not offering. My bravery, confidence, and curiosity leads me down paths that may start out as head scratchers but eventually prove I am in the right place and my creative ability is needed. As a creative, you are absolutely assured of a future because creativity is needed everywhere, every day, in the most unusual places.

"Creativity takes courage."

—*Henri Matisse*

CHAPTER TWO

Creative Personal Branding

THE ESSENTIAL SKILLS

INTRODUCTION

Branding of any kind is not an easy task, but it is made especially challenging for the creative who is trying to figure out what to even brand. If you focus first on the right thing to brand, the journey is smoother. The brands that are often looked at as models are large companies and organizations such as Coca-Cola, Apple, Google, and Craftsman, and that level of branding can feel daunting. Luckily, that is not the type of branding that this chapter covers. This chapter focuses on branding the creative, not the product, goods, or services of you, the creator.

TERMS THE CREATIVE NEEDS

AUTHENTIC VOICE Representing one's true nature or beliefs; true to oneself

AVATAR An icon or figure representing a particular or specific person

CRAFTSMANSHIP The quality of design and work shown in something made by hand; artistry

MID-CAREER A professional who has more than 10 years of professional experience in a specific field

SKILLSET A person's range of skills or abilities

PASSION A strong and barely controllable emotion

TARGET AUDIENCE A focused group at which advertising is aimed

VALUES A person's principles or standards of behavior; one's judgment of what is essential in life

WHAT THE CREATIVE NEEDS TO KNOW

To start the branding process, focus first on your strengths and your skills. You have many; you need only to highlight those. It's likely that you are continually reimagining your creative identity and changing your creative focus. So much of what creatives do is about the process, including the process of becoming yourself. Growing and solidifying your brand is a process to learn more about who you are, what your values are, and what matters most to you. That is your brand. It is not a body of work, nor a project, nor a genre or theme. Your brand is the ever-changing, incredibly talented you!

WHAT THE CREATIVE WILL LEARN IN THIS CHAPTER

Your brand will change throughout your career as you redefine who you are as a creative. You are incredibly lucky that you get to recreate your career as you move along in your journey. Many other professions do not have a path for allowing for this kind of constant reinvention. You will learn how to stand upright and proud as you declare your brand. Once you feel stable about your brand, you are ready to share it with the world. But don't wait for perfection—learn by sharing imperfect actions instead of hiding your talent.

"A product can be quickly outdated, but a successful brand is timeless."

— *Stephen King*

STANDING OUT FROM THE CROWD

What distinguishes your brand is your deep commitment to your passion, your craftsmanship, your skillset, and your authentic voice that only you have. Your aesthetic and style play a great deal into your brand, and creatives get to be more playful than other professions. Trust your gut because your instincts will guide you in knowing the look of your brand. Question it only through your eyes, not the what-will-other-people-think filter. What do you think? If you have a strong aesthetic and that comes through in all areas of your brand, people will feel like they know you before they have even met you. Consistency shows your audience you have everything pulled together, even if you do not—trust the look you love and stick with it for a while.

Even if you are mid-career creative, you can revisit your brand. Not necessarily because it's not working, but during your mid-career point, you have the opportunity to outshine your past self. You can tighten up with a clarity that you now have at this stage in your career. A rebranding can bring attention to your career and your next body of work.

FOCUS ON YOUR WHY

Why is it important to know your why? The idea of the why came from Simon Sinek book Start with Why: How Great Leaders Inspire Everyone to Take Action (published 2009) who inspired others to dig deep and focus on purpose. Therefore, your why is not who you are or how you do what you do, but it is the reason you do what you do. Get in touch with your creative pull, often known as the muse. Ask why the tug is substantial and what is it about the need to create that nags deep within. Understanding that helps you to determine your why. It is your purpose, and you will do whatever it takes to continue creating.

"He who has a why can endure any how."

—*Frederick Nietzsche*

YOU ARE BRANDING YOU!

The first hiccup, with creatives, is often the desire to focus on branding the work produced. You are not branding your work. You're not branding your body of work; you are not branding what your product is. Because, over the course of your career, no matter who you are, your body of work will change and shift. You never want to focus on the product or outcome because you won't want to make the same kind of work your entire career. You will want to make something entirely different, and if you spent all your time branding that product, you have to start all over. That's why you don't brand your body of work. You brand the maker—that's you. People are interested in you as a creative, in addition to your work.

FIG 2-1

Know your why.

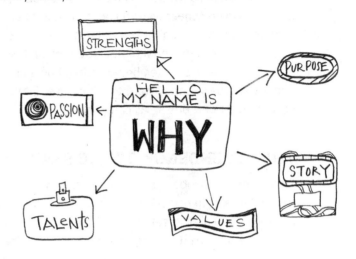

take action

Make a list of all the things you can think of that make up who you are as a creative. Think about your work, your materials, process, style, techniques, tools, and inspirations and make notes of those things in your journal. As you start to see you for who you are and what matters most, you will begin to look at the features to be celebrated and highlighted— that is your brand! Your favorite things that you want to celebrate and highlight.

If you're your authentic self, you have no competition.

—Scott Stratten

WATERED-DOWN BRANDS

Do you sometimes convince yourself that, even if you're not great at something, if it is creative, you'll do it anyway? When you're trying to make a living and build your career, those actions are not beneficial for your brain. It doesn't demonstrate bravery, only fear. If you know what you love and what you are passionate about, then you don't need to take projects on that do not live up to your passion. Also, you water your brand down when you do things that you are not excited about because you don't complete them with the same energy.

If you are struggling with what your real strengths are, ask yourself what you are good at. If you're still lost—that's what your community is for: Ask three to five people you trust, "What would you say I am good at?" And, ask multiple people because your mom will tell you one story and your best friend will tell you another. Ask several people, "When you think about my creative capacities, what do you think I'm amazing at?" Start there. Ask them, and ask them to go deep and be honest with you because it will benefit you. Once you receive input from others, take time to sift through it and determine which things you are most passionate about. Don't water your brand down with stuff you wouldn't want to do every day, all day. As an example, if you are a creative writer, brand yourself as a creative writer, not a technical writer or a grant writer because you may want to focus on a different area in your future and you don't want to be known for only one small category.

THE DEPENDENCY OF THE STARVING ARTIST

Taking small odd jobs, just enough to get by is not your brand, and it gives society permission to say it's okay to pay creatives poorly. Meaning, when someone asks, "Hey, will you do this for free?" you should ask them, "Have you ever had a plumbing problem? Did you ask if the plumber would mind coming to fix that for free because it will look good on their resume?" That is unusually all it takes. You do not need to continue your whole career giving things away for free. The occasional charity auction, one that is personally important to you, or a donation of your work to an organization that you want to give to is fine. Beyond giving because it's a passion point, it will not build your resume, nor will it get you recognition. You have to be compensated; there's an honor in what you do as a creative. Follow this rule, and together we can all make that starving artist idea go away.

FIG 2-2

Honor your creativity.

CLEAR VALUES

If you have never done a personal values assessment using a values list, do that now. Knowing your top three to five individual values allows you to have a quick guide to check in on how you feel about experiences related to you, your values, and your brand.

HOW IT WORKS

Everything I take in as work projects I align with my values. I mostly use my top three as checkpoints. It works like this: A new potential project comes my way; my first step is to check in with my gut because my number-one value is intuition. If it feels good and right and the people I'd be working with feel good and right, then I give it a check in that box. Second for me is fun. I ask, "Will the project and people be fun to work with?" because fun is my number-two value, and if it isn't fun, I won't do it! Finally, my third value is creativity. I ask if I'll get to be creative with the project and people, and if the answer is yes, it gets a check in that box. If any of the three are missing, I usually decline. I also have a few additional values I bring in next, depending on the project.

An example of a project I have turned down in the past was for a government agency. The first few conversations I had with the director left me feeling like something was off (intuition), and the work they asked me to produce for them was standard, without a lot of room for fun. They were not interested in exploring ideas (creative) as a new way to look at producing something different. Without being able to check off all of the boxes, I knew I had to decline the project. And, as an aside, whenever I lead with my values instead of being driven by the dollar, in a short amount of time a much better venture always comes along.

There have been times in the past when a project didn't check all of the boxes, but I took it on anyway because I felt I could learn something from it. An example of this was a project I took on with a technology company. My intuition checked out, and the people were fun, so two boxes were checked, but I wasn't sure up front that the project would be creative. That, however, was outweighed by the opportunity to venture into a new sector for me. It also allowed me to learn about another area of content with which I was unfamiliar. I have a deep love of learning, and the project with the tech company worked out well. In the end, it wasn't very creative, but this time it was okay because I learned so much working with that team that I would trust my gut again in a similar situation.

If you know your values, they can guide everything you do. Your branding becomes clear, and you can tell the story that matters to you. Knowing your values can also help so that you don't go down a detour filled with shiny distractions.

FIG 2-3

Know your values.

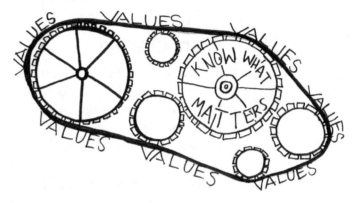

take action

Grab your journal and a pencil. Head to an online search engine and put in "List of values." You will find many lists to review. Read them over and write down a list of values that resonate with you. There are many values to choose from; try them on, roll them around in your mind, and see what fits best. Choose only three to five to focus on; any more than that and it muddies the water. Here are some examples of values, but there are long lists of values to consider.

Authenticity, balance, beauty, community, courage, creativity, diversity, equity, family, fun

You may find values that align with you, or you may need to search a bit more for the perfect match. Look for the words that you consider necessary and essential to who you are. Be creative! Don't choose words you think you should, such as "family" or "teamwork," unless those are rooted in your core. If you cannot imagine making decisions about anything without first checking your alignment with those values, then you will know you are on the right track.

Now that you have selected your top five, you want to spend some time assessing them and determining what they mean to you. Your highest values are also your top priorities, and they should align with your brand.

It's not hard to make decisions when you know what your values are.

—Roy E. Disney

BRAND ENGAGEMENT

For some creatives, being social is where they shine. They're great at socializing, and they can talk about what they do with others. But, for most creatives, being able to meet people when they come to see the art and do business right on the spot feels impossible. Most creatives will choose to hide and not engage at all. There is often a desire to hide out and hope that somebody will buy your work. That is an old-fashioned notion of what it looks like to be creative. It's hard because, in our artistic culture, we don't require creatives to understand all this stuff and learn how business works. Instead, we often sell the myth of "Build it, and they will come." But, for only one in a 10 million does that happen. For the rest, you will have to work harder than sitting around waiting to be discovered. It has happened, kind of, in the past. The painter Jean Michel Basquiat was homeless, living on the streets in New York City until Andy Warhol discovered him drawing on napkins in the park. It was such a romantic story that Julian Schnabel made a movie about it called Basquiat (Miramax Films, 1996). Here is the problem with this idealized version of an artist: There are no Andy Warhol's right now. The idea of patrons who fund individual artists is more of a myth than a reality. Now we must use our storytelling skills to court our buyers.

FIG 2-4

It takes seven different engagement opportunities for someone to learn who you are.

There are very few galleries, small venues, local theatres, or handmade shops left. There are few critics left in the creative fields; there are very few publishers that are just going to discover you while you're writing in a coffee shop. Even if you get that gallery show, prime performance venue, or a book deal, you are still the one doing all the marketing, and you still need a brand. The work is never done for the multi-hat wearing creative. You must sell your brand yourself. If you know your story well and you can tell it in a compelling way, you still must engage and build relationships. You must show up and engage in conversations to build relationships with people face to face. It's the same thing on social media. People need to know you.

If it makes you feel a little sick inside wondering how to engage, the first answer is you must wear multiple hats, have a brand, and be able to do many different things at different times. Sometimes, taking off your creative hat and putting on your businessperson hat, your professional hat, your agent or representative hat is also needed. To make it easier to play these different roles, practice what you will say in your head while pretending you're talking about someone else. Take the attachment between yourself and your work product away and see it for what it is: a storytelling opportunity. If the audience isn't interested, move on to another, and then another, until the story you are telling gets more comfortable and you can remove yourself from it, even if it is about you. That's the confidence and bravery hat. Practice being able to do that with different people you will encounter throughout your career.

Do you know how many times, in numbers of engagements, it takes for people to remember who you are? Seven! It takes most human beings seven interactions of any kind for them to remember who you are. That's a lot of relationship building, and that means you can't meet someone once and expect that they will remember you. Deep relationships are where the sales are, where the hiring is, and where you find opportunities.

TARGET AUDIENCE

Have you taken the time to ask who your target audience is? To build a reliable brand, start by understanding who you are selling to and go deep on the discovery. It doesn't mean your audience won't come from all angles, but when you're trying to figure out how to start to build a brand, make a specific avatar. An avatar is a visual image of a figurehead; it helps you understand which people, companies, or organizations you should be targeting. If your avatar doesn't line up with the customer, you are then hunting for everything, and it will fall apart. You will look in the wrong locations, for the wrong person. Once you commit to the idea of a narrow focus, your time and dollars are better spent. You can always grow and expand later, but start small and focused.

DESIGNED CLIENT

My ideal client avatar is a wise, idealistic, slightly grumpy, middle-aged, or older, man. That client and I are going to work amazingly together because I understand him and I'm going to deliver something wilder then he imagined. I have a clear visual of who I get my checks from, and this gives me a unique niche market. My gut tells me they are good at heart (even if the outside is crusty) and they like to have fun, and I get to be creative because they are wise enough to honor my practice and trust me. But, if I didn't have this very vivid avatar image, then I would spend all my time chasing anyone and everyone all the time in all different directions. Your work can be more relaxed too—figure out who you should tell about your brand first and most often. Now, don't get me wrong, I have women young and old write checks, but they usually find me.

You might be feeling that identifying a target audience makes for a narrow category, and to that you are right: It is intended to be a starting place. For many creatives, you don't need that many clients, only the right clients. The

FIG 2-5

Know your ideal client.

ones who get you, your brand, and your story. Your creative business isn't for everybody. That is okay. Knowing what your avatar looks like precisely, what they like to drink, and where they enjoy eating will help you to see this person and you'll know where to find them. If you know who you are looking to promote your brand to, it is a lot easier to find the right people. That is easier than searching through a crowd, feeling like every person in that sea of people could be a client; that is too daunting.

Think about great clients you may have had in the past—that can be a good starting point for thinking about who you work with best. Make a list of personalities that you've worked well with in the past. This list can guide you to types of people you would prefer to work with on future projects. It also helps to know who you do not want to work with on projects.

"Be so good they can't ignore you."

— *Steve Martin*

READING THE ROOM

Always look around the room you are in and ask yourself who is looking at your work. Once you identify those who appear to be connecting with your work, move over to them and open the communication. They want to get to know you and are excited to meet the creator; that is the part of your brand where you open up and share your gift. Do you know that they have the financial means to take that home tonight or hire you on the spot? No, but it doesn't matter because you are engaging and co-creating a plan to stay in touch and build a relationship. You may not always know who's in the room, but if you see engagement opportunities, take the lead and introduce yourself. This action requires you to bring your bravery and courage hats. Cultivate people when you are most authentic and excited about your brand. Being uniquely true to who you are allow syour ideal customer see you as you. Working the room is changing to fit into what people think you should be; reading the room is identifying who is in sync with you.

FIG 2-6

Be careful with the messaging connected to your brand.

MULTIPLE BRANDS

Should you have several brands for different projects? The short answer is yes. I have three brands that I operate under; I have a brand for my day job type of work, another brand for my speaking and writing, and another for my play. I put most of my energy into the first two, but the third is fun for me, so I use that as well. If you are wondering about different branding options because sometimes you create 3D and two-dimensional art that is still under the same umbrella brand of visual art, you do not need two different brands. However, if you write spy thriller novels and play bells for Christmas concerts, then yes, maybe you want brands. Make sure they are genuinely different enough to warrant the amount of work it will take to manage more than one brand, though. I share this because branding is not something you do and then it's done and you leave it alone. It is a living thing that needs trimming and watering and room for growth and change. It will always have a component of work to it to keep it current and fresh for both you and your audience.

WORDS MATTER

Your brand is what you say about yourself and the things you allow others to say about you. Watch what you say when you talk about your brand. Just as you must watch your social media, watch what you say during conversations, meaning sometimes even if you say something that's not a big deal at the time, it could come back to bite you.

Let me give you an example of something I still battle every day. Out of something that I said for years, I created my own worst pet peeve. People who know me, or who have worked with me, will say, "Hey, I know you're really busy, but. . . . " I feel terrible when people say that to me. Both because I don't want to be thought of as harried and busy, but also because it implies I don't have time for them. So, now I don't use that word. You will never hear me say "I'm busy." Instead, I reply with "No, I'm not busy. I have all the time in the world for you." Because, for me, when someone says "I know you're really busy, but, . . ." it instantly that makes me feel they think I don't have time for them, and that is terrible. When I started my company, I said yes too often, and then I spent my time saying "I'm so busy." In doing this, I created a negative aspect of my brand accidentally. For years I built a workaholic brand, and I was a workaholic. I am not anymore, but I told that story over and over, and it stuck, and now it has taken me years to unstick it and rebrand. If I only had a time machine! So, always be very careful with how you present your brand. Make sure you mean what you say, and you check in with yourself often. Ask yourself if this is indeed the brand you want people to think of when they think of you.

FIG 2-7

REFLECTION

Your creative brand is your promise. It's your promise to your audience on what you will deliver. To show that it is what is important to you you have to be vulnerable and truthful, even when it's hard. Your brand is a guarantee that when a client or customer meets you, you'll be the same person and won't be a surprise. If you can accomplish a brand that is authentic to you and your audience, as promised, then you'll have a successful business. But, if things don't match up (meaning your brand looks fantastic and then you show up and you're a mess), word travels quickly. Make sure you're authentic while being confident and brave; if you're messy, be messy your way and own it. The most important part of branding is to focus on yourself as the brand, not your produced outcome. It is vital to demonstrate confidence, bravery, and passion for your brand because if those things are not there, why would anyone be motivated to buy from you or hire you? Celebrate and highlight your talents, craftsmanship, and skills. Use a clear, authentic voice to tell the story of your brand. For the most impactful brand, allow your values to assist in decision making and learn everything you can about your target audience. Engage and share your brand by offering insight into you, the creative.

HOW WILL THE CREATIVE USE THIS INFORMATION GOING FORWARD?

Directions: Create a brand statement and post it in a location where you will often see it to remind you of who your target audience is, what you do for them, and what you want people to know about you, the brand.

Brand statement

I work with _____(who are)_____

to help them _____

and _____.

Every person, who comes in contact with my brand will know

_____.

With this statement, you offer clarity about your offerings and who you work with. When you take the guesswork out of the who and what, you get to focus on your practice.

BUILDING YOUR CREATIVE NETWORK

Directions: Think of people or other resources that can help you develop your creative brand as learned in this chapter. Write down these creative network connections in the space provided. Write a specific goal for contacting or making use of one of them.

1. _____

2. _____

3. _____

Goal: _____

CHAPTER THREE

Tell Your Story

FIRE UP YOUR BRAVERY

INTRODUCTION

Now that you have a clear handle on branding *you* instead of what you create, you'll focus on how to tell your story. Creatives can be terrible at telling their own story because of lack of confidence, and the lack of confidence leads to lack of sales. The chapter focuses on creating authentic, curated stories that you are comfortable sharing. You don't need to invent or exaggerate your story, just tell it in a way that is more compelling.

TERMS THE CREATIVE NEEDS

ELEMENTS OF A STORY Character, setting, plot, conflict, resolution

CHARACTER A person in a novel, play, or movie

SETTING The place or type of surroundings where something is positioned or where an event takes place

PLOT The main events of a play, novel, movie, or similar work, devised and presented by the writer as an interrelated sequence

CONFLICT A serious disagreement or argument, typically a protracted one

RESOLUTION The action of solving a problem, dispute, or contentious matter

WHAT THE CREATIVE NEEDS TO KNOW

Your story is all of you, all the parts and pieces, both exciting and dull. People want to know more about how you create and why. They want to hear details about your process because it is such a mystery how creatives go from a single spark of an idea to full production on stage. Often, we are even enamored with our discoveries, but we don't share them because we are worried what others in our field might say. However, other creatives are rarely your target audience, so care more about sharing with your clients and potential customers. This chapter will offer insight into how to tell an engaging story by providing only the curated version you feel comfortable sharing, without hiding.

FIG 3-1

Offer an inside look into your process.

WHAT THE CREATIVE WILL LEARN IN THIS CHAPTER

In this chapter, you will discover that the more generous you are through your creative process and products the higher your sales and hiring offers are. People want to know about you and your process. You can pick and choose how much you want to share—this is your brand and your story, but you do have to show up and share, allowing your audience to peek inside your practice and process. You will learn the elements of a story as a guide to help write yours.

TELL YOUR STORY

Your story matters because it is the fabric of what makes up you. No one can tell your background by assessing your clothes or haircut or choice of food; therefore, you have to clue them in, because the most important element of branding is storytelling. Good branding is good storytelling. People who do not see themselves as creative are enamored by your practice. Whatever you make, when people look at your work, experience your performance, read your words, whatever your artistic practice is, they are both enjoying and wondering how it came to be.

If they are engaged, interested, and like what they see, hear, or read, they are more likely to close the deal. Will the client buy a piece, a ticket, a book or hire you for a gig on the spot? Most will not close the deal on site or hire you immediately based on what you produce alone; they want more; buyers love the back story. Knowing more about the creative is what makes most people close the deal. People who do not consider themselves to be creative might say, "I could never sing, I could never draw a stick figure, I'm not creative," because they are enamored by your gift. The reason people buy art, go to music shows or to the theater, or read great literature is because the people who created the work offer a mystery. You carry a mystique that people want to know more about. Tell your story in a way that they get a little slice of how you create. Give them an inside look at not only the completed work, but how did you did it (process), and you are instantly more compelling.

> *"It's like everyone tells a story about themselves inside their own head. Always. All the time. That story makes you what you are. We build ourselves out of that story."*
>
> — *Patrick Rothfuss*

HOW MUCH TO SHARE

As a creative, you have a private world outside of the rest of your life. Most creatives do. You think differently and see the world through different lenses. You do things in ways that make sense to you, but your actions may confuse others. How, then, do you determine what to share and what others might find interesting? Use traditional storytelling tools to develop the stories you want to share about yourself. Throw everything in first, as you are building your story, and edit later, because something you may find to be no big deal could be a tidbit that others find fascinating.

FIG 3-2

CHARACTER DEVELOPMENT

Anytime you are telling a story, such as when giving your elevator pitch, listen and stay alert for the parts that resonate most with the receiver. Watch their body language and eye contact to see how they are reacting. Once you have a sense of the pieces that work best, amplify those parts of the story with more vibrant details. Using your listening skills can help you build a compelling story about yourself. You want the idea of yourself to be authentic, not a shallow cartoon character. Think about roles in movies or books; you don't know absolutely everything about them, just the parts and pieces necessary to move the story forward. Find the parts and pieces of your story you are willing to share and push that character out front each time you need to.

SETTING

The space where you create should also be a part of the story you share. If it's a kitchen table, a laptop, a broom closet, a sound studio, or a great space with natural lighting, share why that works for you. Did you build it? Does the space have a history that is interesting? Offer details and don't diminish the area you have created for yourself, even if you have ideas for a different space in the future. Many people live and work in spaces that do not offer creativity, and sharing how you do it excites and inspires people—let them have that by sharing details. Also, share how you work in the world, meaning do you work while traveling? Do you have to-go studio kits that you take with you? Do you use vintage materials or equipment—share that!

PLOT

Think about the plot of your story as your process. How do you do it? Many creatives do not give much thought to how they create; it is just something they do. Stop and look in on your process, and see your steps and your flow and think about how you can share that. People who do not consider themselves creative might ask you the question, "How do you come up with your ideas?" All creatives, undoubtedly, have been on the receiving end of this or similar questions. The first response can often be "I don't know," or, "It just comes to me." Is this true, though? Spend some time watching yourself and your creative process. Are there nuggets you could pull out to share? Test these ideas on family and friends to see which part of your process is most interesting to them. Start there and grow your story by sharing the process of how you create a spark of an idea to a fully realized production.

FIG 3-3

Include all elements in your story: character, plot, setting, conflict, and resolution.

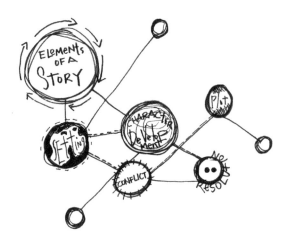

CONFLICT

An example of an interesting conflict you can share might include the hours you create. Many creatives are night owls. Most people you are going to share your story with will likely keep more traditional hours, and your ability to create into the night offers an exciting moment of conflict because many people hearing this part of your story will say, "I could never do that." That is a significant clue for you if they say something along those lines; use that as your opportunity to share how the pull is so big that you can't help but show up whatever the hour. If you have another challenge that fuels your creativity, guide it into a short story that you can share.

RESOLUTION

Unlike fairy tales, the resolution part of your story does not have to be tied up in a bow. The life of a creative is weird and odd, and there is no need to hide that. Share the resolution in your story through the triumph that you have accepted your weird and bizarre self into your story. It can take creatives a long time to settle into their personalities. The sooner you get there, own it, and show up confident, the easier your practice is.

Pause here and write down a few bullets under each header—character, setting, plot, conflict, and resolution—in your journal. Making notes on fleeting thoughts allows you to return and expand the ideas later. When the creative muse visits, she is ready to offer something to you. Turn her down and she'll leave; agree to listen, and she'll come often.

*"Stories have to be told or they die, and when they die,
we can't remember who we are or why we're here."*

—*Sue Monk Kidd*

STYLES OF STORYTELLING

There are many ways to tell your story, as many ways as there are creative expressions. Practice different techniques and see what serves you best; it's your story to show, and the vehicle for telling it needs to feel natural and comfortable for you. You need to be pushed out of your comfort zone a little bit, though, because for many creatives the ideal setting is to be alone, but you can't live like that forever. You have to share yourself and your talent; you can only do this if you develop a story that fits your communication style. You should also control and curate your story to share just the bits you want your audience to know. Curate your professional life in a way that is a specific story, as that storytelling affords you an audience that instantly connects with you.

LIVE STORYTELLING

You can do incredible storytelling with any creative activity. If you're a musician or performer in any way, if you pause and say to your audience, "Let me tell you a little story about this song" or "Let me tell you a little story about how we put this dance together," then you've got them. Now they become a part of your brand and your story because you offered insight into the process. Now they feel they know you. Every time you are at an event, you have the opportunity to gather an audience of one or many and tell your curated story, live on the spot. Live storytelling can include the use of photography, illustration, video, graphics, music, and voice and audio elements.

WRITTEN STORYTELLING

When you have the opportunity to have your story placed in a written or audio form for the public to see, be honest. Visual artists have this with a statement on the wall; writers have this with bios and book jackets; performers in playbills and other creatives in different ways. Make your brand about your passions, the stuff you love, your values, and what you care about most. Don't waste your opportunity on a public statement and try to be smart and use big words. People want to know you, not that you have a vocabulary. Put all the bull away and be real. It is the way to build your brand and to be clear about who you are; gift the real you—messy, flawed, and honest. Curate your message but share honestly. Written storytelling can include the use of photography, illustration, graphics, charts, graphs, doodles and other written elements.

VISUAL STORYTELLING

If you are not a visual thinker, ask for help from someone who thinks in pictures. Don't rely on ineffective presentation tools to tell your story. Put your thoughts together with visuals that are compelling, limit text, and highlight big ideas. Think of slides running behind you as set design. How can images better tell your story and enhance details? Never use a presentation to repeat what is coming out of your mouth. You will lose your audience and an opportunity. Choose images wisely and make sure they relate to your story, and include pictures of your working space and your work whenever appropriate. Visual storytelling can consist of the use of photography, illustration, film, video, and graphics.

MASHUP STORYTELLING

Maybe your creativity is a mix of mediums. DJs are curators, curating music, and I would encourage you to think like a DJ when you're coming up with your story. When you are putting together your story, curate from your own life and experiences. Pull all the parts and pieces together, swirl them around, and create them into this magical outcome. Channel the curator

FIG 3-4

Build a group of people who will be honest with you.

and the DJ who can sample a little from here and there—building a new story altogether. That is how unique stories are created. Don't shy away from creating mash-up stories, because the more interesting you are, the more you will hold your audience's attention.

"We are all storytellers. We all live in a network of stories. There isn't a stronger connection between people than storytelling."

—*Jimmy Neil Smith*

SERVE UP SAMPLE SIZES

When you share your story, do you sometimes not know when to quit? You might not know where to edit or how much or how little to say or share. If you can think about setting up your story and your sharing like a DJ or a curator, and think about it as sampling, it will serve you. That means testing things out and getting feedback. If you choose something for your branding in fonts, words, colors, or visuals and you receive feedback that it doesn't make sense or isn't clear, then revisit the playlist. You can make changes and tweaks as needed. Test things out; try them on for size and see how they fit. If you give a sample of your story, compel the receiver: He or she is likely to ask you to tell him or her more and then you have him or her. You just drew someone in—even while testing things out. It's a great opportunity where you're going to give a little, intrigue your audience, and wait to see if they ask for more. Imperfect action is 100% better than no action at all. And, who knows? What felt incomplete or imperfect to you might be surprising and ideal for your audience. A large piece of telling your story and of creating your brand is to run mini tests to see how things fit on you.

BUILD A TRUTH TRIBE

Surround yourself with people who tell you the truth. Check your brand and your decisions with your truth-telling tribe. These truth tellers will be honest with you because they want you to grow and be your best. Create a list of the people in your life who you can count on to be real with you. Tell them they are one of the few truth tellers you call on. They also need to know that they have permission to always be honest with you. As you bring these like-minded people together, they will then become your tribe. They are passionate people who can't get enough of your brand, and they believe in you. Share your story with them and ask them to help you build it into a compelling tale.

take action

Schedule specific time with individuals in your life who show up for you. Take them out to coffee and share that you are ready to build an official truth tribe and you would like to include them. Choose people with no agenda other than supporting you. Explain the rules. First, how you would like to be spoken to when the truth is required and what language to use. Next, express that they need to be honest with you no matter what because you are ready to show up, and for that you need to grow. Finally, ask them their best mode of communication when you need their support and then honor what they tell you. Meet often and thank them for being a part of your truth tribe.

TAKE A BREATH

Build in pause. Be a creative who follows this one rule of the business. Request time to think it over. Creatives are often so excited to be offered a sale or a gig that the enthusiasm makes them jump before they have had time to weigh things out. Sometimes after you reflect on a project, you will discover you might lose money by doing it, or the commute would be crazy. There are always many things to consider before agreeing to a gig. Take your time and pause. The best thing you can do in your life when presented with a new opportunity is to say, "I will get back to you on that." Use this time while pausing to check your gut and determine if the opportunity aligns with the story and brand you are building. If the answer is a definite no, then decline. While you are making your brand and story, you have to stay on a path. To be scattered all over the place is to be off brand and lost in your story. After you have taken a necessary pause, go to your tribe and ask what they think about it. Asking for a few minutes to think things through makes you look more professional to the client. Be careful because looking too eager cheapens your brand. Take a pause, take your time, and make sure what you are about to say yes to is a good fit for you, your brand, and the story you are telling.

PROCESS OVER PRODUCT

The most significant motto in my creative life is "process over product." I value process over the product much more because that is the fun part—when you can focus on process as play and exploration. For many creatives, this is true, which is why we consistently create new things. When focusing on the product, spend time building your brand, exploring and developing. Develop relationships with your brand by sharing your process. If all you ever show on your social media, in your portfolio, or on your website is finished perfect products, you're not letting people in your process. People want to know about the process. As you are writing and rewriting your story, weave process in, be generous with it, let people peek behind the curtains.

REFLECTION

Creating a brand is a way for you to tell your story. It's beyond simply listing projects or building case studies. It's a way to demonstrate who you are. There are many ways to tell your story; you have to test several out to find a good fit. Always be authentic in the stories you tell and stay true to yourself, sharing only as much as feels comfortable. Write your story well before you ever have the opportunity to tell it. Practice it, so you feel in control when it matters.

HOW WILL THE CREATIVE USE THIS INFORMATION GOING FORWARD?
Directions: Take a few minutes to think through the elements of your story as it relates to your brand. Write down three ideas to tell your story in the space provided.

1. _____

2. _____

3. _____

BUILDING YOUR CREATIVE NETWORK
Directions: Think of people who can be a part of your truth tribe. Write down possible opportunities when you would need to call on your truth tribe in the space provided. Write an immediate goal for contacting or making use of one or more of them.

1. _____

2. _____

3. _____

Goal: _____

FIG 3-5

PROCESS OVER PRODUCT

SECTION II

SPREAD THE WORD

CHAPTER FOUR

Business Cards and Letterhead

YOUR UNIQUE IDENTITY

INTRODUCTION

As discussed during the branding chapter, the items in your identity package, including your business card and letterhead, should all look like they are from the same person. Because this is not a design book, we will not go into detail about designing your professional documents. However, it is essential that you have those items to work with as you begin this journey toward being a creative professional. It matters to have everything aesthetically go together to connect your brand and your identity pieces, to share your story.

TERMS THE CREATIVE NEEDS

BUSINESS CARD A small card printed with one's name, professional occupation, company position, and other contact information

IDENTITY PACKAGE The image in which a business presents themselves to the public

LETTERHEAD A heading on stationery stating a person's name, company position, and other contact information

COLOR STORY A palette of colors used to connect and identify each piece with a particular story

GIG ECONOMY A labor market characterized by the prevalence of short-term contracts or freelance work as opposed to permanent jobs

PDF Portable document format, a type of saved file format

WHAT THE CREATIVE NEEDS TO KNOW

We still need business cards. If you are at an event and do not have a business card to give to someone, that can cause that individual to believe you are not serious or a professional. As a creative, you will likely end up doing many different things because that's what we do. You will make a living doing more than one thing. In the creative fields, it is okay to have several different business cards. It does not dilute your brand if you keep each business contained and do not mix them. I maintain three different brands, and they do not conflict. If you have a couple of different brands, have an identity package for each of them or make them look like connected sub-brands.

WHAT THE CREATIVE WILL LEARN IN THIS CHAPTER

In this chapter, you will learn why a business card is still relevant and why you need one or more to tell your story confidently. You'll uncover creative ways to always carry one or two cards with you. You also learn why the business card is not the place to get overly creative. Keeping it standard aligns you, the creative, with all other professions.

COLOR YOUR IDENTITY

Pulling your identity package together begins with a color story. When you think about a color story, do not choose a palette that is too trendy or overly popular. Be mindful of what is in the zeitgeist right now, meaning if colors are fashionable at the moment, steer clear of them because they won't be as popular in a few years and then you'll look outdated. Don't go too neutral either, because that can be boring. Your color story should have some connection to who you are in some way. The color of your identity package items, including your business card, gives you a way to talk about why you made that choice. Do your colors for your identity package come with a story? Share those connections.

When combining colors on your business card, keep in mind that it is challenging for the eye to read specific colors such as yellow printed on gray. This seems obvious, but some color combinations are terrible to look at in print. Neon and overly bright colors are also hard to read. They look great on clothes, but in print, they can be challenging. A lot of people design business cards in black and white for a reason: It's striking, and it's easy to read.

YOUR IDENTITY TYPE

The next thing when thinking about your identity package is your font choice. Give some thought to this because there are a lot of typefaces and questions to ask before making your selection. Are you going to have access to those fonts always or are you using them in a school, workplace or from a borrowed computer? If your current computer has 12 fonts on it, then use one of those so that you know you'll always have access to it. Then, decide if you should use a serif or sans serif font. Times New Roman, a serif font, is easier to read because the eye can follow the lines along the bottom and top. However, aesthetically, sans serif fonts, such as Arial or Helvetica, can be more visually appealing from a design sense. The other important thing about your font is the size. You will want to do a few test prints of the items in your identity package to make sure the font size is large enough. Never use a font smaller than 12 points for the vital contact information, instead use a 14 or 16 point, so the receiver does not struggle with reading your information. Make it easy for the person you are asking to contact you. If you have barriers such as small font size, you are increasing the likelihood that you will not hear from that person.

FIG 4-1

Your business card is a jumping off point. Always carry it with and prepare to swim once you hand it out.

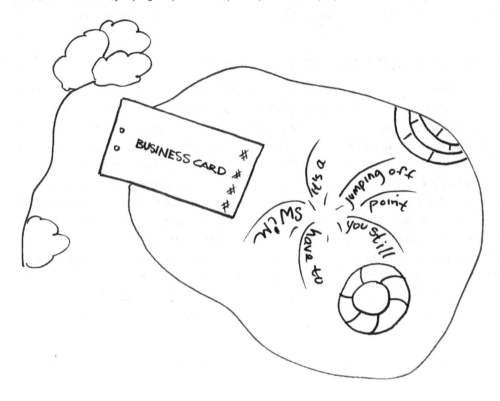

CLEAN, CLEAR CONNECTIONS

Creators try to get too much information on one card. An important question to ask is what key information needs to be on your business card? Don't put everything on there; instead, ask yourself if the recipient could get this information if you sent them to your website. A business card is there to say, "Hi, I would like to introduce myself," not, "Here's everything; ready for me to overwhelm you?" Keep it clean and straightforward. A business card is an invitation to seek more information from social media or a website. You offer it to get more time to discuss projects with them, and for them to learn more. It's also a reminder to stay in touch. Think of a business card as an introductory jumping off point; you still have to swim through the sea of conversation, follow up, and relationship build. Don't overwhelm the receiver with every bit of information you have; he or she will seek out the rest when he or she is ready.

IDENTITY YOUR WAY

If you are a maker, a poet, or a performer, you could use your business card as a mini portfolio. There are many examples of successful business cards to be found through search engines online. What makes them successful? They are clear and comfortable to read, with the right size fonts. Business cards are intended to be your mini billboard when you meet someone and hand them your card. Why not invest a few extra dollars and use the back of the card, too. It's a blank canvas ready for the taking. Instead of leaving the back of the business card blank, add images or text. There are many business card sites online that can print cards inexpensively.

This is the other reason to have more than one card if needed: They are cheap to print. Most of the online sites are the same price or only a couple dollars more to print the backside. Consider the visuals you could share if you added something extra to the back of the card.

RECTANGLE, CIRCLES, SQUARES—OH MY!

The standard business card size is 3.5 by 2 inches. There are a variety of card shapes and sizes on the market, but this is not the time to grab hold of the creativity flag and wave it proudly. The business card is the one place to conform to the standard. Creatives often use the micro-business card, which is 1 inch by 3 inches, or a square business card, folded cards, or round cards. While these are fun and cute, they are not functional. You must take into consideration where you will hand out your cards. Likely it will be at public events, networking opportunities, or openings. It begs the question of where recipients store their collected cards. In their wallets? In their cardholders? In their shirt or pants pocket? If this is the case most of the time, then you must imagine what is going to happen to a tiny micro card or an odd-shaped card, while in a stack with other cards collected at an event. The odd shaped or the micro-mini will get lost. The microcards and the various shaped cards are good for something, so if you already ordered yours and are just now reading this, use them as tags on products or attach them with glue or staples to larger postcards or fliers, but for business cards give away only the standard size.

FIG 4-2

Create a business card using a standard size.

CARD-CARRYING MEMBER

Often, step one to landing a job or getting a gig is attracting the potential client immediately, so have a professional business card with you at all times. It is how you present yourself to the public. Your business card is your public face once you are no longer in the room with the receiver. When meeting people at a conference, networking event, or an opening, there's a short window where you can introduce yourself and offer your card. Have you done enough on your card to attract the kind of attention you want? Will the receiver want to talk with you further or will they dismiss it and determine that you are not offering anything that enhances their business? These questions can be answered if you remembered to bring a card with you.

There are creative ways to always carry one or two cards with you. Tuck a couple into your wallet, back pocket, and glove box and visor in your car. Put a few in your bag, backpack, or purse. Hide one or two in your phone case; pop it off when someone asks for one and hand it to them. Never get caught without a card—find a solution that works for you to always carry one.

HANDMADE IDENTITY

You may want to make handmade business cards. The questions you need to ask are, "Am I making something that serves me, my brand, and my story well? Does it align with my identity package?" Keep in mind most people want your contact information and will dispose of the card after they log your information into their devices.

METAL BUSINESS CARDS

Here is a story of a youthful, creative spirit moment from my past. When I was in college, I handmade my first business cards, and I thought I was so clever. I was in a studio exchange in Manhattan that was next to a factory that had hundreds of old, thin, metal printing plates. In this factory, they used offset printing and were throwing the flexible, metal plates into the dumpster. Like any industrious, young art school student I pulled several of the plates out of the garbage and, using a T-square and tin snips, I cut the metal plates into standard business card size. Then, I printed my contact information on clear sticker paper and stuck it to the small metal plate pieces. I did not ask myself the right questions, such as, "Does that seem at all logical to use cut metal as business cards?" To me it made sense and was artistic. The cards were beautiful and looked old, messy, and so creative that it somehow slipped my mind that people would need to store the cards immediately after receiving them. We had an event at the studio and I handed the metal cards out. They were sharp metal objects! I also had the business cards in a bowl with a sign that read "Please take a card." Then I overheard someone say the sign should read "Warning: By taking one of these cards you might cut your hands or tear a hole in your pants pocket." That was the moment when I realized my target audience is not my fellow creatives. Paper. Standard. Professionally printed. Remember that. Go weird and wonderful in the world, yes, but your business card is the one place to go standard; it doesn't work otherwise. You don't stand out. You get lost.

> *"Metal business cards are a good investment.*
> *Especially if you were to meet Magneto. He would*
> *have no other choice but to be attracted to you."*
>
> —Ryan Lilly

WHAT GOES DOWN ON PAPER?

There is no need to put your mailing address on any of your documents because creatives are often transient and move around frequently. And, people rarely mail things anymore. If someone needs to send something to you, they will ask for your address.

1. Your first and last name
2. Your phone number
3. Your e-mail address
4. Your website
5. If there is space, you can include social media handles

Titles only work at organizations; if you are a solo entrepreneur, don't do it. If you have a title on your business card that says artist or musician ask yourself if that is that all you do. It may not make sense in this new gig economy we live in to limit yourself. Titles often don't make sense anymore or require explanation. Very few people are doing jobs where a title is relevant to what they do. Leave the title off.

PRINT QUALITY

The printing quality of your card matters. You do not want to print your cards from your home printer. If you hand someone a business card printed on text-weight paper from your home printer, the ink can smudge, and if the card were to get wet, all the ink would run. The professional companies use permanent ink and heavy-weight card stock that would likely not go through your average home office printer.

Once you are ready to have your business cards printed professionally, do a little research first. Many of the online sites offer discount codes and alternative links to enter the sites through different portals where the discount will automatically show up at the check-out. This extra research can save you cash. The online sites have a lot of templates for you to use, and this allows you to get even cheaper business cards. But, be mindful, if you choose to use their templates, you might be surprised when you walk into a hair salon and discover that they have the same business cards. It happens because everyone seeking quick, cheap business cards uses the same templates. If you're thinking of using templates, you might be better off to print a plain black-and-white card.

take action

If this is your first time creating a professional business card or you haven't done it in a while, take some time out to refresh your knowledge. Visit a print shop to review samples or go online to business card sites and request mail samples. This act will help you to best determine paper thickness, print quality, and extras, such as embossing or foil stamping.

ONE HUNDRED AT A TIME

It doesn't save money to order 5,000 cards at a time. I did this once when I first opened my business. Indeed, I ordered 5,000! Two decades later I still have some of those cards around. The turn-around time on business cards is so fast, order 100 at a time and when you need more, you will likely be ready to make changes. Then, order a new set of 100.

LETTERHEAD LOGISTICS

Your letterhead is not likely to be printed on paper. Very few people print letterhead anymore or send printed letters for that matter, especially in the creative fields. Design your letterhead knowing you will e-mail it most of the time. Write a letter formatted in a word processing program, saved as a PDF that you can e-mail. When you design your letterhead, if the best you can do is open a word processing program, use Helvetica, and create a simple header, that is fine. Don't get caught up in a design panic because that's not likely what your creative practice focuses on. If you are a designer, then go to town and have fun; your identity package could become a portfolio piece, but for everyone else keep it simple. Do make sure the items in your identity package have some connection—visually link your social media, website, blog, and other pieces you may need for your practice.

Your letterhead should include your name, phone number, e-mail, and website. Some letterheads also include a logo or a headshot, depending on your field and your social media handles.

E-MAIL SIGNATURE

The signature section of your e-mail is your electronic business card. It is also an ad for what you are currently working on and your upcoming events. To create an e-mail signature, place your name first, and then a line in the title section that is thought provoking, creative, or fun. Include all your social media links, as this adds a level of professionalism to your signature and makes it easy for viewers to find you online. Consider including a list of links to all the current things you are engaged in or working on. This part will change as your projects change. You can also embed a video if you have recently done a TED talk, or audio if you were interviewed on a podcast as examples. Your e-mail signature is the new business card, and you need to have both.

FIG 4-3

Add an e-business card known as an e-signature to the bottom of your e-mails.

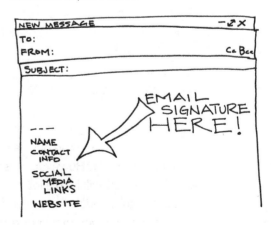

You can search online for templates for this if you want fancier looking images and colors. The most important thing about e-mail signatures, though, is that you see every transaction, with anyone, as an opportunity. It takes a few seconds to go into your e-mail settings and add this. While all e-mails are different, you can do a quick online search for "how to add an e-mail signature." If you do not do this, it's a missed opportunity, because every time you send an e-mail to someone, you never know what they're doing or what they're looking for; this stuff matters; this is your ongoing public business card. People also pull up old e-mails to find websites and phone numbers—make it easier for those chasing you.

> *"The proper definition of a man is an animal that writes letters."*
>
> —*Lewis Carroll*

LETTER WRITING

It's important to know how to write a professional letter. While it's unlikely that you will mail a letter, you will undoubtedly have a call for writing professional letters and e-mailing them.

The best use of your creative energy is to use a cover letter for the things you send formally, either mailed or electronically. Write a creative, fantastic cover letter that genuinely sells all that you wish you could say on your resume. The resume is the appetizer, and the cover letter is the entrée; it is where you're going to tell your story. Show your personality in your cover letter. You need to be professional, but remember you're creative, so you have permission to stand out. Doing this could help you gain an opportunity to sit one on one with someone or with a team in an interview. The interview is like the dessert at the end. In person is when you get to share who you are; that's how you have to think about every opportunity for which you apply. The resume is a little bite, the cover letter is the meal, and the interview is the dessert.

When applying for a job, a grant, a project, or a residency and the application asks to upload your resume, you always upload a cover letter with it, whether they ask for it or not. Do it anyway, and make your resume one page and your cover letter one page; almost everyone allows you to upload a document that is two pages. Have a PDF (portable document format) that is these two pages; you will almost always get both through. When someone sees your salesmanship in your cover letter, you're going to get noticed over others who only send a resume.

If you have had some business experience and you know how to write a letter, great; skip ahead in this book. However, most creatives have never written a professional business letter, and this section will help a lot.

Let's walk through how to write a professional letter. Is there a company, a person, or an organization that you would love to work for or do a project with? Is there an opportunity you want to apply for? Then, channel that as you are thinking about the instructions for writing a good letter. Help form the thoughts for this exercise by having a target in mind. The first step is to research the job, gig, or opportunity. Look it up online and find out the contact person's title and contact information, including their mailing address.

FIG 4-4

Follow a formal layout for your professional business letters.

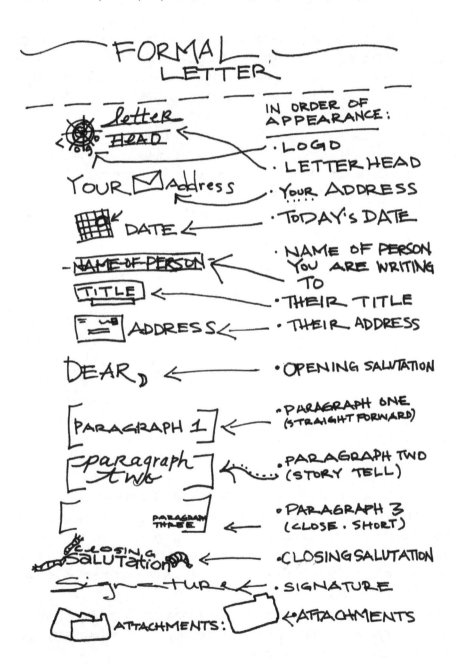

STEPS

1. Use the letterhead you created and place it at the top of the page; even if you're sending the letter electronically, you always want the letterhead at the top because it looks professional. A reminder: Your letterhead should have your name, address, phone, e-mail, and website, and it may contain your social media links and a logo or headshot, depending on your field.

2. After your letterhead, you will return a few spaces and put your mailing address, not your name just your address.

3. Return once and put the current date. An important note about dates: If you are sending out a lot of resumes and cover letters and you're in the cycle for a couple of weeks, make sure you change the date before you send something out. You want to continually update the date because you don't want somebody to receive your cover letter and open it to find a date from weeks ago. They will think it is old news.

4. After the date, double space, and put the person's name that you are sending the letter to. When you're applying for random jobs through human resource (HR) departments, it can be challenging to find a name. When you are first starting out and you're looking at entry-level jobs, find out the director of HR's name for the organization that you're applying to, because that's often who is going to see your information first.

Make sure to use the proper spelling of a name and the appropriate prefix and suffix. It may not seem like a big deal, but it is important to remember that when people are trying to determine how to narrow the field of applicants, they're looking for anything and everything to help make their decision. The best way to get sent to the "no pile" is by not doing your homework. Make sure you know the spelling of person's name, and if you don't have a personal relationship with them, do not use their first name, because you don't know them and first names are casual. Using first names is too social and too conversational; you must earn that.

5. After the recipient's name, you will hit return and add in that person's title.

6. Hit return and add the company's address. Here, I recommend trying to fit it all on one line, but if they have a large suite number or if you are applying somewhere with a long city name combined with a long state name, you may need two lines, which is perfectly acceptable; you can do it either way. I make the recommendation to save space because you only want your cover letter to be one page.

7. Hit return and write, "Dear, [Name of person you are writing to]." Regarding the salutation, you can still use dear as a professional phrase to engage the opening of a letter, or whatever opening salutation you are comfortable with.

8. Now, the first paragraph of the cover letter. Note: A paragraph is about five to eight sentences. Open the cover letter by stating "I am writing to you in regarding." You never

open a professional letter with "My name is"—the reader will figure out your name because you're going to put a signature at the end. The reason this is important is that it allows the receiver to decide from the beginning whether he or she is the right person or if he or she needs to pass the letter along. Also, consider that an assistant may be collecting incoming resumes and cover letters, and that company may have five positions open. The assistant who's doing the intake is not going to read your letter at all; they're going to take one look at it and put it in the bin of the interviewer for that position. They will appreciate that you made their lives easier!

It may also be possible that you are interested in working for this company or applying to a show or a residency and there isn't a defined position. You may like what this company or organization does, or you like a person who works there, and it may not always be possible to say "I'm applying for this position." If that is the case, consider something such as "I'm writing to you because I'm interested in your company and I would like to have a conversation with you about working with you" or, "I visited your website I saw this project which is amazing to me ... ."

9. Share how you heard about the position, the company, or the person.

10. The next thing you want to address in this paragraph is that you've done your homework. If you research the company, the position, the person, you can show that you want to get involved. It is essential to do this briefly and be specific. This is the kind of stuff that impresses people because you come to the door already giving it a little bit more than others who are applying for every gig out there.

JUST LIKE DATING

When you're desperate to get a gig, a job, or a show, it is like you're hitting on everybody and everybody knows it. People pick up on this and think, "I'm not going near that person who is so desperate." The same thing goes when you're applying for jobs. If you use a desperate approach and apply for anything and everything, people can smell it. An example is if you sent a cover letter failing to update the company name, the position, or the person's name—it is like you called your date by the wrong name in the first few minutes. If you are having trouble getting a gig, a job, a show, then consider your dating skills to rework your cover letter. Be mindful and update it regularly and people will pay more attention. Ask your truth tribe to review your letter to look for desperate language.

11. To close your first paragraph, focus on one quick sentence that hits home: your knowledge about this position, this company, or the person. At the end of the paragraph, close it with a bow-tied sentence to insert your personality and your connection with how you see that company, that person, or that position. Close it with a memorable zinger.

12. Double space to begin paragraph two. Paragraph two opens with a hard-hitting sentence to grab attention. In this paragraph, you'll demonstrate why are you qualified. Focus on how qualified you are. This paragraph is also where you can talk about things you wish you could say in your resume. In this paragraph, you'll want to offer what is impressive about you. When talking about your skills, be mindful of what you say. As an example, don't say you're a great team player if you know your creative work is better alone or if you work better in isolation. There are jobs for you; don't act like you are a great team player. Only share what is real and honest. If you are in any activities or memberships that do steer the course of who you are as a human, now is the time to say it; speak up; talk about that. If there's something that's meaningful that matters to you, don't be shy about it.

13. The final sentence of paragraph two is what you must remember to update and change every single time you send a cover letter out so that the person reading it feels like you wrote it just for him or her. Doing this is like a magical love note written just for the recipient; it's not a form letter.

14. Close paragraph two by referencing the company, the position, and the person as much as you can. Changing the name of the person or company in the last sentence of paragraph two will show that you wrote this cover letter just to this company.

15. Double space for paragraph three, which is this shortest paragraph. It's often only four to five sentences. Open this final paragraph referring to what else are you sending with this cover letter. As an example, "I am also attaching, to this e-mail the following items … ." List all of the items individually and do not abbreviate; doing this allows the person receiving to know what else he or she should look for or have in your folder.

16. This sentence is where you let the receiver know what you expect to happen next. Tell them that you will be following up on a specific timeline. If it's a position that you can see the close date, then write "I will be in contact in two weeks" (after the close date), or whatever time frame is appropriate. If you have a structured sentence that notifies them of your intention, also let them know you are interested in an interview. To do this, you might say, "I look forward to interviewing with you." You are not going to say, "I hope you will consider me for this position and I hope we can meet." Having confidence is felt and is desirable, just as passive language is undesirable. You must believe that you deserve an interview because you do.

17. Finally, you always want to close every letter by thanking the person; as an example, you might say, "Thank you for taking the time to consider me for this position." A thank you is another thing that gets you the gig, the show, or the job. Showing gratitude encourages people to see you as thoughtful.

18. Sign off with whatever your chosen salutation is. For this, you might consider sincerely, warm regards, best wishes, or whatever you're comfortable with.

19. Under the salutation, place your signature. It is an easy action if you save a digital file of your signature and insert it when needed.

20. Finally, your first and last name and title should be written under your signature.

BONUS ROUND

The last thing to do at the bottom of the letter, as low as you can go before you fall of the paper, is to write a list of what you intended to attach. Yes, it seems redundant to do it twice, both in paragraph three and at the very end, but, when you write in paragraph three "Please find my cover letter, resume, and so on attached" that is for the person you're making application to. When you put an attachment list at the end, that is for the intake person who collects the resumes and cover letters. He or she is not going to read the paragraphs to see what you intended to attach, but if you list it at the end of the document, he or she may give you the courtesy of looking to confirm that you did, in fact, attach or enclose all the things you meant to.

SENDING IT OFF

In a short e-mail, tell the recipient what you know about his or her company or what it is they do. Attach your resume and cover letter. Tell them you look forward to meeting them for an interview. Reference the point of engagement if you have met in the past or the desire for why you want to connect. Do not go on and on even if your heart is pounding and you are so deeply in love—again remember the dating reference? Don't be desperate. The subject line should be direct. I have a secret for that: If you have met the person or have any connection, put "requested materials" because if I see a subject header on the e-mail that says "requested materials" I believe there is something in there that I asked for, so I pay attention. If it's unsolicited and you haven't met the person, you want to use subject headers that are open and inviting and also don't allude to a job. Think about how you would talk to about an exciting project and craft the subject line carefully. Ask your truth tribe to sign off on your choice before hitting the send button.

REFLECTION

When thinking about your identity package and your business cards, think of it as a marketing opportunity, all the time. If you're handing your business card to someone, what are you saying to him or her? What kind of story are you telling? What does your letterhead say about the story you are telling? Learn to write letters, and create a simple template for yourself that you can use every time. Create an electronic signature for your e-mail and store your handwritten signature digitally to sign documents fast. Your identity, your brand, and your story depend on it.

HOW WILL THE CREATIVE USE THIS INFORMATION GOING FORWARD?

Directions: Take a few minutes to think about how you will create pieces of your identity package. Write down three ideas for getting it done in the space provided. Will you do it? Hire it out? Barter? Trade?

1. _____

2. _____

3. _____

BUILDING YOUR CREATIVE NETWORK

Directions: Think of people, organizations, or other resources that can help you create the elements of your design package. Write down these creative network connections in the space provided. Write a specific goal for contacting or making use of one of them.

1. _____

2. _____

3. _____

Goal: _____

CHAPTER FIVE

Resume and CV
IT'S JUST THE APPETIZER

INTRODUCTION

Your resume is another piece of your identity package. Are you wondering what the difference between a curriculum vitae (also known as a CV) and a resume is? You'll find out in this chapter. You'll also receive some tough love and ideas for making your resume stand out. Your resume is the next document you're asked for, after your business card. Don't feel compelled to load everything in it though—use your cover letter for that. Your resume should include your education, your experience, and your current position with facts with dates on one page. Your CV will be ten to 100 pages depending on your career and will be the place you store your personal history, but you will rarely hand that document out unless you are in academia.

TERMS THE CREATIVE NEEDS

RESUME A brief account of an individual's education, qualifications, and experience, as part of a job application

CURRICULUM VITAE Also known as a CV, this is a career-long list of an individual's education, skills, qualifications, and previous experience, including academic background, teaching experience, degree area, and research

COMMISSION An order or authorization for the production of something, such as a building or work of art

GIG ECONOMY A labor market of short-term contracts or freelance work as opposed to permanent jobs

WHAT THE CREATIVE NEEDS TO KNOW

Think of your resume as the appetizer to begin to entice a potential client or job. Then the cover letter is the entrée, and the interview is a delicious dessert where you are going to give it your all and show off your chops. If you put everything on your resume, then you have nothing left to give. Resumes should not be a catch-all for hobbies and skills—put all that in the cover letter.

FIG 5-1

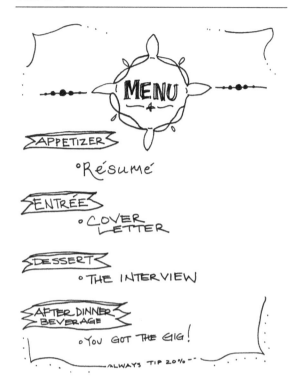

Your resume should read like a biography of facts for things you have done. It is not a place to talk about what you could do.

WHAT THE CREATIVE WILL LEARN IN THIS CHAPTER

You will learn what you should and should not include in your resume and what the difference between a resume and a CV is. Your resume is a place to show your confidence, as evident by your editing ability. More is not better when it comes to a resume. More, however, is the name of the game when it comes to your CV; load everything you have done into your CV.

RESUMES AND CURRICULUM VITAE

There are a couple of differences between curriculum vitae (CV) and resumes. First is the length: A resume is a summary of experience, skills, and education in just one or two pages. A CV is intended to be detailed, without limits on the number of pages. As your career grows and develops, you will likely end up with a long CV, between ten and 100 pages, depending on your career path, listing everything you have done over your career.

The next difference between curriculum vitae (CV) and a resume is the purpose. Most people never need a CV, as it mostly represents academic accomplishments, where a resume represents skills and experience such as inclusion in shows, anthologies, or compilations. Most professions do not maintain a CV as they drop jobs and experiences off their resume as it becomes outdated. The creative, scientific, and academic fields mainly use CVs.

BUILDING YOUR RESUME

If you are a student or are just starting out, you may struggle to get even a one-page resume pulled together; that it is okay, because you're just getting started in this field.

At the top of your resume, place your letterhead, including your name, phone, e-mail, and website.

Never abbreviate on your resume, or on any professional documents; instead, write everything out. With all categories on your resume, put the most recent first and then the oldest.

If you are early in your career, then the first category listed is your education because that is the most prominent thing. As you move along in your career, it is often the standard that you place your education near the bottom of your resume. List what you earned your degree in (e.g., Fine Art). If you are currently a student, put what your pending date of graduation is and then remember to update that when you enter the workforce.

If you went to another college or university other than where you received or are receiving your degree from and you feel it was relevant, put it on your resume, even if you did not earn a degree; include the dates of attendance in parentheses. That allows the reader to understand that you did not receive the degree but you attended during those dates.

If you participated in a study-abroad program or have traveled extensively, you can put that on your resume by also putting the dates in parentheses.

MAINTAINING YOUR CV

FIG 5-2

Why take the time to maintain a CV your whole career? The simple answer is when you have your retrospective, get published, or you have significant exhibitions you will be asked for your records as reference points. If you do the work of adding new items a couple of times a year, you will quickly maintain your professional history. Keep track of everything you are involved in professionally; this can include volunteer work that is relevant to your field. Maintaining a CV is also very helpful when you are applying for jobs and projects as a reminder of all you have done throughout your career. It can be a confidence boost to read every so often as a reflection of all the work you have accomplished over your career. It is also an excellent refresher to read over your comprehensive CV before any interview. Do this to remind yourself of dates and categories you may want to reference.

DATES

You do not want to put months, only years. If you had a gig that lasted four months or four weeks, you still just put the year. In the interview, you can say, "This project span was from June to August." You do not need to write that on your resume. In this new gig economy, it's understood that creatives are project based. And another reminder: For all categories, you want to list most recent to oldest.

TOUGH LOVE

This is a crucial tough love moment if you are just starting out: You must let go of high school or your irrelevant past. No matter how glorious you're bygone days were, captain of a sports team, high school class president, all of it needs to go. Let go of the stuff you worked on in college, too. As an example, rarely is anyone in a creative field is asked their GPA because it's not what matters. If you are proud and want to share your GPA, save it for the interview. For the most part, though, level the playing field and join in as if you have been in the area for a while. Do this, and you will discover no one asks about grades or GPAs. Step into the confidence of who you are now; your past is just that.

If you are first starting out in this career field, you may feel compelled to beef up your resume by putting duties under each employment list. Save this too for the cover letter or the interview. Just say what the position was, list the dates, and leave it at that.

Seasoned professionals know what your duties included; they get it and realize you had additional responsibilities because all jobs do. Save the "let me tell you what else" for when the opportunity permits. Wait until asked because listing duties on your resume is unnecessary, and professional creatives don't include that.

FIG 5-3

LANDING A GIG IS LIKE DATING

You want to treat the first encounters like flirting and reveal a little bit at a time.

Note: Don't actually flirt; this is a metaphor! A resume is, again, just the facts. A cover letter is a place where you storytell a bit, making connections to reference later. The interview is where you share your personality. Be you throughout the whole thing; if they don't like the goods, well, then, good for both of you to know early on. But treat each encounter as building on the next, referencing but not repeating, and don't be desperate. That doesn't work on a date, and it has no place in the professional world.

DON'T FILL UP SPACE

If you asked most professionals if they have time to read everything on a resume, they will most likely admit to just glancing at it. You'll get a glance at best, and if you ask people to read paragraphs, you're not going to get that. Once you're invited in for an interview, then the professionals across the desk are ready to listen. They have time for you. Don't waste people's time by writing unnecessary things on your resume. Choose the most recent highlights to share on one page only.

"The challenge of life, I have found, is to build a resume that doesn't simply tell a story about what you want to be, but it's a story about who you want to be."

—Oprah Winfrey

Include only the things that tell the best story of where you have been and where you are headed. Some editing is always required.

Don't include hobbies on your resume. Resumes are essential factual documents, so including things you enjoy is irrelevant. People want to read about skills and experience. You can add fun stuff to your cover letter or even your extended bio, but leave them off your resume. Also, save the tricks for the interview or during a networking opportunity where you just might get asked about your special skills. That is the time to bring up your hobbies, extracurricular activities, and your unique abilities.

THE BIG LIST

The following is a list of things that you might include on a resume. Please, however, don't write down the categories and then write "none" underneath. It is just a suggested list. If you do not have anything to put under a category, just put it away for the future knowing that you may fill in something later.

Letterhead, including name, address, phone, e-mail, website
Education
Professional experience
Teaching experience
Military service
Workshops
Residencies
Exhibitions
      Solo exhibitions
      Group shows
      Collaborative projects
Showroom or gallery representation
Collections
Commissions
Curatorial projects
Performances
Panels
Jury
Committees
Boards
Volunteer work
Articles
Publications
Reviews
Book inclusions
Published photographs of work
Lectures
Speaking engagements/Talks
Radio
TV
Grants
Fellowships
Awards
Recognitions
Specialties (technical writer, programmer, languages)

take action

Grab your journal and write down as many things you can think of for each category listed (if relevant to your field). Just be clear if you were paid or were a volunteer.

VOLUNTEER

If you have done volunteer work in your field, include that in a separate category. On a side note, consider volunteering because it often leads to internships and gig opportunities. Volunteering at organizations in your field allows you to network and build your contacts list. It will, in turn, help you build your resume. It is a place to be confident and brave. Join in volunteering and use the time to connect.

> *"We make a living by what we get, but we make a life by what we give."*
>
> —*Winston Churchill*

FIG 5-4

Volunteering can lead to internships, gigs, and connections.

BUILD YOUR CATEGORIES

With the gig economy, new fields are continually developing; to stay up on these developments you will likely have new titles for new categories on your resume or CV. Always follow the current requests to remain relevant. Also, you may want to pull types into their header if they are significant enough to warrant. An example of this might be teaching. If you have a lot of teaching experience, you will pull out your teaching experience as a separate category from your other professional experience.

COMMISSIONS

If you offer commissions, you might pull those commissions into a separate category and include, if you have permission, the client's name. Include the commission for a custom song, mural painting, a personal story, and so on. It is a particular category for people who prefer to work on things that are custom for specific clients.

NAME AND LOCATION

If you are a maker, under exhibitions, you will list if your show was a solo show or group show. For musicians and performers, this category will be performances, and you will include the name, location, and if it was a group or solo performance. If you are a writer and have anything, including your thesis, published, you want to have a "Published" category that also includes the publication name.

AWARDS

If you received awards or scholarships while in school and you are just starting out in your career, you can include those on your resume for now, with the recommendation that as your career grows, you will eventually take those off. Then, add only awards received during your post-college professional career. If you received awards or significant grants, list them on your resume.

MEMBERSHIPS

Include any memberships and affiliations on your resume with which you are currently active. If you are a card-carrying member of any organization related to your creative field, list it on your resume. However, if it was in high school, don't add it. As with all areas of your resume, list only years when referring to dates, not months.

take action

Once you have your one-page resume complete and your multi-page CV, have a close friend or family member review them. Ask individuals who are familiar with your career and might notice if you forgot to list something. Ask several people to review for you, if possible.

INCLUDE LINKS

At the end of your resume, consider including links to your social media, and, if relevant, your website or your online portfolio. Including links allows the viewer to learn more about you. It is a generous action that makes the viewer's life more comfortable because he or she does not have to search to find further information about you.

REFERENCES

Leave references off your resume. They are a different professional document, and if your viewer would like your references, they will ask for them. Do not include the line "references available upon request." It is obvious, and it takes up precious space on your one-page resume. Leave your references off your resume.

FIG 5-5

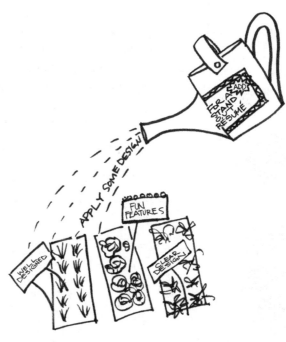

> *"The design of your resume is the first way to let one know more about your aesthetic."*
>
> —Brit Morin

APPLY SOME DESIGN

The layout or design of your resume can be creative if appropriate for your field. With most creative job offerings, you can be playful. Catch the eye of the viewer by including images, colors, or a logo to represent your artistic aesthetic. Make your resume stand out for all the right reasons. Again, this is where editing is needed. You want just enough but not so much that it looks messy or unreadable. Clear, well designed, and with fun features is your goal for a standout resume.

If you are delivering a hard copy of your resume in person or posting it at an event, consider better paper quality, colored paper, or a color printed version. Those little details are sometimes all it takes to stand out.

REFLECTION

Your resume is your opportunity to share your education, your professional experience, and your skills. Be confident enough to know that your resume will receive a quick glance. Know that you have other opportunities to add in the extras, but neither your resume nor your CV is the place to do that. A keen eye for editing is essential for a clean resume.

HOW WILL THE CREATIVE USE THIS INFORMATION GOING FORWARD?

Directions: Take a few minutes to think about how you will use the information from this chapter on your professional resume or CV. Write down three ideas in the space provided for making your resume stand out.

1. _____

2. _____

3. _____

BUILDING YOUR CREATIVE NETWORK

Directions: Think of people who can help you by reviewing your resume or CV. Write down these creative network connections in the space provided. Write a specific goal for contacting or making use of one of them immediately.

1. _____

2. _____

3. _____

Goal: _____

CHAPTER SIX

Biographies, Statements, and Philosophies

USE WORDS THAT MATTER

INTRODUCTION

Your biography (bio) is a small introduction to the greater story of your life. Share only the things that feed and fuel your practice. If you don't want to share certain parts, don't. You get to bravely curate your story and how much of it you want to share in your bio. It is the place where you get to leave off things that you do not feel are relevant and include only the things that you are most proud of in your life and career.

TERMS THE CREATIVE NEEDS

BIOGRAPHIES Referred to as a bio. It is an account of someone's life written down

PROFESSIONAL BIO A summary of who you are. It is the art of presenting yourself in the best possible and most interesting light

SOCIAL MEDIA BIO A short intro about who you are, why you're on that platform, and anything else that you want to always be in focus when new visitors find your page

CATEGORY-SPECIFIC BIO A history of your experience as related only to that field (such as a teaching bio)

STATEMENTS A brief written or verbal representation in support of the creative's work to give the viewer understanding

PHILOSOPHY STATEMENT A self-reflective statement of your beliefs about the specific area of focus, such as teaching, including concrete examples of what you do or anticipate doing in a classroom.

WHAT THE CREATIVE NEEDS TO KNOW

Bios are short, factual, and written in the third person because it's vital that anyone cut and paste into whatever document they need, without editing. Your bio should be straightforward in the telling of your personal history. Bios are generally one paragraph to one page, never longer.

FIG 6-1

Your bio is a small sample of the greater story of your life.

WHAT THE CREATIVE WILL LEARN IN THIS CHAPTER

In this chapter, you will learn what the purpose of biography (bio) is. You will learn how you might expect to use your bio and how to write it for easy consumption. A bio is a tiny, short story of a portion of your life, so you want to collect and offer information that is factual and not embellished. Weave the information into a story that is compelling to read.

SHARE, DON'T TELL

Reveal honest, thoughtful information so your audience feels they are a part of something, not isolated from it. Listen to your gut, ask yourself what you are trying to say, and give yourself time to pull it together. Creative's statements can sound jumbled and confusing due in large part because the creative is often hiding, or they have no idea why they are making the choices that they are. Reveal fun facts about yourself and the things you like; never hide who you are. That is not fair to your viewer. When you're writing a statement, dig deep: get to know yourself better and share your story with confidence and bravery; don't just get caught up in the end product. Each decision you make connects to your unique why, and that could be very inspiring if shared. If you get to know yourself well, and put in the time, effort, and energy, then you will be able to articulate what it is you do and what it is you want to do. There is no prescription or recipe for being a creative.

> *"The mistake ninety-nine percent of humanity made was being ashamed of what they were; lying about it, trying to be somebody else."*
>
> —*J.K. Rowling*

tip: Make It Easy

Most of the professional documents you will create are written in the first person because you're the author. Write your bio in the third person, however, because it should be easy for anyone who needs your information to copy and paste it into a new document. If your bio is easy to use without having to edit it, you are the hero for providing it in a user-friendly format. Bios serve many purposes throughout your career and will need to be frequently updated. Create a list of organizations or individuals who have requested your bio; if it significantly changes every few years, send it to the names on the list (if still relevant). Add a note that notifys them that your bio changed and you wanted them to have the most current copy. You can do this with your resume as well.

FIG 6-2

Get a five star review.

BUILDING YOUR BIO

Your bio begins where your story begins. Open your bio with your name and where you were born. If you moved soon after or raised somewhere else, still list your place of birth—your future biographers will thank you. Represent where you were born and where you grew up to include both if that is an essential part of your story. As an example, if you were born in one country and moved to another as a child, talk about the impact that had on you concerning languages and cultures. If you moved around a lot growing up, you want to share that because it becomes a part of your story. A bio is a tiny, short story of a portion of your greater life, so you want to offer information that is factual. You will also share where you live and work currently as well as highlights from your career.

You have a story to tell, so use this opportunity to make yourself sound incredible while still being factual. That is the purpose of a bio: to tell your story in a shortened, condensed version using narrative that lifts your story.

BUILD YOUR NUGGET

If you completed your bio, listed all your pertinent information, and yet still have room, use the space to build your story nugget. That is a part of your story that is incredible to tell and enhances who you are in your bio. As an example, if you had some heralding situation in your childhood or you moved from a place, that is impactful in your storytelling. When you describe where you are from, you can get a little more colorful with your language. As an example, instead of saying what city, territory, or state you were born in, you could say you "grew up in a small, rural mid-western town, outlined by Amish country." As long as it is still factual, it can be a little more colorful. Be brave with your language.

FIG 6-3

Use a visual language to elevate your bio.

If you are a student, talk about your major or your area of focus because that's an essential part of who you are in your life right now. Eventually, however, that highlight will fade as you transition into your career. In your future, your education, in your bio, will become a simple line, such as "received a BFA or BA from this or that university."

DON'T DATE YOURSELF

On your bio, you never want to say what year you were born, nor do you ever tell your age because it screams you are young or still in college. Once established in your career, age is no longer a topic discussed in the workplace. The only time you would ever say what year you were born in your bio is when you're ninety and used for a retrospective. For now, no dates or ages.

HIGHLIGHTS AND HITS ARE THE RULE

You want to highlight education, military service, outstanding professional work, volunteerism, internships, study abroad, residencies, essential exhibitions, publications, awards, or performances, on your bio. You don't want to include that you've worked at a coffee shop for five years; it's not crucial to the story. Unless your time at the coffee shop was research for your next significant project, then include it. Otherwise, make sure the items listed in your bio are noteworthy. Offer information on accomplishments of which you are proud. Your bio includes only your career hits!

THE SHORT AND LONG

The length for a standard bio is one to two paragraphs. For publishing or significant exhibitions, a bio can be up to one page. Each time your bio is requested, however, you will be asked to provide a specific length. These requests can come as a number of paragraphs, sentences, words, or number of characters. Also, know that you may be requested to submit your bio using a specific type style, font size, or other accommodation. It is essential to alter your bio to meet these particular requests. If you have a call for a more extended bio beyond one paragraph, think of the layout in the next section.

LONGER BIO FORMAT

1. Paragraph one is your history, including a line or two about your education.
2. In paragraph two, add other professional accolades that are relevant to your practice. Examples may include diving into a job or a position much deeper because it is related to the work you're doing in the world. If you are self-employed, you'll use the second paragraph to talk about that journey and how you got there. If you are applying for a teaching job, you may have a second paragraph to your bio that leans more in that direction, or, if you're applying for an exhibition or auditioning for a performance, you may have more about previous shows or performances or your work. But save the deep "why it altered me" content for your statement.

3. Close a long bio with an ambition statement. An example of the last sentence might be "I am a designer, and my life's ambition is to bring the dinosaurs back to life"; that is a big goal and gives the reader insight into what you might be working on currently.

In case you tend to get carried away with the use of colorful language, take the time to ask several people in your truth tribe to review your bio. It is a good practice to do this before ever sending a professional document out. If those who care about you don't understand something, listen to them and change it. Do this because all types of people will read your bio.

CLOSING

End your bio with one sentence about where you believe you are heading. You will alter that line frequently as your goals change. As an example, you might say, as a closing sentence, "And my future holds interior designing the first shuttle to Mars." That is confident, attention grabbing, and aspirational. Your closing statement is an opportunity to show your ambition, your interests, and where you think you're heading.

WHO IS YOUR AUDIENCE?

You need a bio for your website and each of your social media accounts. These may be slight variations of your bio. Each will vary in details depending on who the audience is, but the bulk of the facts will remain. A common practice in social media bios is to use a bulleted list. It is a way to get more concepts in when the number of characters or words are limited. The press will request a bio from you, and if you are going to present at a conference, you will need a bio. Always tweak your bio depending on your audience.

> *"A good teacher, like a good entertainer, first must hold his audience's attention, then he can teach his lesson."*
>
> —*John Henrik Clarke*

LOOK FOR EXAMPLES

As you begin to write your bio or update an outdated one, look for examples of bios online or ask members of your truth tribe to see their bios. Find good examples for your specific field and use those as models. Our community of creatives is connected: You need only ask for help. Modeling your bio after a well-written example lifts everyone up in our industry.

SEVERAL BIOS NEEDED

Most creatives have two to five different bios because we all do so many different things; we need several bios to list the variety of work. You will need a professional bio, a social media bio, and possibly a category-specific bio, such as teaching. Most creatives have several different bios at any given time. It is necessary due to working on varied projects.

Examples of each biography include the following:

A professional bio is a summary of your professional history, highlighting your career accomplishments.

A social media bio is a short introduction to who you are and what you want new visitors to know when they visit your page.

A category-specific bio, such as a teaching bio, is a history of your experience as related to that field.

STATEMENTS

All creatives need a statement or philosophy statement, depending on your career path. If you are a maker, producer, or performer, you'll have a creative or artistic statement. If you are a historian, administrator, curator, event planner, project manager or educator, you'll have a philosophy statement.

If you've had the privilege of writing a statement before, how did you feel about it? Very few creatives enjoy writing statements because they were trained to believe that statements matter so much that they must bleed for them. You may have been taught to bring out the thesaurus and use big impressive words throughout your statements. Here's the thing, though—most people are not interested in reading them, and I'm not interested in you wasting your time writing that way. Put your thesaurus away; nobody's going to read your perfect statement that you worked so hard on if it doesn't come from your heart and gut. Very few members of the public want to read a statement that is cold and lacking in emotion because they know those are written only for others in the field. Save the jargon-laden statements for the conferences that only others in your creative area attend. For public statements, offer information that is digestible.

BE GENEROUS

You have a gift as a creative and should be generous with your written words. People who do not consider themselves creatives have no idea what you do. They wonder how you came up with your ideas, and they are curious. They have no idea how your brain functions, how you go from here to get to over there; they will be the first to admit that they don't get it. How your brain functions can be very confusing, so why write a statement that is overly complex and jargon-laden that leaves people more confused? When they look at your work, watch your performance, read your piece, whatever your practice is, and then look at your statement; they are looking for answers. When they read it, do they find answers and not more questions? Or, are they left with confusion?

Write statements that are generous and that answer questions. Creatives often like to remain a mystery. You may be thinking you want the audience to think for themselves and so you don't want to reveal everything. Humans are intelligent

FIG 6-4

Answers vs. Mysteries.

and will place meaning on your work, right or wrong, but your viewers are still going to ask further questions and ponder more in depth, but they need something have an entry point into the work you create. Being generous can significantly help you get across what it is you do in the world. A lot of creatives struggle when speaking to people; you can create all day long, you can jam in your dark room, make music, or you can build something, write something, and then the minute you have to talk about it, it feels scary. Leading with generousness can take this pressure off. Have confidence in what you do and how you do it and in your decisions. Share the pull of why you must create and how the ideas come to you. That is a starting point and is an excellent offer to your viewer.

> *"Generosity is giving more than you can, and*
> *pride is taking less than you need."*
>
> —*Kahlil Gibran*

YOUR STATEMENT STANDS ALONE

Your statement is a stand-alone document often in place of you—it is your voice. You will not be in the room when an audience is reading your statement 99% of the time. If you are in an exhibition and your statement is on the wall for the run of the show, make sure it speaks for you when you are not in the room. If your statement is in a book or a playbill, it will be read without any interpretation from you. So, what would you want to say to someone who is excited about what they are seeing? If you're a performer, the audience member may not have a chance to come up and talk with you; what would you want to say to them? Can they find it in the playbill? What would you want them to know? This where you have to be honest and make sure people know about your process, your practice, the work you have made. Think about a statement as a means of communication; it's a conversation. Imagine the questions you've been asked in the past; were you able to answer them? If you can now explain the answers, write them down and build them into your statement. Run your statement past your truth tribe to ensure you aren't leaving anything out and that your language is not confusing.

BUILDING YOUR STATEMENT

Share what inspires you. As an example, if techniques or textures are what lights you up, then share that. If you are into formal elements, collaboration, or solitude, then share that. Get real on your why's because for most creatives, what we like is the process of making; you need to be able to talk about your process. If you are a researcher or curator, you may like putting together collections or groupings. If that's what lights you on fire, tell that story. Share the deep pull inside of you, not what you think others want to hear. Be the one who is refreshingly honest in your language and information offered.

Statements are around three paragraphs long, or less than one page. Your statement will cover things you reference, or source, things you look at, and inspirations you have. Share what you are looking at and how you use that. Share how you get inspired or mad or excited or responsive or curious.

"I always say that my artist statement is not to be afraid to talk about the messiness—the unpleasant feelings and happenings around my life. I also try to convey what it feels like and sounds like and smells like and looks like inside of my particular skin."

—Morgan Parker

STEPS TO WRITING A STATEMENT

1. PARAGRAPH ONE

Begin with what your work looks or sounds like, or what movements you incorporate if you are a performer. Reference the work on site. What does the audience see? Share what your inspirations are. Reveal the sources you're pulling from, what are you looking at? What are you reading? Where are you traveling? Are there historical references? Share how you're translating that inspiration into your creative practice. Use generous language that is that is for everybody, including the public, the curator, the academic, and your grandmother. Write a statement for the critic. If you share things that everyone can learn from, it creates a more exciting, dynamic community. It takes bravery to be vulnerable enough to share what matters deeply to you and your creative practice. Many creative fields hold things too tight to their chest, and that creates a community of scarcity. If you are worried about revealing something that you think others may steal from, let it go! You are creative; you will create more new things.

2. PARAGRAPH TWO

Talk about the emotional feelings connected to your practice. What is a story you are burning to share? What is it you want your audience to feel? It's okay to say emotional things in your statement. Things are sometimes left off a statement because creatives feel odd about sharing challenging things that happen. However, if your work is about angst or deep feelings, you have to share that information to complete the picture of your process and practice. It can feel scary to say it out loud, and you may worry if your audience will feel a certain way when they look at your work. That is not something you can control, but if you give them all the information they need, they are more likely to feel what you are trying to express. Without that information, your story as a whole falls flat. If you share emotions in your statement and someone reads it, he or she may go back to take a second look because you just gave them more to see.

If you have a repeating or a central image or a very strong conceptual through-line that is relevant to your practice, also add information to your statement about that concept. Let your viewer know why your work references a specific image and what your intention is for including it. Offer connection points to your viewer; if your work is incredibly conceptual or abstract and someone is trying to figure it out, give a little insight. If you are working hard not to be a starving artist, try providing more insight into your work, practice, and process—that may help drive sales. You cannot be afraid; your statement is where you get to tell your story completely; you own that space. Use it to be honest with yourself and your audience. Mystery rarely produces sales, meaning sales are much higher if you tell the purchaser what they're buying.

"Smart art galleries know it's not the words on paper but the emotion in the piece that makes clients pull out the credit card or checkbook. The gallery's number one concern is will this stuff sell? What your bio, artist's statement or resume articulates will be of no help if you don't make art that connects emotionally with buyers."

—*Jack White, The White Stripes*

3. THIRD PARAGRAPH

Use the third paragraph to talk about the elements of your work. As an example, what are the methods, materials, tools or techniques you use? Explain why you are pulling elements together into one piece. Share methods, materials, tools, or techniques used in your practice. Close the third paragraph by sharing your working process. For the audience reading this statement, think about how you go from idea to execution. What are your steps, how do you express your process, and how do you know when it is complete?

This notion can be challenging for students or those just learning because most of your work is assignment based; you often don't have time to create your practice or make your own work yet. Even with beginner work or assignments, think about how you go from the initial idea to your prep work, to outcome. Do you doodle or write notes first? Do you get right into the technique or materials? Do you research? Do you seek inspiration? Do you have to go for a walk? Share what your process is so that people understand how you came to create what it is they're experiencing.

take action

Grab your journal and work on your statement. When you're done, sit back and take some time away from it, then come back, read it, and ask yourself if it feels like you are generously sharing. Does it feel like you are answering questions that may arise from viewers? Obviously, you can't answer every question, people ask strange stuff, but if you read it and feel you are offering a sense of who you are as a creative, then you're on the right track. You might have a statement that someone wants to take the time to read, and you can feel proud of that. A well-written statement is a confidence booster.

PHILOSOPHY STATEMENT

If you are an academic, educator, curator, producer, administrator or event planner, to name a few service area examples, you will have a philosophical statement. Most of the items listed are similar to the statement; you will alter the elements to be experientially focused, meaning the first paragraph of your philosophy statement, instead of talking about what it looks like or sounds like, you'll share insight into the experience. It's your practice, but the visual, audio, or tactical aspects may be the work of others. When you work in this way, you are taking elements from other people and bringing them all together as a creative curator, and what you want to

FIG 6-5

Share all of the places and things that inspire you.

talk about is the visual, audio, or tactile experience. Share what you want your audience to get out of your statement, so they better understand your philosophy.

You will also share inspirations in a philosophy statement. Share what inspires you, what you are looking at, reading, listening to, or where you are traveling. Alter the middle paragraph, especially if your practice is services such as event planning. Talk about the emotional experience. The last thing on the philosophy statement is your working process or your ideation process. Your clients want to understand how it is you create ideas, produce things, or teach things.

If you are an educator, a teaching philosophy is a statement focused on your ideas, thoughts, and values about teaching and learning. It should also include examples of what you do in the classroom.

REFLECTION

Bios are short, factual, and written in the third person. Your statement is your chance to tell the story you most want to share and to offer insight into your practice. Don't get lost in dense jargon or mystery share why you are passionate. Be generous when writing a statement and provide answers. Follow directions, never hand over the bio or statement you have on file, and always prepare time to alter as needed.

HOW WILL THE CREATIVE USE THIS INFORMATION GOING FORWARD?

Directions: Take a few minutes to think about your bio and statement. Write down three items to explore further in the space provided before writing your final bio.

1. _____
2. _____
3. _____

BUILDING YOUR CREATIVE NETWORK

Directions: Think of people who can help you by reading your bio or statement before you put it out to the public. Write down these creative network connections in the space provided. Write a specific goal for contacting or making use of one of them.

1. _____
2. _____
3. _____

Goal: _____

SECTION III

ASSERT YOUR VALUE

CHAPTER SEVEN

Portfolios and Presentations

STYLE RULES THE ROOM

INTRODUCTION

Throughout this chapter, we will discuss putting together a professional portfolio. This necessary documentation of your work and practice goes by many different names and refers to visual, audio, and written forms. Names such as portfolio, collection, demo reel, deck, playbook, and dossier can mean different things, but they are all used to reference the same general idea throughout this chapter. That idea is a record of what you have created, in a format sharable with others.

TERMS THE CREATIVE NEEDS

PORTFOLIO A range or record of work by a person

DECK A presentation tool used to provide your audience with a quick overview of your work plan and a record of previous projects

PLAYBOOK A book containing diagrammed steps or plays for a specific project

DOSSIER A collection of documents about a particular person

RFP A request for proposal (RFP) is a type of bidding solicitation

RFQ A request for quote and qualification (RFQ) is a business process to invite suppliers to bid on a project

PUBLIC ART Art in any media staged in the public domain, usually outside and accessible to all

PHOTOGRAPH SLIDE FORMAT A single transparency frame that has been placed in a slide mount

WHAT THE CREATIVE NEEDS TO KNOW

Your portfolio should always be your absolute best. It should be images, words, or audio clips that highlight the very best you have to offer. Choose pieces that are the best representation of what you want to present. This chapter will provide a checklist to realize this.

WHAT THE CREATIVE WILL LEARN IN THIS CHAPTER

You will learn how to build a portfolio, what should go in it and what shouldn't, who is likely to review your collection, and what you need to know about the review process. You will learn why you do not want to put anything in a portfolio that is unfinished, poorly photographed, or recorded, along with tips for creating a strong collection to represent you, your work, and your practice.

PULLING TOGETHER YOUR PORTFOLIO

If you are applying to a gallery, for consideration for an exhibition, for graduate school, for an artist's call, for an RFP, or for an RFQ you will need a portfolio. Visual portfolios are often put together in slide format, such as a PowerPoint. A collection either focuses on your work personally (because you're a maker) or pulls together images and copy for a curated project or to sell a concept that you want to be funded or approved. Portfolios can also be called a collection (fashion and writing) or a reel (film and video); audio portfolios are called demo reels.

FIG 7-1

Your portfolio speaks for you.

The order of your visuals, audio clips, film clips, or written pieces matters. Never put your absolute best first. It seems counterintuitive, and you may be wondering why you wouldn't want to grab the attention of the reviewers by putting your very best first. Portfolios are reviewed by a committee. Imagine a committee is sitting in a space reviewing portfolios; they just finished with the previous applicant, and it's your turn. As your first slide begins, the committee is probably still talking about the last applicant's work. You don't want your very best to be the first one because the committee is not with you yet. They're still thinking about and talking about what they've just seen. So, show a good piece first, a better piece second, and your best third, then go from there.

You're probably not in the room during the review process. There are exceptions to this rule, but, in general, you are not there to represent yourself. You send your documents off, and the project manager organizes your materials, along with all the other applicants. The project manager may have spoken to you about your work, but because he or she does not get to vote, he or she can only say so much on your behalf. It's also important to understand that portfolios are often reviewed without any written information. It may be accompanied by information that feeds that portfolio, however. Nine times out of 10 the organization presents the slide or the clip with no informational copy on the first few rounds; therefore, your portfolio must speak for itself.

"Art is not what you see, but what you make others see."

—*Edgar Degas*

REVIEW PANELS: WEIGHING THE ODDS

Review committees are designed to give the fairest outcomes to the applicants, meaning the makeup will be a representation of ages, background diversities, gender, and disciplines. There's an odd number of people on the review committee who will vote, meaning the committees will have three, five, or seven people reviewing portfolios so that ties are not possible; with an odd number of people, someone will always serve as a tiebreaker. Also, sometimes your collection is reviewed blind. That means you may not get to put your name on your work when it is evaluated. This occurs because sometimes there could be bias or they don't want the individuals on the panel to know who made the work. So, they review blind or without names. They're choosing the work on what they see, hear, or read and not on what they know about the person. That can benefit you if you're unknown.

YOUR PORTFOLIO: TWENTY IMAGES STRONG

For the most part, a visual portfolio is always 20 images and no more. Why 20 images? Because before the digital era, images were taken in photograph slide format. Slides were presented or stored in a slide jacket that fit 20 slides inside the pockets. This became an industry standard to present 20 images or put 20 concepts in your deck. Writing samples are often limited to five, depending on the length.

WHAT SHOULD YOUR PORTFOLIO INCLUDE?

The images, audio files, or film stills in your portfolio should include half full original images or sound. The other half can be close-ups or short clips. You can also do less than 20 if you do not feel you have 20 strong pieces. You could include 15 images or film stills in your portfolio, and 10 of those pieces can be full, with five close-up or clips.

Read directions, and if they state that you can only submit five audio files, film stills, or images, do precisely that. If you are submitting a demo reel or audio file, keep it short. Slate a film reel in the front and end.

It can be difficult sometimes to select which pieces to include in your portfolio. One reason this can be a challenge is that you may create many different things, as so many creatives do. In that case, group audio files, film stills, or images by like things next to each other in the presentation. As an example, place all black-and-white drawings together and then all the paintings together and then all the sculptures together, because most people who are going to review portfolios will be experts in your field and will make the leap and understand you are attempting to show variety. Jumping around mediums is likely to confuse your viewer. The same thing goes for demo reels—don't bounce back and forth with different aspect ratios in the same string of clips. Review panelists will look at hundreds of collections, so don't create confusion around the work you are presenting.

LOOK GOOD SOUND GOOD

You can take a good photograph of anything with a smartphone. The most important thing is to be mindful of the lighting and the surrounding space. If it is an audio file, compress it so that it's easy for the reviewer. Sometimes your submissions are reviewed by the panelist at home before

FIG 7-2

Use the collection you are showing to highlight only your best work.

they come together for voting. Never include an image where you've sat a painting on the ground, as an example, and then you took a photograph of it, and you can see the grass poking up at the bottom of the painting, or of a sculpture up on a stool where you've placed a wrinkled piece of fabric.

People notice and it is instantly disappointing. It's better to crop in on a piece and not show the whole piece to get rid of any distracting elements.

Learn to use photo editing programs. This will save you time, money, and the embarrassment of having to submit subpar work. Learning a photo editing program means you will know how to crop and color correct. Learn audio and video editing software that will allow you to showcase your practice. It is important because it is the little things that separate the finalists from those in the no pile.

THE LOOK OF YOUR PORTFOLIO

You may have some images that are horizontal and some that are vertical. If this is the case, create a border to the edge of the frame. If you create a border, do it on every slide, meaning some full-bleed images should have the same border for consistency. The edge should be neutral; always use a middle gray or a black as your background frame because it highlights the image no matter what it is. You won't know what kind of projector they have or what the lighting in the room is like, so you don't know what that's going to look like. You don't want to use white as the border frame because it can blow out whatever work you're trying to present. Your work is going to be presented by a large projector and depending on that quality of light, if it's white, it will blow out.

If you have the opportunity, test run a projection before sending your portfolio out to see what it looks like on a wall. Take the time to review it and ask others what they think. Project your best and your most common images with no border, a white border, a grey border, and a black border to see which showcases your work best.

"It's not what you look at that matters, it's what you see."

—Henry David Thoreau

COMPANION LIST

If you make it past the first few rounds, or if the panel has questions, they are likely to then ask the project manager for additional information. This means you have to create a companion list. It is created in case the reviewers have questions; they can then refer to this list to see a title, medium, and date. Do not include pricing on this list. If your portfolio includes visuals, include thumbnails on your companion list.

DEMO REELS

Demo reels are video and audio portfolios. They include five to 10 examples, depending on what the application calls for. Video and film clips should never run over two minutes and 12 seconds per clip. Audio clips should also be short, and the entire audio reel should not run over four minutes and 12 seconds. These times restrictions exist because industry standards have revealed that human attention spans are only available for that amount of time. Looking at a still image, the human brain stays engaged for just eight seconds. Anything beyond those numbers, humans lose focus.

When you look at many YouTube videos that have gone viral, they are around two minutes because that's how much capacity we have. You'll have to change your reel sometimes if you are given specific parameters. If you do not follow application instructions, you will likely be removed from the applicant pool before the reviewers even get to experience your work.

FIG 7-3

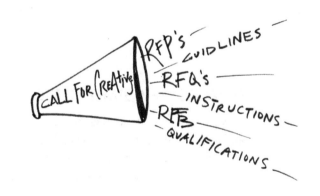

You have to do your homework regarding formatting. Because technology changes rapidly it is impossible to suggest a specific format, software, or cloud location. The best thing you can do is have clips fully edited as ready-to-go compressed files. It will allow you to place, drop, or drag them wherever requested. Be the one who can apply to anything quickly because you have everything ready. Spending time, every time, on prep means you are less likely to apply to a call. If you are ready, you can apply to everything.

CALL FOR ARTISTS/CREATIVES

A call for artists or creatives is used in public art, education, and museums to ask creatives to apply for projects. A request for proposal (RFP) or a request for quote and qualification (RFQ) are types of bidding where a company announces funding is available for a specific project or program and companies place bids for the project's completion.

No one project, program, or organization has the same guidelines; they all request a little something different, and if the application is coming from a governmental agency, there will be an even more in-depth reading of instructions required. There are many sites online to find calls to artists and RFP and RFQ requests for creatives. It is essential time spent because sending unsolicited reels and portfolios will not get you what you are looking for. Mostly, they will go ignored.

FIG 7-4

There are many stages to a review panel.

HOW REVIEW PANELS WORK

Once the review panel assembles, they work through all the submissions, one by one, until each applicant has been reviewed several times. They take a vote, recorded by the organization staff, to select finalists and alternatives. The panel then makes recommendations to the project manager. Often, the finalists will come in at the second round for an interview or an expanded presentation. An RFP in public art, as an example, allows you to apply with something you've done in the past or apply with a proposal concept. If this is the case, then in the next round they will ask you to flush out your ideas further. The next step after the review panel concludes is to get full approval of the finalists from the governing body. This could be a board, an appointed committee, a city council, or a dean's department, to name a few. It can take time, which is why it is essential to read the guidelines to learn about the estimated timetable. Once approval happens, the selected creative is notified and then give a timeline for funding and completion of the project or the event date; follow all guidelines and payment procedures.

> *"Be who you are and say what you feel because those who mind don't matter and those who matter don't mind."*
>
> *—Dr. Suess*

Because the review panel will make recommendations to the project manager specifically for the no votes, you can learn a little bit about what was on the minds of the panelists. It is a generous thing the creative community does. Feedback and notes are often available to the applicants to create a better application in the future and to make it a stronger, more competitive community. Take advantage of this and always ask if recommendations were collected to help improve your practice.

BECOMING FEEDBACK FRIENDLY

Get in the habit of building in intentional feedback on your work, and applying for opportunities will give you that. It can be uncomfortable, as creatives, to hear feedback. The way to be a professional is to get another set of eyes and ears on your work and then listen to other people's opinions to make your work stronger. If you apply for a lot of things and nothing is happening, ask for feedback from people you trust. Be brave and show confidence by admitting you don't know everything; welcoming input from others could lead to better outcomes. Sometimes you need to get another set of eyes or ears to see what you're not seeing. Be mindful of who you ask for feedback. I am sure your mom is lovely, but if she is not trained in your field, she can't offer a useful opinion. When someone is critiquing your work who has similar training or more, he or she know what to look for. Keep those members of your tribe close and request their assistance often.

Confidence is showing up, taking in feedback, saying thank you, and processing on your own time. Just say, "That's excellent feedback. I'll take that in. Thank you!" If you're the one person who does that, you are humble; you honor the experience and the panel of experts' time—they will remember.

take action

Always get a second set of eyes or ears to review your documents before you send them out. If you receive feedback that something does not make sense, listen. Pause, regroup, and rework. Choose something you are working on right now and ask someone you trust to review it. Buy them a cup of coffee or make them dinner and ask them for their honest feedback.

PRESENTATIONS

There are many different presentation software and tools, with new ones popping up every day. Presentation software, in its traditional use, is outdated and overused. If you find yourself in a position to pitch a project, a conference, a talk, a lecture, or presentation and you are requested to present via a presentation program, there are nontraditional ways to do it. Imagine an opportunity to use a presentation program as a background or as set design. You could ask if the projection could flood the whole space you are presenting in and immerse yourself and your audience in a landscape or an environment that will tell your story much better than numbers or statistics.

take action

Do you pay attention to talks using projected presentation programs? Would you if it were a more immersive experience? Next time you create a presentation that stands out, design an experience that is projected behind you and that offers a deepening of the content you are presenting by setting the stage for the journey you will take your audience on.

FIG 7-5

Use your presentation slides as a background set design.

REFLECTION

As creatives, putting our portfolio, collection, demo reel, deck, playbook, or dossier out there for all the world to see can be intimidating. Remember, we are often much harder on ourselves than anyone else ever would be. We see all of the flaws and imperfections. With bravery and confidence, however, you can change your fears into learning lessons. If you can stay open to input and feedback, you can grow and adapt to the point where you see each application as an opportunity. If you know ahead of time that you will receive feedback for improvement, it will be easier to release your work into the world. Even if you don't get the gig, there are always new things to learn. Stay open when sharing your portfolio; this isn't personal, it is professional.

HOW WILL THE CREATIVE USE THIS INFORMATION GOING FORWARD ?

Directions: Take a few minutes to think about how, specifically, you will create a unique and memorable portfolio. Write down three ideas in the space provided.

1. _____
2. _____
3. _____

BUILDING YOUR CREATIVE NETWORK

Directions: Think of three to five people in your life who know your work and practice and who will support you as an extra set of eyes and ears. Write down who these connections are in the space provided, followed by a specific action.

1. _____
2. _____
3. _____

CHAPTER EIGHT

Pricing and Sales

CRUNCH THE NUMBERS

INTRODUCTION

How to price your creative talents can feel very personal. This chapter will focus on a professional approach to treating your creative practice as a business. The most important aspect of your creative practice, after the act of making it, is getting paid, which means knowing what to charge, how to bill, and how to sell. Throughout this chapter, you will receive guidance and concrete steps, with details on how to get paid, promptly, for your creative work.

TERMS THE CREATIVE NEEDS

EXPENDABLE MATERIALS Supplies that are consumed in use and must then be replaced, such as paint

REUSABLE MATERIALS Supplies that are used again and again, such as rulers

KEYSTONE One hundred percent mark up selling at twice the price it was bought or produced

WHOLESALE PRICING The cost of a good sold where the wholesaler charges a price higher than he or she paid to the producer

RETAIL PRICING The total price charged for a product sold to a customer, which includes the manufacturer's cost plus a retail markup

INVOICE A list of goods or services provided, on a written a statement as a bill

REPS Act as a sales representative for a person, company or product

AGENT A person who acts on behalf of another person or group

BRICK AND MORTAR STORE Traditional street-side business that deals with its customers face to face in a building that the company owns or rents

MERCHANT SERVICES Authorized financial services that allow a business to accept credit card or bank debit card transactions using online ordering or point of sales systems

MINIMUM ORDER The smallest amount or number that may be ordered in one delivery, usually to spread delivery costs over an economical number of units

WHAT THE CREATIVE NEEDS TO KNOW

To have a successful business as a creative, you have to, at the very least, understand the payments process. If you can hire out the actual work of it, that is all the better, but you should have a basic grasp of the mechanics of how it all works as a starting point.

WHAT THE CREATIVE WILL LEARN IN THIS CHAPTER

This chapter will provide steps for developing pricing, details on creating invoices, insight into using reps and agents, and tips for avoiding pitfalls when it comes to billing and payments.

"If you wrote something for which someone sent you a cheque,
if you cashed the cheque and it didn't bounce, and if you then
paid the light bill with the money, I consider you talented."

—Stephen King

FIG 8-1

START WITH YOUR HOMEWORK

When you're determining pricing, it is essential to do research, beyond anything you will receive in this book. This book can offer tips and strategies, but the market changes regularly and to keep up you must do homework. To figure out where prices for your category/industry are currently at, you'll want to jump online and run a few searches to get a sense of pricing. Use online search engines as a starting point to determine retail costs of the goods or service you provide. Are you just starting out? Then you may need to lower your prices a bit from the average you find in your research. Are you a mid-career creative? Then stick to the higher end; you've put your time in and can command higher prices. The highest rate will always go to the creative who is both well established and has a record of sales to prove value. You must build up to that.

Never price your goods or services too low. It is not a good idea to go so little as to try and compete with big box stores or large online companies. If that is your focus, you'll likely fail because you're not a massive billion-dollar company with thousands of employees and you don't have 20,000 widgets to sell. Eventually, you'll discover that you're not making any money and it's not worth it. Another thing with going too low is that it negatively impacts the entire industry that we all work in. If you decide to be the cheapest one, you're taking the work away from the field, but only for a short term. If you're the cheapest one and you get lots of work, you probably have less experience, and something you wouldn't expect can derail your whole operation, and/or it is likely that you won't be able to keep pace. So, plan on pricing in the lower-middle road as you are starting out and moving to the upper middle as your career progresses, until you achieve the fullest pay possible.

It's also vital that you don't think you deserve the highest pricing as you are beginning your career. If you do that, if you're always stuck at that price point without much room to go higher, you can't grow. Because you're selling to clients at a high price point, you limit your market right away and flood it with only those high price points; you can't go back and lower prices. You should never go backward. The only thing that you can do in that scenario is make different work. Then you can say, "This is different work. This is the different material. The lower price point is because of this reason." That's the only way to work around that. You always want to be mindful that you don't put the too-high price too soon, and you don't let anyone do that to you (meaning a gallery or an agent). You always want to leave room for growth.

> *"People are willing to work free, and they are willing*
> *to work for a reasonable wage but offer them just*
> *a small payment, and they will walk away."*
>
> —*Dan Ariely*

WHOLESALE VS. RETAIL COSTS—EXPLAINED

Wholesale is the manufacturer's cost, you being the manufacturer. You made the product or object. As you read further, you will find steps for identifying how to determine your wholesale costs. If you are selling directly to the consumer, such as through an online shop, then you will price at retail. Retail is what the end customer pays who is buying your product or object. When you walk into any store, you can pretty much bet that that store purchased whatever item you are buying for half of what it cost, if not more. To keystone is when you take your price (wholesale) and the buyer or rep marks it up double. An example is if you are selling products or objects for $1 to a buyer that has a store, and they price the product or object at $2. That is a keystone markup.

FIG 8-2

Offer wholesale and retail prices.

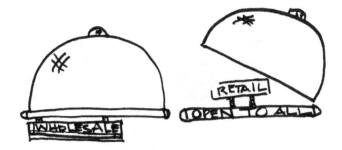

You never want to publicize your wholesale costs. Those are between you and your buyers or your reps. You never put that out publicly because you don't want people to know that the actual cost. You want them only to have the retail costs in their minds.

THE BASIC PRICING FORMULA

Here is a simple formula that you can start with and expand to fit your needs. Begin understanding what your costs are so you can keep track of them and so you know how to bill people. This formula breaks down pricing objects and services separately.

STEPS FOR SELLING OBJECTS

1. You total your material costs first. These are expendable materials, not renewable. If only a portion of your materials are used, divide the price by the percentage and use that number. As an example, one tube of paint is $10 and you used half; your materials cost would be $5.

2. Add your labor cost. This is not you; it is others you hire.

3. Will there be shipping costs? If you need to ship or deliver, add those costs.

4. Add a 15 to 20% administration fee on all work to cover those costs.

EXAMPLE:

Suppose, for an object you made, the materials cost $100, then you hired someone to make it and you paid them $100, it cost $100 to ship, and you add 20% (in this case $200), and, with all these fees, charge a total of $1,000. Admin costs can include things such as insurance; office supply costs (paper and printer ink); and your time to write the invoice, prepare the shipment, and respond to e-mails and phone calls from the client. This means you would pocket $500 for the object; that is your fee as a creative.

BUT WAIT; THERE'S MORE

Are you sure $500 is enough? An additional step before pricing the object at wholesale is to add a 40% artist's fee on top. That means step five is to take your $500 spent on materials, labor, shipping, and administration and add 40% or, in this case, $400 to the total. To the $1,000 price, we add $400, making the wholesale cost $1,400. This leaves the creator with a $900 profit. Your object is offered at $1,400, then would retail at a keystone mark-up of double. Now your object is for sale at $2,800 with you receiving $1,400 and the gallery, agent, or rep earning $1,400.

As a creative, it is crucial to understand why the gallery or rep takes 50%. Creatives can feel frustrated with agents, reps, and galleries because they will take your wholesale price keystone. The frustration comes in because creatives often feel the rep or gallerists isn't doing the same amount of work as the creative, yet they offer you something that you must pay for. You're paying for the access to all the potential buyers that, without your gallerists' connections, wouldn't know you exist.

They put you on their website, give you space to show, they create and mail show cards, and, most importantly, they talk about you with clients. For all of that, they deserve equal pay.

BASIC PRICING FORMULA FOR SERVICES

Creative services might include things such as photographers, curators, event planners, speakers, producers, or musician gigs, to name a few. Again, you must research what the industry standard pricing is and what the market will bear.

STEPS FOR PRICING SERVICES

1. First, total your cost of labor (industry standard dollar per hour) and multiply that number by the number of hours worked.

    NOTE: The hours worked can be yours, but sometimes it is not. If you must hire subcontractors, you also need to calculate that into the total bill due.
2. Next is your admin costs. This can include insurance, overhead, office supplies, and so on.
3. Often service-based work means the additional costs of presentation materials, as with graphic and interior designers, architects. This anything you have to print for the client.
4. Once you have a total of the first three steps, then you are going to do an automatic keystone before you give the price point, because in services, there is not a wholesale/retail; there is just a cost.
5. Add on 40%. This is important because in the service industry you may be asked to offer a discount or a finder's fee if you are brought in by another service provider.

As an example, if you are a wedding photographer and you got the job because the event planner recommended you, it is industry standard that you would give the planner a 10% appreciation fee. If you are going to work in the service industry, you need to capture kickbacks on all fronts. There is nothing wrong with it. There is nothing negative about it. It is a loyalty-based system. So, if you are, say, an event planner, you always use the same caterer, the same venue, the same DJ. It is kind of like when you work in restaurants, and even though you are the server, you tip out the host and the bartenders and cooks. You do that because that's how it works. You have to be loyal because if you are not, nobody is going to kick back to you. What comes around goes around, and if you kickback 10%, then the next time you recommend someone they will do the same for you.

That is the simple version of how you do the math on being a service provider.

FIG 8-3

Creating pricing means experimenting and moving options around until there's a good fit.

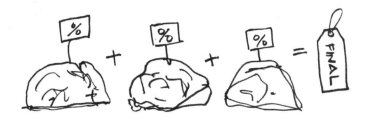

THE MATH ON SHIPPING

Most of the time, you're going to pay to ship any products, goods, or artwork to the showroom, gallery, agent or rep. If it doesn't sell, they'll cover the cost of shipping it back to you.

Know that you're usually responsible for the shipping. You have to factor that cost in. Shipping is expensive. It's something you have to investigate frequently so that you do not lose money. If you know someone's ordering something or requesting something and you know they're out of the state or if they say at any point, "I'm going to need it shipped here," jump online and investigate. Get an estimate on the cost and factor that into the price.

Shipping might also include local deliveries. For this, you will factor in if there is a truck rental, the cost of fuel, and if any additional rental equipment is needed, such as a dolly or packing blankets.

FIG 8-4

There are several factors in determining shipping costs.

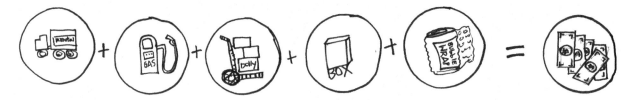

DISCOUNT REQUESTS

If you have an agent, a rep, or anyone who is selling your work on your behalf, your contracts will include information regarding discounts. An example of when a cut might be requested is if a gallery or a showroom is working with an interior designer who comes in and says, "Hey, I'm a designer. I want the designer's discount of 20%." This is the same as the kickback loyalty program with service providers. What a 20% discount means for the creatives is you're going to have to eat a 10% loss, and your agent or rep is going to eat a 10% loss. This is another reason to add the 40% markup: so that you do not have any surprises when your payment arrives. Because you signed a contract agreeing to the terms of discounts, they will have permission to offer a discount without contacting you, and it will be reflected in your payment.

A discount is an appropriate business to business transaction. A discount is not appropriate, however, if you are a maker and are a part of an open studio and you allow retail customers to buy at wholesale or at a significant discount. If you sell direct to a retail customer, you are still required to cut your agent, rep, or gallerist. This, too, is likely written in your contract.

If you have an agent, a rep, or anyone who is selling your work on your behalf, always read your contracts from them and ask them to explain or get advice, if needed, to ensure you understand all of the terms.

INVOICES

If you didn't get an e-mail stating your bill is due or something in the mail that said this bill is due, would you forget to pay your bills? Likely, you would; we all would. Invoice is the system by which creatives and freelancers get paid.

It is important for creatives to recognize that just because you do work and you deliver on time, no one is going to have a check ready and waiting for you. Instead, they are going to say, "Okay, send me a bill and I will pay you." The use of an invoice is important for both your records so that everything is trackable. People need invoices because that is how they remember their bills, but they also need invoices for their tracking system. There are certain ways you need to create invoices for the people who work in accounting, purchasing, and procurement; they can't just look at something think, "Yeah, I get it; that's cool. We will just pay that." Nope. They are going to request specific items on your invoice.

You never want to deliver anything without an invoice as proof or evidence. Your invoice is your agreement between you and whoever you are delivering or providing service to. It is an agreement that you will give them what you say on the invoice, and they will pay you what you are requesting.

Use cloud software to manage your invoices and bookkeeping. There are many versions you can purchase. It makes an end-of-year tax prep so much more comfortable. In fact, ask your tax preparer what software they would recommend for making their work easier when it comes to doing your tax work.

STEPS TO CREATING AN INVOICE

1. Letterhead: When creating an invoice, you always want to have your letterhead at the top.

2. The word "invoice". NOTE: You can also use this same system if you are giving someone an estimate, and it is not an invoice you need to pay on. Then, you can write "estimate" in big, bold letters.

3. Your contact information: After the word "invoice," you then want your name, your company name, and your address, so they know where to mail the check.

4. Your contact information continued: You must always have a phone number and an e-mail address. This is required to process the check.

5. Client contact name: Name of the person you are submitting the invoice to comes next. If you don't know the contact person's name, then you need to ask. This should be written on the invoice as "Attention to:"

6. Client contact information: The name of the company, individual, or organization that you are sending this to.

    NOTE: If you are working with an event planner, they are likely not the bill payer. They are the intermediary. So, find out the contact name of the end client who is paying the bill.

7. Client contact information continued: Include the client's address, phone number, and e-mail address.

8. Date: The date of both the event (if relevant) and the invoice submission date should be included.

9. Terms: Your payment terms should be written on the invoice, such as Net 30, which means that means from the time the invoice is received, they have 30 days to issue the check.

10. Description: You want to write either the scope of work for service providers or product delivered. Note: If you are a maker and it is a product or object, you want to include item description and quantity.

11. Total: The tally of costs and total payment due.

12. Invoice number: Many companies will request an invoice number, so get in the habit of creating one and on the top portion of your invoice include a numbering system.

FIG 8-5

Create a template for invoicing clients.

13. Client ID number: Assign your clients an alpha or numeric code and then always use that same code as the client identification number.

Create a template invoice right now, in the program of your choice, so that when you are ready to bill next, you will have everything in place to fill out the areas and ship the invoice off quickly. Fast turnaround time is impressive!

tip

Payment terms of Net 30 are industry standard, unless you work for a government agency because government agencies can only pay you when they get every signature required and the invoice goes through all the proper channels. It can mean payment at Net 60 or up to Net 90. It is just part of doing business. You have to accept that. By government agency, I mean universities, city, state, county, or federal entities.

PAYMENT TYPES

Depending on what industry you work in, a lot of people won't mail your checks. They will want you to run their credit card, which means you have to get a merchant services account, which is easy now, because of products such as Square and PayPal. Before you set up your business and begin to work for others, have a plan on how you will take payment; you don't want to get caught off guard.

MINIMUMS

If you are a small goods maker, do your homework and find out, for your industry, about minimums. If you are going to work in stationery, gifts, tabletop, accessories, or clothing, to name a few, no one is going to call you and say, "I want to order just one." This is obviously not the case for original works of art because there is only one. But, if you are having anything mass produced or manufactured, people order in minimums, usually by the dozen or half dozen. Be brave by asking other people in your industry what they do regarding minimums; those who are generous will offer up that sort of information in a minute. You can also ask friends you might know, who are on the buying end, what they see industry minimums being. If you are a service provider, this isn't normally something you concern yourself with.

WHAT IF THEY DON'T PAY YOU?

Working to get paid is one of the worst things you will have to deal with as a professional in the creative fields. This is where confidence up front will make it easier for you to keep the checks coming on time. One way to avoid having to chase down payments is to tell the client they must place a credit card on file that you will run if their payment is late. You can also use this credit card to collect a deposit because you never want to start work on a project without at least 25% (nonrefundable) down. Make sure you are paid before you deliver or ship.

REPRESENTATION

Representation doesn't mean you had a show at a gallery once and they sold a piece for you. It says you have signed a contract with an agent, a rep, or a gallerist who has a legal binding agreement with you. One thing it lists is where their region is, which means once signed, you cannot sell through anyone else in the state(s) or territories, and you should honor that. As an example, if the contract you signed with your agent states you cannot sell or work with anyone else in the state of California, then all sales or gigs must run through that agent and that allows them to receive the cut they are due.

Before jumping directly into working with reps or agents, do your homework. Research your industry to determine who the people with the right level of experience are. And, if an agent or rep contacts you directly, don't get caught up and excited before you pause and investigate their background, their pricing structure, and their current and past client lists. It takes bravery to sit still and educate yourself on their practice, but in the long run that upfront work will pay off as a payday because you found the right agent and you won't have regret because you didn't work with someone soliciting you.

REFLECTION

Everything discussed in this chapter shifts and changes depending on many market variables, and there are templates available for all types of pricing for creatives. What is most important, though, is to create a network of industry-connected people. You will need them throughout your career to ask advice from and discuss industry trends. It is essential to have these connections both locally and nationally, as pricing varies widely, depending on location. That isn't always something captured by going online alone. Having relationships in the markets you want to work in will give you fair market pricing. Be brave and demand deposits, require credit cards to be on file, enforce your Net 30 terms, and always provide an invoice within one week of delivery of goods or services.

HOW WILL THE CREATIVE USE THIS INFORMATION GOING FORWARD?

Directions: Take a few minutes to think about the steps you will take to use the information from this chapter in your creative practice. Write down three ideas in the space provided.

1. _____

2. _____

3. _____

BUILDING YOUR CREATIVE NETWORK

Directions: Think of people, organizations, or other resources that can help you by allowing you to ask questions that came up for you in this chapter. Write down these creative network connections in the space provided. Write a specific goal for contacting one of them.

1. _____

2. _____

3. _____

Goal: _____

CHAPTER NINE

Contracts and Coverage

A HANDSHAKE ISN'T ENOUGH

INTRODUCTION

It seems a simple thing to have two parties sign an agreement for the delivery of goods or services, yet for creatives this can be a huge barrier. This chapter shares the positives and the pitfalls of creating and requesting contracts for projects. A lot of creatives lose money, deals, and opportunities because they were too uncomfortable to ask for a signed agreement. Like all professions, creatives need coverage too, and a handshake is not enough of an agreement. This chapter also covers types of insurance you should consider as a creative.

TERMS THE CREATIVE NEEDS

CONTRACT A written agreement concerning employment or sales, enforceable by law

COMMISSION Authorizes the production of something such as a work of art

CONSIGNMENT Agreement to pay a supplier of goods after the goods are sold

ELECTRONIC SIGNATURE Data in digital form attached to an electronically transmitted document as verification of the sender's intent to sign the document

BID Offer (a certain price) for goods or service

BROKER A person who buys and sells goods or assets for others

QUOTE To give someone an estimated price of a job or service

ESTIMATE An approximate calculation of the value, number, quantity, or extent of something

SCOPE OF WORK (SOW) The area in an agreement where the work to be performed is described

WHAT THE CREATIVE NEEDS TO KNOW

It is essential to know how to put together a contract or a basic agreement so that everyone understands the terms before goods or services are exchanged. Contracts are a necessary part

FIG 9-1

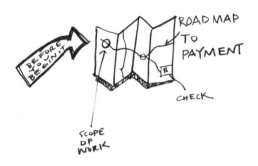

of working as a creative. Even if you work for someone else, you will likely be involved in the process of contracts if you are in the creative fields.

WHAT THE CREATIVE WILL LEARN IN THIS CHAPTER

If you're going to choose a career as a creative, you'll work freelance, which means you will deal with contracts. In this chapter, we will cover how contracts work, why they're essential, and why, if you find yourself with a large-scale contract, you may need a lawyer to assist you.

BEFORE YOU BEGIN

As you begin any new project, pause before jumping right in to ensure you are protecting yourself, your practice, and the work you produce. Make sure you are clear on the scope of work that you have agreed to deliver. Take this on because sometimes people won't even think to offer you a contract or an agreement. The reason it's beneficial that you take the initiative and put together a contract or a basic agreement if one is not offered is so that everyone is on the same page. Often, creatives are excited to receive a commission or a paying gig and they fail to ensure payment. This must be the first step before you begin any work at all.

Think of your practice like that of a handyman. No one would come into your home to repair something without having you sign an agreement for a quote, an estimate, or a bid, so why would you do work without the same? Create a sample agreement including terms. Search online for samples for your field.

COMMISSIONS

If you produce work on commission, always sign an agreement before you began working on a project; this ensures both you and your client agree on the details of the project. It will not offend clients to sign an agreement—all other professions do this, from plumbers to dentists to lawyers.

DEPOSITS

If you produce through commissions, custom work, or consignment, always get a deposit. If it's a more significant project, the industry standard is to get one third down at the beginning of the project, then one third at the halfway point, and the final third at delivery. If it's a smaller project, then get half down at the start and the other half at delivery. It can depend on what you're doing, if it is a service or good, but always get a deposit in the beginning. Note that the deposit is non-refundable. If they pay a deposit and you spend time working on their project and then they change their minds or want to cancel the rest of the project they can. But you did work on it and took time, so you need to be compensated for that. You cannot work on a project and allow it to be canceled or changed without being paid. You can build in a process where the client could eventually exchange it for something else but not for a refund because you would be out of that money. Instead, you say to your client, "Potentially I can resell this. I can make you a new one, but the deposit stands."

AGREEMENTS

For the contract or agreement to be legally binding, you must include a few essential elements:

1. All parties must agree to an offer made by one party and accepted by the other. This is the "what will be delivered" section of the contract.
2. Something of value (goods or services) must be exchanged for something else of value (money, as an example).
3. Specifics should be provided. This is where you can fill in the scope of work. If it is a product, then you want to include the size, shape, and color. If you are offering a service, then you want to be clear about what exactly you will deliver.
4. The agreement must be signed and dated by both parties.
5. Both parties' names and contact information should be included.

"Thoroughly read all your contracts. I really mean thoroughly."

—Bret Michaels

Always read any contract given to you before you sign it. If you are creating the contract, proofread it yourself and ask someone else to read it, too; this ensures there are not any typos or general errors. If the contract feels complicated, hire a lawyer to review it for you before signing.

ELECTRONIC AGREEMENTS

It is possible to create a contract by piecing together several e-mails exchanged between the creative and the client. An example might be to request the client to reply to the e-mail, agreeing that they understand everything written and that you wish to make no changes. Once they reply "agreed," you can use that as a contract, but it is still better to have a specific signed agreement. This may feel like a step that you don't have time for, but you also don't have time to chase payments or recreate something because you misunderstood or didn't get specific enough. Take the time to write down what you agreed to ensure that the client knows they owe you for the work you are doing for them and you're going to get paid. Without written documentation, you have no proof and no guarantee of payment. Never start any of the work until everyone agrees. This will save you a lot of headaches and heartbreaks.

FIG 9-2

BUILD FOLDER FOR EVERY PROJECT

If you create agreements through e-mail exchanges instead of writing up formal contacts, get very organized with your inbox. Create folders with each different project or client name and put all e-mails related to that project into that folder so that you have them as back up should any part of the agreed-upon terms go south. Create a plan to always get everything in writing.

"Verbal contracts are about as useful as a fart on a treadmill."

—Robert Rinder

tip

Use your e-mail system and set up folders or another method for yourself to be professional and organized. You can file thousands of e-mails and keep everything so you have a paper trail. You need that as evidence if anything ever goes wrong. Set up this system now before you are too busy.

WHEN TO HIRE A LAWYER

Understand what you are signing, and if there's any confusion about a particular passage ask the person who sent you the contract. There's no shame in admitting that you don't know what a sentence or section means. If you still don't understand, especially if it's a multiple-page contract, have a lawyer review the agreement. Hire a lawyer who is an expert in contracts and explain it to you in layman's term. Pay legal experts to advise you for your peace of mind.

If you have already delivered work and are awaiting payment, it's worth the investment to have a lawyer look into why your payment is delayed. Demand that you are treated like any other professional who deserves to be paid for their goods or services. Getting brave and showing your confidence strengthens our industry and eradicates the phrase "starving artist."

INCORPORATING

One of the smartest things you can do as a creative is to set up a limited liability corporation or LLC. Corporate status gives you a better return on taxes because you can write a great deal more off as deductions than you can if you are a sole proprietor. Incorporation offers access to more contracts because many companies and organizations will not hire sole proprietors due to liability. You also gain access to group rates on insurances. You can do it yourself if you feel comfortable with paperwork and governmental processes. If not, hire a lawyer who can help you incorporate.

take action

Research the procedures where you live for incorporating a business. Start online at the Secretary of State office or the Corporation Commission; the office that handles this will be different depending on where you live. Research it now so when you are ready you will have all the information at your fingertips.

BUSINESS INSURANCE

Why should you, as a creative, carry a business insurance policy? For starters, with insurance coverage, you will get more work, more contracts, and more gigs because clients want to know you're covered for certain liabilities. Business insurance will not only cover your practice, should you get sued, it will also cover the loss of property or equipment. As an example, if you have a studio fire, or if your computer were stolen, a business insurance policy offers protection and peace of mind. If you host an event, such as an open studio or a show and you invite clients or strangers, they could injure themselves on your property. If they were to harm themselves in any way, just by stepping a foot on your property, you'd need insurance to cover that. Talk to an insurance broker about the best business insurance in your area as your needs and requirements will vary based on your location. Business insurance cost very little compared to what you could get out of it, such as lucrative contracts and coverage in case of a lawsuit.

BROKERS

There are different levels, types, and costs of insurance for your business and you should let a broker help sort it out. A broker will find several insurance policy offerings; it doesn't cost you anything. Once you explain the scope of work you're doing and what you need insurance to cover, they will do all of the hunting for quotes. You just have to tell them what your needs are. They'll give you options. You pick how much you want to spend, what kind of services you want. Then, you pay the insurance company directly. The broker will then contact the insurance company you choose and help walk you through the setup. They are paid by the insurance companies, not you. Use a broker and get the coverage you need and deserve.

FIG 9-3

A broker helps identify insurance options.

HEALTH INSURANCE

Another kind of insurance to think about is health insurance. A lot of creatives can find the idea of obtaining health insurance overwhelming. Another benefit of having an LLC is you can buy insurance as a group, which is less expensive than buying as a single person. You will also receive many more options of plans to choose from. If you are married, you can purchase group policy and put your partner on it and your children. Again, look for an insurance broker who will do all the work for you. Carry health insurance because if you are self-employed as a creative and something happens to your health leaving you unable to work for a while, you'll have limited options.

OTHER INSURANCE TYPES TO CONSIDER

If you use a vehicle for your business, in any way, discuss vehicle insurance with your broker or insurance agent.

Include property insurance in your business policy in case you have to stop work due to property damage. If you work from a laptop in a home office, your homeowner's insurance will often cover loss or damage, but it is worth double checking.

FIG 9-4

If you create products for sensitive user groups, such as children, then you need product liability insurance. This insurance protects you and your business against claims of personal injury or property damage caused by products you made. As an example, if you make baby bibs with ribbon sown on them and a baby rips it off and chokes, you need insurance for that. This insurance covers your practice if you have to pay out, but it also covers your legal fees and court costs.

Business Owners Policy (BOP) is insurance that combines several things and provides interruption insurance, which covers the loss of income from an emergency that disrupts your ability to run your business.

If you have employees working with you, then you must carry workers' compensation insurance. The laws requiring coverage vary from state to state, so it's important to learn what the specific laws are in the state in which you are operating. In most states, you can get workers' compensation insurance from the same insurance carrier as your business insurance, or you can get it from a payroll company if you choose to use one to pay your employees. Research or ask your insurance agent about the laws and requirements for your business's location.

REFLECTION

If you want to have a successful career as a creative, request contracts, agreements, and deposits. Have the confidence to demand that you get paid on time and the right amount—it will make all the difference to your practice. Carry the necessary insurance to cover yourself and your practice. Know that you do not have to do it alone; consult with lawyers, brokers, and anyone else willing to help you.

Professionals in other industries would never dream of trying to do things such as contracts and insurance on their own, so why should you as a creative? You shouldn't; get support and get covered.

HOW WILL THE CREATIVE USE THIS INFORMATION GOING FORWARD?

Directions: Take a few minutes to think about how, precisely, you will prepare yourself with the knowledge you need for contracts and insurances. Write down three ideas you will take away from this chapter in the space provided.

1. _____

2. _____

3. _____

BUILDING YOUR CREATIVE NETWORK

Directions: Think of people, organizations, or other resources that can help you act immediately to get the coverage you need. Write down these creative network connections in the space provided. Think about lawyers, brokers, and other creatives who have gone through this already. Write a specific goal for contacting or making use of one of them.

1. _____

2. _____

3. _____

Goal: _____

CHAPTER TEN

Nonprofit vs. For Profit, Plus Grants

THE MISSION IS THE DIFFERENCE

INTRODUCTION

Nonprofit and for-profit business models are useful for creatives to explore. This chapter will lay out the difference between nonprofits and for-profits. This chapter also examines grants, steps for writing them, and tips for increasing your odds of receiving them. Funding is out there and available, but there isn't a quick way to access those funds. This chapter does not go over setting up a for-profit nor a not-for-profit because this varies by state and you will need to research and investigate where you live.

TERMS THE CREATIVE NEEDS

APPLICANT POOL The group of applicants applying for a specific category to a particular organization

CONSTITUENTS Individuals, families, and communities that benefit from programs that not-for-profit organizations provide

CONTINGENCY A provision for an unforeseen event or circumstance

FOR-PROFIT An organization focused on maximizing profits and forwarding profits to the company's owners and shareholder

FOUNDATIONS Non-governmental entity established as a nonprofit or a charitable trust, with the purpose of making grants to individuals and organization

NOT-FOR-PROFIT A type of organization that does not earn profits for its owners. The money collected by or donated to the organization is used in pursuing the organization's mission

PHILANTHROPY Promotes the welfare of others, primarily by donating money to good causes

SHAREHOLDERS An owner of shares in a company

INITIAL PUBLIC OFFERING (IPO) The first time that the stock of a private company is offered to the public

> **501(c)(3) STATUS** The most common type of nonprofit status. Refers to tax-exempt under section 501(c)(3) and its primary activities are charitable

WHAT THE CREATIVE NEEDS TO KNOW

There are pros and cons to both not-for-profit and for profit. There are extra steps you will have to take with either. Searching for funding and grants and making applications requires time. If you are interested though, you will find funding opportunities, and this chapter will help you prepare. Know that nonprofit work and grant writing is about hard work and time, not mystery and magic.

WHAT THE CREATIVE WILL LEARN IN THIS CHAPTER

In this chapter, you will learn the difference between for-profit and not-for-profit. You will learn information about grant writing, step by step. There are many terms covered in this chapter that you may not have previously been familiar with; review those and research deeper on your own if more clarity is needed. In this chapter, you will learn about review panelists, timelines, and final reports.

FOR-PROFIT VS. NOT-FOR-PROFIT

The main difference between for-profit and not-for-profit is the mission. For-profit gives earnings back to their shareholders, and nonprofit organizations put earnings back into programs and services for their constituents. Both can turn a profit.

FIG 10-1

The mission is the difference between for-profit and not-for-profit organizations.

"Stay focused on the mission."

—Naveen Jain

It is confusing to call a business not-for-profit because nothing prevents a not-for-profit from being profitable; it is just a matter of what they do with the profits.

Not-for-profit is classified as 501(c)(3), which means it has exempt status and does not pay under the same tax base as a for-profit. This exempt status enables it to operate as a charity and receive discounts and pay fewer taxes. Not-for-profit organizations have a governing board that approves decisions and determines how money is spent. Both for-profit and not-for-profit companies create an end-of-year report for either shareholders or funders and donors. Not-for-profits have employees but no owners. The board hires the director, and the director hires the employees. A for-profit business is owned by an individual or group, the CEO is hired by the board, or the company is run by the founder or owner. A for-profit company can remain private indefinitely, never "going public" if they are not looking for funding. Going public refers to a private company's initial public offering (IPO), meaning they are publicly traded on the stock market. Companies often go public to raise capital to expand. A private company that is not public does not have to have a board to answer to and can make their own decisions. You have to submit annual reports to the state you live in to maintain your business status. If you have an LLC, S corp, or C Corp that you run your business transactions through but you would like to apply as an individual for grants, you can still do that as a creative, under your personal name. Most grants are offered to 501(c)(3) not-for-profit organizations or individual creatives who meet the criteria. There are different kinds of grants including project grants, organizational grants, travel grants, and professional development, such as for attending conferences, to name a few.

FINDING FUNDING

If you are a not-for-profit organization or an individual looking for funding, there are different places to look. Start by investigating government entities such as city, state, county, and national offices. Look to other not-for-profits as well as local and regional organizations in your field. Service organizations in your area are a great resource. Another place to look for funding is philanthropic arms of corporations; even small companies sometimes provide seed money. Foundations are another place to look for funding. A foundation is a nonprofit with the purpose of making grants to individuals and not-for-profit organizations. Operating solely from grants, however, is unrealistic. Use grants as part of the income stream, including things such as product sales, ticket sales, donors, and classes, to name a few ideas. You will need several streams of revenue to be operational, never just one.

> *"An entrepreneur without funding is a musician without an instrument."*
>
> —Robert A. Rice Jr.

FIG 10-2

Multiple revenue streams are a must for all creatives.

take action

Many websites post lists of grants for creatives and their deadlines for application. Search online using the keywords "grants" and your discipline. Create a document with links to grants you might be interested in applying to in the future.

COMPLETING THE APPLICATION

1. When you receive the application, read it thoroughly. Don't read one part and jump in to get started. Read the whole thing. The first thing you need to identify is if you qualify. Funding sources have unique qualifications allowing for a specific gender, background, or age bracket only to submit an application. Review the qualifications before moving forward.

2. Follow the directions. If the application states to organize your documents in a certain way and format everything specifically, do exactly that. As an example, the application may call for 1-inch margins, black ink only, a specific font, one page only, or other requests. Listen to these instructions and follow them because there is a reason for the request. It is also respectful to the project manager, who is taking in the applications, processing them, and putting them forward to the panel. If he or she is processing hundreds of applications, you make his or her life easier by following instructions; you want the project manager on your side.

3. Tell your story. When writing the narrative on the application, see it as your opportunity to tell the story you want the grantor to hear. When writing your narrative section, give a broader overarching description and save the technical for an interview. You can express that you want to do this project with technical elements that are cutting edge but state that you won't go into the technicalities. Include a link in case someone is interested in understanding the technical aspects, so they know where to find that information. Share the passion part of your story on the application instead. Spend your narrative telling your story and how fantastic your project is.

The narrative section of an application is an opportunity to tell your story and sell the project's qualities. That's the most significant component of seeking funding—how well you can tell your story. If you're terrible at it, get support because you won't be funded if you cannot communicate what it is you want to do. Edit the statements in your narrative to explain exactly what you want to do. If there are elements you still need to figure out and that would become a part of the grant, then say that.

4. The budget section of your application holds a secret. With any application, there is a limit to the number of words, characters, or pages. Whenever you submit a budget, you will often have the space of a single page. What most applicants do is create a bulleted

list of the items and provide cost, but there is a better way to use the page to the fullest. If you wanted to explain, in your narrative, how a piece of equipment works but ran out of space, include it in your budget. Under each bulleted item listed, you could add one to two short, descriptive sentences. It is a way to extend your narrative and further explain a few elements. This idea won't always work because some electronic forms do not have space for it, but if you have the room or are submitting the budget as a PDF, include more and use the budget for more than just numbers. Be careful to fully edit the additional copy added to the budget, so it does not read as a continuation of the narrative.

Pay yourself as a creative. If your budget does not have a line item of funding for you, the application looks like an amateur. How are you going to eat during that project? Do the math, know the dollar amount of the funding opportunity, and give yourself a portion of the proceeds. If you have a job and feel you don't need funding for yourself but want it for materials you wouldn't typically afford, fund yourself. Even if you end up using the financing on materials, you look more professional by requesting to be paid. Your budget should include things such as hired labor, materials, rentals, travel, transportation, and training, to name a few.

FIG 10-3

Always create a line in the budget to fund yourself.

5. Once you total the overall amount, add, at the end of the budget, what is referred to as a contingency amount. A contingency dollar amount or percentage is your acknowledgment that unforeseen events or circumstance could occur. The standard contingency amount on a grant application is 10% of the overall budget. Include that, and if it isn't needed for that purpose, you will keep the remaining funding.

6. A request for support materials may be your application, so pay attention. If the application allows you to submit support materials, do not miss that opportunity. You may only submit the support materials on their list, things such as your bio, resume, and brochure; adhere to those rules and directions. If the application instructions do not provide a list of support materials, throw it all in there. If you submit electronically, build a multi-page PDF filled with scans of show cards, posters, brochures, event images, or any additional items to best tell your story. The project manager with the organization will sometimes send the images of support materials in advance of the panel meeting.

PIXIE DUST

Grant writing does not have woo-woo magic to it. There's no fairy dust to sprinkle on grant applications, but there's a formula. The reason most people do not get funded through grant applications is that they are unable to articulate what they're going to do with the money. Grants are not a free pot of money. Put in the work ahead of time to determine what you need money for. The first step is to ask what you will do with the y funding. Get clear on that, and

FIG 10-4

There are many elements that go into applications. All are needed.

your chances of receiving a grant are significantly higher. You can't say I don't know, but when I get it, I'll figure it out. Seek funding only when you are ready and have a project that fits. Don't make your project fit the funding, as that will cause frustration for everyone. Sprinkle just the magic of your story on your grant, use honesty and enthusiasm to sell your passion for your project. Never use desperate or passive language in a grant application; instead build the application from a place of confidence and clarity.

PANELISTS AND TIMELINES

Most funding agencies have little funding, so when reviewing grant applications, they're often going to group all creatives into one applicant pool. Once you submit the application, there is a timeline for granting organizations. If you submit an application to a not-for-profit or a government agency, it may take a month or more to convene panelists to review the applications. When the panelists convene, they've generally already read your application, in advance. After reviewing all the applicants, panelists make the recommendations as to who should be awarded funding. The project manager takes recommendations back to their team, the executive director approves, and then, if they are not-for-profit or a government agency, they seek approval from their board. If a city, state, or federal agency is involved, the recommendation has to be approved by the governing bodies. It can take up to six months before you hear if your project is funded. The staff project manager will keep you updated on where the process is along the timeline. You usually have one year to complete your project. Get to know the project manager before the review because he or she does not get to vote but can offer information about you to the panel, and if he or she shares that you are easy to work with, you are more likely to be funded.

It's okay to shift from your original application proposal to something new. The time of application to completion can take a year or two. The organizations know your project will likely change. It's okay to shift, but if it's a radical shift, have a conversation with the project manager and make sure that it's okay.

FINAL REPORTS

Do your project within the approved timeframe. Then, when your project is complete, one of the most critical steps still must be done. When you receive funding for any project, you are required to submit a final report. The agency that gave you the funding will tell you what should be included in the final report. They may also provide forms to complete for inclusion in your final report. You must do these promptly, both so you will be considered for funding again the future and to show support for the organization's project manager who has to do all of the work to process your grant. Final reports are to understand the value and the importance of the project. They give the organization information to pull for their reports, and they need your feedback on your plan to continue to get funding in the future. Take the time to share that you valued receiving the funding and how the project turned out. If you do not turn a final report in, that agency will blacklist you, and they will tell their friends in the industry that you made them work harder. This is no way to build relationships; help them out and do what they ask of you—cooperate and stay in good standing in the creative community.

FEEDBACK

When applying for funding or grants, if you are notified that you did not receive the grant, ask the program manager if he or she has feedback for you to improve. If so, respect how that feedback is offered, meaning if it is by letter, e-mail, or phone call, take it the way it is delivered and don't make additional requests. There is a reason for that, too. Most funders, not all, will give you feedback on why you were not funded. They take notes, especially if it's public dollars from a government agency, because it is public information if public resources are involved. If you ask for feedback, listen to it and improve next time. You could also get feedback in advance of submitting your application, but give the program manager enough time, and schedule it; don't spring it on him or her.

COST

Some grant applications can come with an application fee, but they are always nominal—between $25 to $50, although government agencies applications will be free. If a granting organization asked for several hundred dollars to start the process, they are not legitimate. The most significant cost involved in grants is time. It is a great effort to put them together and even harder if you do not know exactly what you want to do with the money. Sometimes you may also have shipping costs, if you need to mail hard copies, or carrier costs, if you have hard copies delivered. Most applications are submitted electronically, though.

There are also slight costs associated with filing both for-profit and not-for-profit businesses. There is a filing fee to the Corporation Commission or Secretary of State, depending on your state. If you can complete the application for not-for-profit yourself, you will save money; if not, you will need to hire help to fill it out and the cost will vary depending on the firm you use and where you live.

take action

Investigate setting up your not-for-profit and for-profit online with your state Corporation Commission or Secretary of State. What steps do they have for filling both not-for-profit and for profit? What is the timetable? Who else can help you file?

REFLECTION

The difference between for-profit and not-for-profit is the mission, and that should make it easier for you to determine which category you want for your business. Also, consider that it is possible to have it all. You could have a private for-profit company and donate your time and a percentage of your income to charitable causes. You could also create a philanthropic arm of your company if you want to offer charitable contributions on a larger scale. If your focus is to spend close to 100% of your time on charitable work, then not-for-profit is likely your path. Do your homework, see what fits your desired outcomes, and then plan accordingly.

> *"Every good act is charity. A man's true wealth hereafter*
> *is the good that he does in this world to his fellows."*
>
> —*Moliere*

HOW WILL THE CREATIVE USE THIS INFORMATION GOING FORWARD?

Directions: Take a few minutes to think about how, specifically, you could research either for-profit or not-for-profit companies. Write down three ideas for ways you could investigate both to determine the best fit in the space provided.

1. _____
2. _____
3. _____

BUILDING YOUR CREATIVE NETWORK

Directions: Think of people or organizations you could meet with about the ideas in this chapter. Write down these creative network connections in the space provided. Write a specific goal for contacting one of them.

1. _____
2. _____
3. _____

Goal: _____

SECTION IV

READY YOUR TOOLS

CHAPTER ELEVEN

Creative Tools

KEEPING YOUR PRACTICE ALIVE

INTRODUCTION

The most creative tool you have is time. It's worth a lot more than money. Time can be traced back to why you are not accomplishing as much as you'd hoped, or, if you are a slave to time, why you get a lot done but feel tied to your clock. This chapter focuses on tools for the creative—tools such as managing time and building micro-moments as well as stress reduction tactics such as visualization and meditation. We also explore how creative playdates can aid in keeping your creative practice alive and healthy instead of limping. Throughout this chapter, stay open to new possibilities that can increase your confidence and your bravery.

TERMS THE CREATIVE NEEDS

> **MICRO-MOMENTS** To act on a need (e.g., to learn something, do something, discover something, watch something or read something in a spare moment)
>
> **VISUALIZATION** The formation of a mental image of something
>
> **MEDITATION** Contemplation or pondering over a written or spoken discourse expressing considered thoughts on a subject

WHAT THE CREATIVE NEEDS TO KNOW

You are in control. It may not always feel that way, but with the right tools, you can create an environment where your personal life and your creative practice co-exist in balance instead of in competition for your attention. Demand this from yourself, and for that, you will need to be brave and confident enough to challenge yourself to make things better, more comfortable, and less stressful. This chapter will offer tools designed to make the creatives life less stressful.

WHAT THE CREATIVE WILL LEARN IN THIS CHAPTER

Whether you are just starting out or you have a stable career, giving thought to what's next is essential. This is a question all professionals should be asking, but even more so for creatives because so much of what we do is a daily hustle; we can get lost in the long view of our futures. This chapter will offer tools for the creative to use during stressful times, creative blocks, or when you're frustrated with calendars, schedules, and obligations that keep you from your practice.

TIME CHECK

If you could stop the clock, what would you use the extra time for? Maybe use the extra time to create your next brilliant something. Perhaps you have an idea within you that you have wanted to do for a while, but you haven't even started because you tell yourself every single day that you don't have the time. What could you create if you stopped allowing time to control you and instead you took the reigns back from the ticking clock? The first step in making time work for you again is to find windows of time, little nuggets or gems. They're laying all around you.

FIG 11-1

Find gems of time everywhere.

*"A man who dares to waste one hour of time
has not discovered the value of life."*

—*Charles Darwin,* **The Life & Letters of Charles Darwin**

take action

Spend a few days that you would call typical for your personal/professional schedule. Grab your journal and watch yourself for a day or two. Take notes on how long everything typically takes you. It is an interesting exercise, as you watch yourself be honest. Do you waste time in certain areas more than others? Note that observation and those become your nuggets of free time. Keep your eyes open; you're watching yourself to see where time is available that you are currently wasting.

You may need night scope to see the nuggets of time that are there waiting for you. Could you go to bed a little later? Get up a little earlier? Get up for a few hours during the middle of the night and then go back to sleep? Why fight insomnia? If you have trouble going to sleep or difficulty staying asleep, then get up; there's a reason that keeps happening: It's a window of time that remains open for you to use. As creatures of habit, we think there is only one way to do something, but if you are passionate about being creative, you will find a way. Set your alarm for five minutes earlier. Getting back five minutes every day for a year gives you 1,825 minutes, which equals thirty hours. What could you do with 30 hours a year? I like to tell people I am a time inventor and I can create time. I say this because I am intentional about every waking minute of my day. I can identify where I will have spare moments and I plan accordingly to use them wisely.

STEAL TIME

Sometimes you just have to steal time by robbing Peter to pay Paul, as my mom would always say. All creatives need to set a schedule with loved ones and work to allow for creative time, no matter the hour. If you are a night owl, then consider negotiating to go in later to work and offer to stay later. Be slightly selfish and schedule your creative practice time in, just like any other responsibility or appointment. Scheduling the time, even if you just sit in your creative space listening to music, becomes habit forming.

All creatives need to delegate. Are you a control enthusiast? Stop! You do not need to do everything yourself; in fact, if you are doing tasks that are outside of your strengths, you are wasting time. Relinquish control and allow others to step in and do the things that you are not interested in or that slow you down. Freeing up minutes a day or hours a week by hiring others is a perfect way to steal those minutes back for your creative practice. Steal time by shutting off from outside distractions and putting your life on airplane mode. If you're not

FIG 11-2

Creative time can occur at any hour—embrace that.

inundated with pinging notifications, you are more likely to stay focused. Studies show that it takes an average of 23 minutes to return to your original task after an interruption (see https://www.fastcompany.com/944128/worker-interrupted-cost-task-switching)

Even if you schedule just 45 minutes of airplane mode a day, you'll get over four hours of uninterrupted work a week. That is a lot of time stolen back for your creative practice. If you remove the time-sucking things, such as going down the rabbit hole that social media can sometimes be or binge-watching TV shows, you could potentially have hours back.

GO AHEAD AND PROCRASTINATE

No really, procrastination can be right for you. If you are focused on your messy house and using that as an excuse as to why you can't focus on the creative practice, you are permitted to put off scrubbing the toilets. So many creatives love to clean and organize before they can pick up a pencil and focus on their practice. If this sounds like you, ask yourself why you are doing that. Ask yourself if the other tasks must get done right now. Could you do a lot of your tasks smarter or more efficiently? Working smarter means finding ways to cheat. Well, sort of cheat; it's more about planning. You can put tasks off knowing you are going to group them up once a week or once a month. An example of this would be to do your social media posts one day per month and then use schedulers to have them auto-post, or setting up automatic bill pay with your bank. Creating systems that automate your business practice allows you to ignore tasks that can run without you. If you are putting off your creative practice, though, you need to get back on track by inviting your muse to inspire you.

FIG 11-3

Sometimes procrastination can be good, depending on what you are delaying.

MAKE KITS

As a creative, you have likely heard that you should never go anywhere without a notebook or sketchbook because you don't know when inspiration will strike. The same goes with keeping a note pad next to your bed in case you awake in the middle of the night with an idea. To do this is to be prepared. Always make sure you carry a writing utensil and pad of paper.

You create confidence in many areas of your life without even realizing that is what is occurring. You do this with your streaming services by adding movies to your cue and audio files to your devices in advance so that they are ready when you want to watch, read, or listen to something. You can create kits for all areas of your life to make everything available right when you need it. Instead of surfing your phone when you are in a line or waiting for an appointment, why not carry a reading or creativity kit with you? Carry books, documents, articles, or other items you have wanted to read in a bag with you. This gives you time back to use minutes gifted to you when you are waiting for other things to take place. You may have a gym bag always ready in your trunk or at your desk at work; you are familiar with kits. If you receive the gift of time to spend on your creative practice, you don't want to waste it with more getting ready time.

Prepare meals and snacks in advance maybe once or twice a week. Why are we talking about meals in a book for creatives? Because creatives will use any excuse to put off getting to our practice. If you know you're going to have a window of time for your creativity, having your snacks or meals in place means you don't have to stop to prepare. Creating kits for every area of your life gives you more time back, even if it's just time freed up to think. Imagine that!

Prepare meals and snacks in advance maybe only once or twice a week. Why are we talking about meals in a book for creatives? Because creatives will use any excuse we can to put off getting to our practice. If you know you're going to have a window of time for your creativity, having your snacks or meals in place means you don't have to stop to prepare. Creating kits for every area of your life gives you more time back, even if just time freed up to think. Imagine that!

FIG 11-4

Create kits for every category of your life.

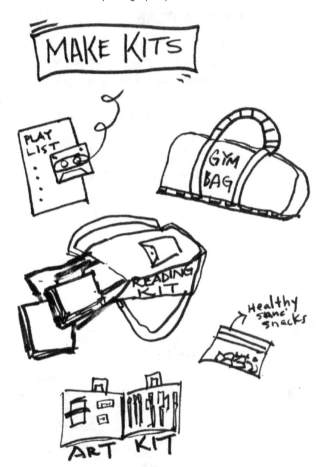

CREATE MICRO MOMENTS

Another tool that can prove very useful is called micro-moments. The first step in building micro-moments is to identify where you leave spare time and waste it. Once you have discovered where the extra moments of time are and you've prepared your kits, you're ready to make a note of what you would do if you had an extra few minutes. Keep a running list of small five- to 10-minute tasks. With a few minutes, could you send one -email? Glue something together? Make notes about a new idea? Micro-moments happen as tiny bursts of time. The idea is to make sure you always have projects ready and in the cue, so you can feel accomplished by doing small things, incrementally, until you complete whole projects or tasks.

take action

Start a micro-moments log filled with tiny tasks to complete. Keep the log somewhere near your creative space so that when the minutes of gifted time arrives, you will know how to use them. Do this and notice how much time you normally waste.

HAVE A PLAN

Here's the tricky part: You can't use the extra time you discover to take a nap. Time is a gift; use it for something that makes you feel amazing. If you want more time, do something with it and prepare for when your newly found time shows up. If you create goals, write down your ideas and have all supplies needed on hand so that you will be ready when the magic moments of time show up. All too often, unfortunately, when the time arrives, creatives run errands to get everything they need and the time is lost. Carve out time for prep work and supply runs. Build into your plan plenty of time for play and experimentation. As a creative, you know that creativity does not come with an on-off switch; it has to be given time to grow and develop.

> *"Without leaps of imagination or dreaming, we lose the excitement of possibilities. Dreaming, after all, is a form of planning."*
>
> —Gloria Steinem

FIG 11-5

Have tatics at the ready to help relieve stress.

STRESS-RELIEF TACTICS

Stress from outside sources plays a massive role in how productive you are in your practice. If your load from your day job or family life is a lot to carry, it will shrink your creative time. So, how do you compete? How do you take care of those responsibilities while maintaining your creative time? Using visualization methods won't take all your stress away, but it can aid you in transitioning into a calmer state before you enter your creative space. There are many styles and methods for visualizing available online, such as apps, audio files, and videos. This is something to explore if you are struggling with the transition process. The basic idea behind this method is to close your eyes and see yourself doing exactly what you want to be doing, with ease and support. As an example, if every day when you drive home from your day job you took the time to see yourself engaging with your family and then a few hours later walking into your creative space, alone where you are free to create, if you build this image into your process, then you are more likely to experience it because visualization helps to bring what you want more of in your life, be it calmness, freedom, happiness, or creative time.

Meditation is another method you can use to calm your mind, and it can assist with the transition process as well. If you find a guided meditation that you enjoy, follow it for a while, repeatedly listen to it until you have the technique down. Practice using meditation as you transition from work to home life and from home life to your creative practice. As an example, can you steal a few extra minutes to do a five-minute meditation that allows you to take deep breaths and feel calm before entering your creative time? This small act can ensure you leave everything else at the door and give the creative muse everything you have at that moment. Guided meditations are online as downloaded audio files, videos, and apps. Experiment a little and try different things to see the best fit for you.

FIG 11-6

Meditate and visualize for an easier transition from day job to creative time.

SCHEDULE CREATIVE PLAYDATES

Schedule creative play dates with your practice. If you are fortunate enough to have a career consisting of your artistic practice with no other daytime job, you are lucky. However, so many creatives often need another job to participate in their practice. This is why you have to use a calendar and schedule in play time. If you have a particular body of work that you make money from, it can become tiresome to have to work on the same thing over and over. Giving yourself time to play frees you from feeling like you do not have time for yourself. It can benefit you to schedule time with other creatives as well. This doesn't have to mean working side by side; it can mean meeting for a coffee or a creative space visit just to check in to share techniques and details about each other's practice. If you are a natural collaborator, create intentional play dates with other creatives to see how your outcomes might change if you included others in your process. This can also be beneficial for accountability, meaning if you schedule a connection with another creative you are more likely to commit to being creative during that time. This can be an excellent tool to ensure that you make new things, play, and explore.

"Time is a created thing. To say 'I don't have time' is like saying, 'I don't want to.'"

—*Lao Tzu*

REFLECTION

These tools can help keep your creative practice alive and well but you have to put the exploration time in to see what fits best for you and your lifestyle. These tools are opportunities that will grow if you encourage them. The first step is a willingness to try different things, even if you have tried them in the past. Maybe today one of these tools will feel differently to you because you are using it differently or because you are now open or more receptive. Gift yourself time to pause, play, experiment and reflect on your practice.

HOW WILL THE CREATIVE USE THIS INFORMATION GOING FORWARD?

Directions: Take a few minutes to think about how, precisely, you will incorporate the tools from this chapter in your own professional life. Write down three ideas in the space provided that you can start doing today.

1. _____
2. _____
3. _____

BUILDING YOUR CREATIVE NETWORK

Directions: Think of people, organizations, or other resources that can help you take action right now to include tools discussed in this chapter. Write down these creative network connections in the space provided. Write a specific goal for contacting or making use of one of them.

1. _____
2. _____
3. _____

Goal: _____

CHAPTER TWELVE

Pitching Products, Projects, and Plans

SHARING YOUR PASSION

INTRODUCTION

There are different kinds of pitches you will encounter during your career. This chapter will focus on the two most common for creatives to encounter: the business (capital) pitch and the elevator pitch. The first thing, when it comes to pitching, is to focus on what is coming out of your mouth. When you're presenting, it doesn't matter what it is, a product, a process, or a service, acknowledge that you are selling something to someone. Anytime you are pitching, you are trying to sell something to someone, and this could include a lecture at a conference or a presentation at school. Treat it all as a pitch focused on sales, and you will have it down in no time!

TERMS THE CREATIVE NEEDS

ELEVATOR PITCH A succinct and persuasive sales pitch. A very short pitch that distills the idea into a summary; it should take only as long as a short elevator ride

BUSINESS PITCH A presentation by one or more people to an investor, group of investors, funders, such as venture capitalists, or possible partners

INVESTOR A person who puts money into financial opportunities with the expectation of achieving a profit

POSITIONING STATEMENT An expression of how a product, service, or process fills a need in a way that no other competitor can

PRODUCT PLAN The foundation of a product, process, or service that you are looking for support on. It is one page, 8 ½ x 11", that is an execution plan for demonstrating next phase development

VENTURE CAPITALIST An investor who provides capital to startup ventures or supports small companies

WHAT THE CREATIVE NEEDS TO KNOW

An elevator pitch allows you to quickly spit out who you are, what you're currently working on, what you're interested in, and upcoming projects, and it provides a little nugget to express your personality. You must do this with confidence in a semi-memorized but exciting fashion. A business pitch is an opportunity if you are looking for investments, partnerships, or help with taking your product to market. Investors will zero in on defined target audiences and financials along with the who of the project. That's you!

WHAT THE CREATIVE WILL LEARN IN THIS CHAPTER

You will learn how to prepare, write, practice, and deliver a pitch with confidence. You will learn what it means to read an audience, the steps for creating an ideal pitch, and tips for pitching to a single person or a full audience. You will learn steps for both elevator and business pitches.

ELEVATOR PITCH

An elevator pitch is 60 to 90 seconds long and to deliver it well you have to practice. It is an opportunity to share highlights from your life and career. Don't write this pitch as formal nor deliver it formally. An elevator pitch should show off your personality. Start to develop language that describes you and your practice. Build a language into your pitch that becomes part of your storytelling. This makes it easier to remember your pitch and share it. As an example, I frequently say my creative career is filled with weird and wonderful projects. This simple line gets attention; it is true and often inspires people to ask that I share more. What words would you use to describe your projects or practice? The elevator pitch comes from the idea that you've met somebody and you're stepping into the elevator with them. You only have from the time you step into the elevator until that person steps off the elevator. That means in a minute or less you have to give a precise pitch, with the goal of he or she asking to hear more.

STEP ONE
"Hello, my name is (fill in the blank), and my company is (fill in the blank)." That sets it up with the person you're engaging with; they know your name, and they know where you're from.

STEP TWO
Next, launch into what it is you do creatively or are interested in. If you make or do all different things, start there and, in your own words, explain that you wear many different hats. Then lead to sharing what your current favorites are.

STEP THREE
Share where you work if it is relevant and if you own your business. If you are working somewhere that you don't care to talk about and it's not appropriate to who you want to become, don't talk about it. However, if your business or place of employment matters, then share that.

STEP FOUR
Finally, share a little bit of who you are, in a creative way. An example might be to say when you are not creating you like to (fill in the blank). Travel? Bake? Hike? To share a bit of your whole

human personality can be an asset to yourself. This works well if you know something about the person you are pitching to and you have something in common.

You should prepare a pitch that is 90 seconds long because you're likely to be nervous and you'll speak faster when you're nervous. You want your elevator pitch to pour out easily over 60 seconds.

> *"We are the gift. We are giving ourselves to our audience. We're giving them the product of our thoughts, efforts, and personality. We're giving them who we are. We're telling them our truth. That's our gift to them."*
>
> —Ben Rosenfeld

You are going to have a lot of requests, in your career, for sharing a few seconds of who you are. This is how most professional meetings begin. If you can become skillful at the elevator pitch, you are light years ahead. The way to make things happen in your career is to get yourself in front of the right people. That adds up to a lot of networking, and for those in the creative fields, that can sound like you are being asked to put pins in your eyeballs. It can feel tough to pitch yourself or your ideas, but when you have a script, which is your elevator pitch, it's much easier. It's like speed dating; you've got it down, you know what you're going to say, you are confident, and you are comfortable in who you are and what you're going to tell the world.

FIG 12-1

Your elevator pitch is a chance to quickly introduce yourself, kind of like speed dating.

take action

Stand in front of a mirror, full length if you have one, and look at yourself while you say your pitch a few times. Set your phone or camera up (or get help) and record yourself giving your elevator pitch. Notice your body language, hand gestures, and facial expressions. Do you need to make changes? Use a clock or timer to see how long it takes you. Do you need to make your elevator pitch longer?

You'll only know how long it takes if you practice. It will also give you more confidence when asked on the spot at a networking event.

Did you know a higher percentage of people are more afraid of speaking in public than they are of death? Many people would rather die than speak in public. Talking to others or speaking in front of others can be an uncomfortable thing for a lot of people, which is why even more preparation and practice is needed. Work on finding techniques that work for you to get through times when you must network. Create a system for yourself that makes it easier and practice to build confidence.

When you're doing your pitch, talk about what you're passionate about. You can also throw in the other stuff you feel connected to because you never know where it might lead. If you can get to the point with your elevator pitch where you're confident, you will start to collect people who are interested in working with you.

When delivering your elevator pitch, you don't want to memorize it in such a way that it sounds rehearsed. Let it be a little bit organic and flow from you a little differently to each person you meet. Prepare 90 seconds because when you stand at home in front of the mirror, and you're talking to yourself, or you're practicing it with family, you're comfortable. This means you want to time yourself and make sure it's longer because when you are sharing your pitch live, it's going to fly out of your mouth. If you only practiced 30 seconds, you'll say everything in 12 seconds. If you are in an elevator, finished your pitch early and you didn't yet hit the floor where that person is getting off, then what happens? Then you're feeling awkward, and you say things not on the script. You never want to be in that place, so have more ready to share in case time allows.

If you are attending a networking event, a conference, or an opening do the following things before heading out:

1. *Carry current business cards on your person.*

2. *Make sure your social media doesn't have anything embarrassing on it.*

3. *Look through your website to make sure everything is up to date and is without typos.*

4. *If you have a portfolio online, double check that it has your best highlights, featured front and center.*

Do all this because you never know if the person you are shaking hands with is going to look you up right there on their phone or tablet.

AN EVER-CHANGING PITCH

Your pitch will grow as you grow in your field. It is also an excellent idea to alter your pitch based on your audience. As an example, if you are a dancer and are looking to create new partnerships in senior citizen communities, you don't want to give the attendees at the senior conference your pitch from last year when you were attending school-age conferences and were working in that filed. Practice your pitch because you may need to alter what you were going say. As an

FIG 12-2

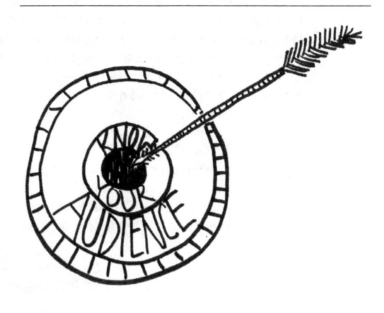

example, you might have thought the audience at a networking session was going to be from a particular industry only to discover people from other areas of your interests. You must be able to switch it up on the fly. There is no one-size-fits-all approach, and it's not possible to create a magic elevator pitch that is done forever and will never have to change.

After you have the moment of engagement with somebody where you can express your pitch, the very next thing you say is how great it was to meet them, then reach into your pocket for your business card, shake his or her hand, and offer your card. This is why you have business cards with you at all times.

"If you can't explain it simply, you don't understand it enough."

—Albert Einstein

THE BUSINESS PITCH

You may be interested in seeking an investor or venture capitalist or want to take a product to market. This means you need to become comfortable with how to pitch. The first thing to understand about pitching is it is only 50% of the product. The other half is about you, the pitcher. This means figuring out how to pitch yourself and see yourself as just as necessary as the product you are pitching. The first thing is to play the part, and looking like a professional doesn't mean khakis or a business coat. Dress the part as the present audience expects. Do your homework; find out if you can find other companies who have pitched to the same individual. This could gain valuable tips on expectations and protocols. A big part of looking professional is demonstrating that you are prepared and have practiced. Wear something that feels good on you but isn't stained or wrinkled.

STEPS

The standard business pitch requesting investments has six steps, they are as follows:

STEP 1: THE PROBLEM, ALSO KNOWN AS THE PAIN POINT

When pitching, consider what is coming out of your mouth. It doesn't matter if you are pitching a product, a process or a service; in any pitch you are trying to sell something to someone. The first step of any pitch is to show that you're solving a problem. Ask yourself where the pain point for those you are pitching to is. This pitch may be a single individual or a whole room full of possible investors or partners. Fulfill something for them that they desperately need, convince them that they have a deep, burning, painful problem and that you are the key to fixing it.

If you start with the pain someone has, you can then get creative. Let's say you're applying for a residency and making a pitch is part of the application. What is the pain that needs fixing? Is the residency lacking in technology-based artists and you happen to be exactly that and can solve a problem for them? Offer to not only be at their residency;,expand your offerings to help set up a studio for tech-based artists and guidelines for next year's application. Now you are showing them they had pain they didn't yet feel until pointed out. The pain point is the first section of your pitch.

STEP 2: THE SOLUTION
The next thing, after you've shown the pain point and you've demonstrated that it profoundly matters, is to show your solution. Your solution is your service, your product, or your process, and you want to say that clearly, but without going on and on. When you're talking about the solution, know that that is called the positioning statement.

take action

In your journal, write a positioning statement like the following:

I provide _____(fill in the blank) to my core customer. I provide this to _____(fill in the blank) your target market for (fill in the blank) _____.

If you can get your words into that sentence, you're ready to pitch.

Once you have your pain point identified and your positioning statement ready, you can then go into further details if additional time is allotted, meaning sometimes you cannot go into further details because many pitch competitions only allow three to five minutes per pitch. If you have more time, however, prepare for it and use it to the fullest to further sell your product, process, or service.

STEP 3: TARGET MARKET
The third section of your pitch is the target market that you want to reach. This is the section to cover who needs you and who should invest in you. Ask yourself who needs your product, process, or service. Are there not enough of what you are offering in the market already? What makes your offering special? The way to know who needs your product, process, or service is to know your target market. Ask yourself, why do they need this? What makes products like mine successful? Is there is a market for you're your process, and, if so, will your avatar use your service regularly? See your target market avatar using and living with your product, process, or service.

STEP 4: THE COMPETITION
The fourth section of a pitch is focused on how your product, process, or service dominates in the marketplace. This demonstrates that you know who your competition is. Name your competitors either by name or by related industry. Talk about what you do that is unique and unlike others in your industry. Why is your product, process, or service better, stronger, or more creative?

FIG 12-3

STEP 5: MAKE THEM BELIEVE

The fifth section asks why they should believe you. In this section, you will share who you are and what values you bring to your product, process, or service. Talk about your character, experiences, skills, strengths, and values, and how you show up. Tell them exactly what to expect from you. Make them believers. Sell your amazing product, process, or service. Remember, a pitch is more than the product or service, it is the personality!

STEP 6: THE ASK

The final step of your pitch is the ask. Before you close, tell your audience what you are asking of them. Are you asking them to buy your product? Are you asking them to hire you? Are you asking them for a partnership? Are you asking to collaborate? Be specific. Sell it. Be clear about what you are asking of those in the audience. As you close your pitch, leave very few questions. Leave room for questions and be ready to give answers but be so succinct that the audience will need to think hard to come up with questions.

Remember a pitch is short, often just minutes. Therefore, make sure your pitch hits the allotted time. You do not want a buzzer to go off and you haven't gotten to the ask yet. This means to practice in advance to ensure you hit the allotted amount of time. Don't leave minutes on the table, but also don't run out!

The more prominent audience for your pitch extends beyond who is in the room. Often there are up to four voices to consider with any pitch. These include your end-user, the person you created a vision of an avatar for; think about how they use your product, process, or service. Second is a potential partner, likely someone who isn't investing capital but possibly services or facilities. Next is the investor, the person who brings the money to fund your project. Finally, the fourth voice to consider is the media that covers your industry. You always want to "sell" to the press to get attention. These voices are all critical, and they are each uniquely different. Be ready to adjust your pitch to the needs of your different audiences.

take action

Before you head out for your pitch, prepare a one-page pitch plan and have it ready to go. This is a digital 8 ½ x 11" sheet with a brief description of your product. Consider also adding a logo and a short tagline. Add graphs or charts of your market summary and your financials. For any remaining business activities, use bullet points. Include your contact information and a list of your team's names with headshots.

To deliver a pitch with confidence, practice a lot. Having confidence means you are prepared and are in control. If your audience only notices you and the words you are sharing, then you will have them hooked. On the other hand, if they see you fumbling with papers, technology, or clothes, or if you fidget or stand rocking back and forth, then you have lost their attention. Look the part and come ready to deliver no matter what. Don't do any of that and no matter how fantastic your idea, product, service, or process, no one will notice.

For success in both pitching and public speaking, learn to read your audience. The first question to ask is why they are there. Learn who is attending and why are they motivated to be there; find out ahead of time as it may alter your practice sessions. Do you need to be humorous based on your audience? Or maybe you should you be calm and straight in your delivery. Next, listen to what you hear about your audience, including side interests, sensitivities, and specific industry connections. If you ignore this information, you could end up offending or losing their interest. The third is to look at your audience. Make eye contact as frequently as you can, as this encourages trust. By assessing what resonates with your audience and what falls short, you will have guidance to make quick shifts to your pitch. Fourth, check out body language. Are they shifting in their seats? Checking their phones or watches? Crossing their arms. Pay attention to how your audience is feeling and change your pitch to get their attention back. This is when you may want to have a joke ready or a great tip. Finally, throughout your pitch ask questions. An example might be, "How many of you have ever had a hard time with (fill in the blank)? Engaging your audience allows for a more participatory experience, which will enable them to remember you and your ideas more than a pitch where they are simply talked at.

FIG 12-4

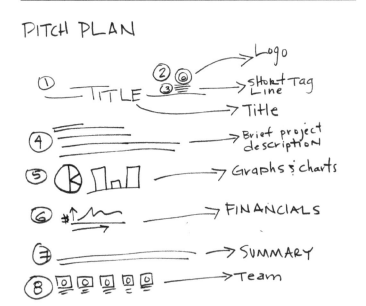

FOLLOW UP

After you make your pitch, follow up immediately with any contacts you made by sending them your plan via e-mail; include links to videos or press when appropriate. Write a warm but professional e-mail reminding them where you met and what you pitched. Let them know you have attached your plan. Tell them it was great to meet them, thank them for their time, and offer to answer any questions. Send this e-mail within 24 hours of your pitch. Do this even if a pitch winner was announced at the event and you didn't win. This is a perfect opportunity to reach out and ask for feedback. Often you will receive a helpful reply.

REFLECTION

A pitch is an opportunity for you to quickly share your project, process, or service, what you're currently working on, what you're excited about, and a little nugget to express your personality. Be remembered—pitch with confidence.

You have now learned how to prepare a pitch, steps for writing a pitch, how to practice a pitch, and why you want to deliver a pitch with confidence. The most important thing to remember whenever writing, rewriting, or adjusting a pitch, is to practice drilling the details into your head so that you are always prepared. Remember that any time you are pitching you are trying to sell something to someone; it doesn't matter what it is, it's all the same, be it a product, process, or a service. Treat it all as a sales pitch.

HOW WILL THE CREATIVE USE THIS INFORMATION GOING FORWARD?

Directions: Take a few minutes to think about when and where you need to use an elevator pitch in your own professional life. Write down three times you will use an elevator pitch in the space provided.

1. _____

2. _____

3. _____

BUILDING YOUR CREATIVE NETWORK

Directions: Think of people you can practice your elevator pitch with. Write down three people you can practice with or pitch directly to in the space provided. Write a specific goal for contacting one of them.

1. _____

2. _____

3. _____

Goal: _____

CHAPTER THIRTEEN

Organize Your Business

THIS WILL CHANGE YOUR LIFE!

INTRODUCTION

In this chapter you will see examples of how asking for help makes you stronger in your creative practice—how to call up your bravery to hire help and get the things off your plate that are not your strong suit. You'll uncover tips for getting and staying organized and protecting your practice. The chapter closes with legal and tax information, especially for creatives.

TERMS THE CREATIVE NEEDS

ASSISTANT A person who helps with particular work

VIRTUAL ASSISTANT (VA) A self-employed individual who provides professional administrative, technical, or creative (social) assistance to clients remotely from a home office

APP An application downloaded by a user to a mobile device such as a phone or tablet

BARTER To exchange (goods or services) for other products or services without using money

ETHICS Moral principles that govern a person's behavior or the conducting of an activity

PARETO PRINCIPLE Also known as the 80/20 rule, which states that, for many events, roughly 80% of the effects come from 20% of the causes

SOLE PROPRIETOR A person who is the owner of a business, entitled to keep all profits after taxes but is liable for all losses

LLC A limited liability company (LLC) is a corporate structure where the members of the company are not held personally liable for the company's debts or liabilities

C Corp A C corporation is a business term that is used to distinguish this type of entity from others, as its profits are taxed separately from its owners

S Corp An S corporation, for United States federal income tax purposes, is a closely held corporation

WHAT THE CREATIVE NEEDS TO KNOW

Stay open minded. To get through the journey of setting up your practice, show up ready to try new things. Ask questions and ask for help. Don't tell yourself you can't afford to hire help; suspend that for now, while we run through how, where, and why to hire help.

WHAT THE CREATIVE WILL LEARN IN THIS CHAPTER

You will learn that asking for help is the answer to obtaining your creative career. You'll learn tools that allow you to be more professional, get to places on time, and get your materials together and organized so You will learn how to set up a practice that is professional and legal, and this means more work, gigs, and projects.

ASK

Are there people in your life who offer help only to be turned down? What would it look like to say yes to their offer? Let's unpack why it is so hard to ask for help. Creatives are often afraid to ask for help because asking for help looks like we are not independent. Creatives place high importance on independence, so asking for help goes against the natural grain. I once learned a valuable lesson from my friends who taught me that allowing others to help you feels great for them. Denying their support makes them feel like you don't trust them. Allow yourself to say yes when others offer their help. Remind yourself that you weren't asking—they were offering. Build to a level of comfort where you can ask for help directly. Creatives need each other; build a helpful tribe that can ask you for help and you in turn them.

> *"Expose yourself to your deepest fear; after that, fear has no power,*
> *and the fear of freedom shrinks and vanishes. You are free."*
>
> —*Jim Morrison*

take action

Grab your journal and write down a list of important people in your life. Next, to their names write down at least one thing you know they would be willing to help you with. In a third column, write down one thing you could help each person with. Keeping this list handy will remind you it is okay to ask for help.

THE PARETO PRINCIPLE

The Pareto Principle also known as the 80/20 rule. It states that roughly 80% of the effects come from 20% of the causes. This means if you spend 80% of your time on that which you are brilliant and which comes natural and only 20% of your time on things that you just need to get done, even if you're not that great at the 20%, you will still be exponentially more successful than the person who flips these two. The problem is lack of confidence. If you're struggling with your confidence and with knowing what you're amazing at, it will be hard for you to commit 80%

of your time. Eventually, the goal is to get to 100/0. If you find yourself veering off and spending more than 20% on things you shouldn't be doing, then reevaluate ways you could hire, trade, or barter more of the 20% off your plate. You can also use this ratio to think about spending 20% financially for an 80% return on time—hence the phrase "money equals time." If 80% of your life is spent doing the things you love, your confidence will grow, your bravery will expand, and you will have the energy to create and build our creative community.

HIRE HELP

There are many ways to hire people to help you. If your career takes off the way it should, then you will hire subcontractors to help you. Creatives are often thrifty do-it-yourselfers, and while admirable, if you are spending your time doing everything that must get done for your practice, you are losing income. The secret to making money is doing less work yourself. Truly. People who make money do not do all the work. If you can get your head around that, you will start to understand how to make money as a creative. Think of the hierarchy of a major company—what does the CEO at the top do? Do they build the chips with their hands? Do they file payroll? Do they sweep the floors? Do they order supplies? The answer to all is no; they hire people to do all those things. If you think of yourself as the CEO and talent for your business, then you can quickly start to eliminate items from your to-do lists by paying someone else to do them.

FIG 13-1

Spend 80% of your time on the things you are passionate about and only 20% on things you are not.

> *"If you hire people just because they can do a job, they'll work for your money. But if you hire people who believe what you believe, they'll work for you with blood and sweat and tears."*
>
> —Simon Sinek

ASSISTANTS

Hiring an assistant for your practice can take many forms. They could come frequently and help you with things in your practice, or they could be on call when you need support. You know your personal best; if you don't like others in the morning, then don't have help come then. If you work best late at night, then hire someone who also works well with those hours. Or, hand over the things you do not want to do or don't have the skills to do and allow the assistant to meet with you once a week and work from his or her office or home. It is nice to have a person who can run errands and sign for things when you can't. It is also nice to have an extra set of hands to lift things or make phone calls for you. When putting out a request for an assistant, I recommend calling him or her a personal assistant and explaining during the interview that he or she will also pick things up for your personal life, too. As an example, if you don't have to run to the copy shop or art supply store, that gives you more time to focus on your practice.

VIRTUAL ASSISTANTS

Virtual assistants, also known as VAs, are self-employed individuals who provide administrative assistance to clients remotely from a home office. They can help with administrative things you do not want to do such as cataloging, scanning, databases, newsletters, and social media, as well as with developing processes for your practice. There are many online sites to hire VAs and people for short-term gig work such as building websites and creating graphic design templates. The beauty of a VA is that he or she doesn't need to live near you because all exchanges happen electronically. You can find people who are not expensive and who love doing this type of work. It is hard to imagine people loving the type of work you do not. There are always people of different personalities who enjoy all different kinds of work. They can take on your small five-hour project because they have a lot of clients and doing your job fits into what they are already doing for all their clients. You can't give up, though: If you hire some people who do a less than perfect job, recognize that was just that person, not the system. Try again and maybe tweak your instructions or spend more time with him or her up front. It is still a person, and you will need to take the time to build a relationship, but it will be worth it. As an example, I have a VA who I have never met in person nor spoken to by phone; she has been transcribing all my audio recording for years. I have another VA who does all of my scannings. She lives in my city and swings by my front porch when I text her that I left a box to be scanned. She scans them, returns the drawings, and drops the files into a cloud for me to retrieve. The costs are nominal compared to the time I would have wasted on those projects, and, instead, I spent my time working on what I love to do.

FIG 13-2

A virtual assistant works from his or her home office. You can accomplish things with out hiring full-time help.

"The best boss is the one who has sense enough to pick good men to do what he wants done, and self-restraint enough to keep from meddling with them while they do it."

—*Theodore Roosevelt*

BARTER AND TRADE

Creatives are naturals at sharing and trading work or services. We start this early on and continue throughout our careers. If you need help, the first place to look is to other creatives who will likely need your help sometimes, too. You might also find people in other industries who are willing to trade. If you are not sure who is willing to accept alternative forms of payment, ask. Try bartering with them. Maybe pay half in cash and half in exchange for goods or services you could provide. Not sure what you could offer? What are you good at? Start there and contribute what you can do, create, or produce. Try it out on your dentist, at the farmer's market, or for tickets to a show. First create a list of offerings with specific details, such as the good or service you are offering, the retail value, the expected date of delivery, and the type of things are you

FIG 13-3

Look for bartering opportunities everywhere.

looking for in exchange. By asking your dentist if there is an opportunity to trade part of your bill, you might discover that he or she has been looking for a private music teacher for his or her daughter and you happen to play the piano. Bartering is not a form of begging to pay less; it is a community service that provides for everyone. You just solved a task for your dentist, and because he or she knows you already, he or she will likely hire you to continue working with his or her daughter long after your bill is paid.

APP SUPPORT

If you are a techy creative, then do a bit of homework to find apps for your devices that will help with organization, keep a schedule and calendar for you, track pending projects, and hold your ideas and lists. There are many organizational-style apps that are free. Read the reviews and find the right fit. Experiment with them, see what they can do, test them, and, if you love one, keep it. If, after experimenting, you are still not impressed, delete it, and there is no harm done. Testing and experimenting are never a waste of time because they give you valuable data points: You learn quickly what you do not like and what you like a lot. You can then go forward with that criteria and look for a supportive app that better meets your needs. If you are not into technology, it's fine to stick to notebooks and pencils or find a balance of both.

take action

1. *Grab a device and jump online.*
2. *Search using the keywords "virtual assistant." Learn all about the many options now, before you need someone. Preparing allows you to move quickly once you are ready to hire someone.*
3. *Search apps that help you organize. You don't have to commit to any right now, but when you feel ready, you will have a sense of your options.*

LEGAL

SOLE PROPRIETOR

A sole proprietor means you're receiving payments under your name and social security number, just as you would with any other employment. It is okay to become an employee and receive a paycheck under your name and social, but it is never a good idea to take contracts and run a business as a sole proprietor. If you're a freelancer picking up gigs and you're accepting money as a sole proprietor, you leave your personal assets vulnerable and unprotected. You are personally responsible for all debts and liabilities. You also limit your savings on your taxes. If you submit an invoice for $100 as a sole proprietor, you will pay hirer taxes than if you submitted that same invoice as a company. Incorporating protects your personal assets and earns a hirer income due to deductions on your taxes and percentages paid for taxes.

TYPES OF CORPORATIONS

There are several different types of corporations, but for creatives, there are three main options, LLC, C corp, and S corp. A limited liability company (LLC) is a corporate structure where the members of the company cannot be held personally liable for the company's debts or liabilities. An LLC is an ideal for creatives because it is the easiest corporate structure to maintain with less annual paperwork. C corp is the standard corporation, either privately held or publicly shared. S corp has special tax status with the IRS and has limited benefits for creative companies. If you operate as a sole proprietor, you will get fewer gigs than someone who is incorporated. This is because for legal and productivity reasons, it is easier to hire someone with coverage that a corporation provides. It is less work to hire someone who carries all the legal documents and can provide them quickly. People prefer to work with companies because the risk of liability is lower than with an individual who carries the burden of personal liability and may lack insurance.

FILE AN LLC

If you're going to do any freelance or gig work, then it is essential to set up an LLC, which is a relatively simple process. You can hire a lawyer to do the process for you, but if you set aside the time, it is something you could read through and apply for yourself, saving money. Also, consider setting an appointment with a resource organization in your community such as S.C.O.R.E, which is the nation's largest network of volunteer, expert business mentors, with more than 300 chapters. Search online for small business service in your community. To apply for an LLC, you start by going online to either the Secretary of State or Department of Commerce wherever you live. It can vary by state, province, or territory, so research that small part. Also, depending on where you do business, you may need to file federally. All the application paperwork is online; download it and read through it to determine if it is something you could do on your own or if you need the help of a lawyer. Follow the instructions exactly. It is an inexpensive fee to file for an LLC and a small annual fee to renew. If you can complete the application yourself, fill everything out and submit it electronically. You may be required to list the articles of incorporation in a local newspaper for a specific amount of time depending on the state, province, or territory in which you live. The organization you file with will give you the details of approved papers and number of days the articles must run. The purpose of this is in case you owe money to another business, they can stop you from filing a new business until they are paid.

Consider becoming an LLC because you will get more work, be protected legally, and it is much easier to pay you.

take action

Jump online and search for information about setting up an LLC in your state, province, or territory. Read through it, bookmark the page, and save it for when you are ready to commit. You will know the costs, the timeline for processing, and what to expect. Waiting until you need it can cause undo stress—jump online and investigate it now.

TAXES

As an LLC or corporation, you might get hired for the same gig as a sole proprietor, but in the end, you will make more money. That's because as a corporation you get to write off more deductions on your taxes than a sole proprietor does. As a sole proprietor, the percentage rates on what you get to deduct are lower, and the categories of what you get to write off on your taxes are less than a corporation. That's a big difference between people who make money and people who don't. If you have a day job, you're never going to amass as much as if you work under a corporate structure. If you have less of a tax burden, you will stay in business longer, invest in new equipment, and possibly employ more people. You may think not writing off toilet paper or car tires is a big deal because you're just going to work. But, if a corporation maintains a fleet of vans, they need to write off tires because they buy so many so often. If you're a small business owner, you want that tax benefit to stay financially viable.

Once you set up your LLC, find an accountant by recommendation from other friends in creative fields. Once you are a professional company, you can no longer use quickie tax services; you'll need someone experienced in tax law and deductions in your industry. This tax accountant will cost more than the quickie places, but you will pay less into the IRS because these accountants understand the tax code and your business.

Once you set up your LLC, find an accountant by recommendation from other friends in creative fields. Once you are a professional company you can no longer use quickie tax services, you'll need someone experienced in tax law and deductions in your industry. This tax accountant will cost more than the quickie places, but you will pay less in to the IRS because they understand the tax code and your business.

BOOKKEEPING

Consider hiring a Bookkeeping if you submit a lot of invoices monthly and if you require software to keep track of your expenditures (money going out). You are creative; focus on what you do best and hire out the rest. Having a bookkeeper to help sort out the requests your tax accountant makes is a life saver. You can contact him or her and ask questions and ask if he or she will complete the required task. You never even need to learn what all the related terminology means.

PAYROLL

If you hire employees, don't write paycheck and submit paperwork for unemployment insurance and social security and taxes. Leave that to people who know how to do that easily. You can hire a company who will set everything up for you and your only task will be to type in the number of hours someone worked and a check will automatically issue to their bank account. Payroll companies also communicate with your bookkeeper and your tax accountant on your behalf, making your tax season that much easier. They issue your employees' W-2s for you. The cost, if you have a couple of employees, is under one hundred dollars a month. Your time is worth more than that.

DON'T BUY RETAIL

Buying wholesale instead of retail saves you money and prevents you from paying taxes twice on the same product. You can purchase all your supplies wholesale, even as a sole proprietor; you do not need to be a corporation. Go to the Department of Commerce, or the equivalent, in your state, province, or territory and apply for a resale ID. A resale ID is a certificate with an ID number that you use to set up accounts with your vendors. Anywhere you buy your supplies, buy at wholesale, or buy it tax exempt. If you are a painter and you buy supplies at retail cost, that means you are paying sales tax when you make that purchase. Then, you paint the painting with those supplies, and when your gallery sells the painting to the end buyer, they must charge sales tax. So, now sales tax is charged twice. Even if you're selling directly to the customer at a fair or a festival, you're required to charge both the city and state sales tax percentages. You must then submit those taxes collected monthly or quarterly, depending on how your accountant set it up. Set up vendor accounts with all the companies you purchase from to receive wholesale benefits where possible. This is more savings into your pocket.

"Never pay retail".

—*Warren Buffett*

GRAMMAR CHECK

I cannot spell to save my life, so I must always do extra work to make sure I check my spelling. If you have a similar problem with letters, as many creatives do, consider paying for a spelling and grammar check program. If that sounds like you too, be cautious when writing anything that another set of eyes will see. Before shipping any document off, permit yourself to pause, take a breath, slow down, and always give yourself enough time to proof written documents. Get in the habit of asking someone in your truth tribe to look at your documents. If no one feels qualified to copy edit, then pay for a software program to support yourself.

STORING DOCUMENTS

Creatives are known for being slow at delivering requested documents and paperwork. What a lousy reputation our industry has; we can change it through preparation. When items are asked of you, it is not that you are too lazy to ship it immediately. No; likely you are working hard, scrambling to produce an updated version, or possibly recreating it altogether because you don't remember where you put it. You need a game plan for updating your professional documents frequently and for a convenient storage plan so you can always find what you are looking for. Consider using a cloud service and storing your documents that way so you can retrieve them from any computer, anywhere. This gives you great freedom and flexibility. A cloud service is also excellent if your computer breaks or gets stolen so that you don't lose everything. You also need a plan for updating your professional documents often. As an example, consider noting "update docs" on an electronic calendar. If you update quarterly, and if anything should happen, you would only be outdated by three months, you can make that up quickly. Stretch beyond a quarter, and you must recall too much.

take action

Create a "dump document." It can be handwritten or you can use software on your computer to make an electronic document. Your dump document is a bulleted list of updates to make to your professional documents. The method is to jot down gigs or activities completed as things occur. Use this to quarterly update your professional documents. Having a list that is ongoing means you don't have to take the time to recall when what you have done over the last year when your resume is requested.

ETHICAL CHECK-UP

Your ethics are the moral principles that govern your behavior and activities. Whether you are just setting up your practice or you're established, it is equally important to invest time to review how your choices and processes stand up ethically. Make sure your values and principles guide the projects you choose. Never be lead just by money; demand more from yourself and lead with your creative passion. The money will follow. Never work on a project or in collaboration with someone if it compromises your ethics; it is never worth it. Never do something to get ahead if it is behavior that makes you uncomfortable in any way. Take actions in your personal and professional life that harm no one because stepping on others, in any form, to get ahead is inexcusable. Stand up for others and yourself; our creative community needs each other.

take action

Grab your journal and write down or review your values. Use those to make a list of ethical compromises you are never willing to make. Use this list to guide your choices of gigs and projects. Taking the time to do this means knowing in advance what you are and are not comfortable with and helps with decision making when requests arise.

FIG 13-4

Show your bravery by asking if you can pitch to people you admire.

REFLECTION

The creative cannot create in a bubble; you need support, and you need to learn to ask for help. Create systems for your practice that make maintaining your professionalism easier. Seek legal advice when needed and search out mentors and service volunteers to support you. Use a professional tax accountant and a bookkeeper if you are running many invoices monthly. Use a payroll company to pay employees and assist with tax preparation. File for an LLC, buy wholesale, and learn to barter. Lead your practice with bravery, confidence, and ethical awareness.

HOW WILL THE CREATIVE USE THIS INFORMATION GOING FORWARD?

Directions: Take a few minutes to think about one "take action" from this chapter that you will do immediately. Write down three steps for that action in the space provided.

1. _____

2. _____

3. _____

BUILDING YOUR CREATIVE NETWORK

Directions: Think of people or networks whom you can ask for help. Write down these connections in the space provided. Write a specific goal for contacting or making use of one of them immediately.

1. _____

2. _____

3. _____

Goal: _____

CHAPTER FOURTEEN

Social Networking

THE HUMAN CONNECTION

INTRODUCTION

Social networking is humans connecting. It may look a little different because we are exchanging images, videos, memes, and written words, but it is still one human sharing with another or with many. It is a fast-moving industry, so specific social media sites, platforms, tools, and companies are not mentioned in this chapter because it is impossible to predict who will stick around and what new rising social media start will emerge. Research all items related to this topic to investigate the latest, most exceptional social media platform options. Learn your social habits to consider how you can translate to an online social experience.

TERMS THE CREATIVE NEEDS

FLASH SALES Sale of goods at reduced prices, lasting for only a short period

FOLLOWERS In a social media setting, a follower refers to a person who subscribes to your account to receive your updates

HANDLES In the online world, a handle is another word for a username

HASHTAGS Keywords that can be used to search messages with given hashtags

NETWORKING Interaction between people exchanging information and building contacts

PLATFORM The software or service that you use to publish your content on the internet

SOCIAL NETWORKING Electronic communication through which users create online communities to share information

TESTIMONIALS A public tribute to someone and their achievements

TROLLS Someone who creates conflict on social media sites by posting messages that are controversial

VIRAL Refers to the sharing of a video or a website link to a mass audience in a short amount of time

SOCIAL MEDIA CALENDAR A calendar to plan social media posts for regular posts on a variety of topics

WHAT THE CREATIVE NEEDS TO KNOW

Social media is not something you set up once and leave it to run on its own. Social media is designed to create connections and build your network. If you are anti-social in real life, you will have to work hard to maintain online profiles. Find what authentically matters to you and share that, then follow like-minded people. It takes time to build a community, and this extends to online.

WHAT THE CREATIVE WILL LEARN IN THIS CHAPTER

You will learn how to build your social network, ideas for what to post and publish, when to post, and how to post most efficiently. You'll learn why negativity and trolls are a waste of time and are to be avoided as well as why it matters that you show up to the social party and engage once you are there. Building your business, brand, and practice requires that you build a community.

Human beings are social by nature. We always have been—out of necessity. We need each other. What is changing is the way we socialize, both in person and virtually. Social networking is how we keep in touch, how we share our comings and goings, and how we announce events, milestones, and life changes. If you are a business and a creative, you must have a social media presence. And you want to be active by being a participant and not a lurker or loiterer.

"Human beings are social creatures. We are social not just in the trivial sense that we like company, and not just in the obvious sense that we each depend on others. We are social in a more elemental way: simply to exist as a normal human being requires interaction with other people."

—Atul Gawande

FIG 14-1

Show up authentically and creatively on social media platforms.

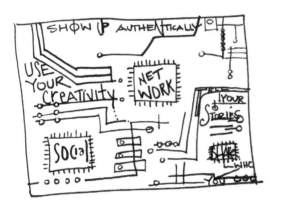

MULTIPLE ACCOUNTS

Set up at least two accounts on all social media platforms. Doing this allows you to post family photos and events with friends on your personal account and professional posts on your business account. All platforms make it easy to toggle back and forth between your accounts once signed in to both. If you are also posting for clients on social media, you can pay for services that will let you run several accounts at once and post across multiple accounts. Research services that offer free posts and those that require payment. Determine if you need one to make posting easier for you. If you have different brands, post separately for each.

ELEMENTS OF POST

There are different primary features of social media posts depending on the platform you are using, but there are elements to consider:

1. Use headlines. What you choose as a headline for a post is what people will see first. Like a newspaper, does it grab the reader and encourage him or her to check out your post?

2. Use language and phrases that become stand-alone quotes, sound bites, memes, or audio or video quick share files, meaning they are short enough that people will share with their friends.

3. Statistics matter if you are interested in sponsorship or need to use your numbers for funding. They can also help you review the posts that you received the most likes or comments on. Take a look at your stats frequently and use that information to post more of what is liked or less of what isn't.

4. Tips and how to's are the most searched thing on the internet. If you can offer either a tip or a tutorial in your post, more people will connect with you and seek you out.

5. Sharing quotes is a popular social media activity. If you have quotes that are meaningful to you, share them. People will follow along if quotes are something they also enjoy. Consider sharing your quotes, written by you.

6. Images and pictures. If you are creative, you should have a lot of images at your fingertips. Share not just finished things, but also those in process.

7. Audio/video. Share audio clips of your work and snippets of a video you have created.

8. Share infographics, charts, and other non-text formats, as they can be a fun way to express ideas. When appropriate, include them in your posts.

9. Re-post other people's posts; it builds relationships with others when you share their post, and they are more likely to share yours in the future.

take action

Grab your journal and write down ideas related to your practice that you could post about in each category from the previous list. As an example, list people you follow and whose posts you've enjoyed. Start to take note of who they are so you can re-post when you are out of fresh ideas. Having running lists can help so that you do not go long stretches without posting anything new.

IT'S A PARTY

It's important to think about networking over social media as a party where people get to know each other. You must attend, participate, and engage. You can't watch the party from your bedroom window across the street. Make your presence known and chat with people. Use social media to share what you are working on, but also take the time to comment on other people's posts, so they know you are present. There is no formula on how all people engage, nor would you want that. What is most important is that you be you; post things you love and that matter to you. Be authentic. The content, the people, and the platforms will all change and shift. How you connect with people matters and should stay consistent. Building relationships across platforms is the reason you are spending time on social media. Don't just build personal relationships; grow professional ones too.

"Engage rather than sell … Work as a co-creator, not a marketer."

—Tom H. C. Anderson

SHOW UP AUTHENTICALLY

When you show up authentically and are comfortable, people will meet you there. Share what you are proud of, open yourself up, be brave, and know that your information will be received by the right people. With that said, don't gut yourself and revel everything because that is too much for a social media post. Your followers want to see what you're excited about; they want to know what gets you out of bed in the morning, and they want to see you share more than work. If your passion translates into your career, tell people about how that came to be and how you keep it. Use social media exchanges to act just like you would face to face with a person. Never say anything you wouldn't say to their face, and if you love something, tell that person. That's authenticity, and if your followers meet you face to face, they will be pleased to find out you are the same person online and off.

"Don't say anything online that you wouldn't want to be plastered on a billboard with your face on it."

—Erin Bury

Don't put anything on social media you wouldn't do in front of your grandmother. When deciding to join social media, your next thought must be about how to behave in cyberland. It is important because if a future or potential employer looks up your social media accounts, you want to be seen as well behaved.

GOING VIRAL

Don't get caught up in what other people think you should post to social media. Marketers will offer tips on how to make something go viral online, but the success of that is wildly unpredictable and depends on everything. There is never a guarantee that something will go viral. Therefore, you can't worry about posting things that might get attention or hope that the post will go viral. It doesn't work that way. If something you love doing goes viral and gets the attention that is great, but it is not the only way to get noticed. Do good work, share more than just your work, and show what inspires you and what you are looking at; that will get you more attention. The only way to gather a following is to be your authentic self; that is when you make a connection—only when you are real.

HANDLES AND HASHTAGS

When selecting your handles for your social media accounts, choose something you can stick with for a long time. Consider using your name to make it easier for clients to find you. If your handle name is taken or doesn't make sense to use, choose something connected to your practice, such as a shortened version of your name. Then use the same handle or one with a slight variation on all platforms for consistency. A hashtag is a searchable word or phrase that allows anyone to see what else is posted on the same topic on all social media platforms. When incorporating hashtags, consider what you would want to be known for. Don't just choose popular or trending hashtags. Choose things that you would want people to know you for. Just to give a sense of the count on popular hashtags, here are the top ranking: #love has over a billion and a half posts; #art is close to 500 million. Do a little homework and see what hashtags would fit your posts and make some new ones up—why not be a trend setter yourself?

FOLLOWERS

As you are visiting social sites, posting and engaging, people will see your handle and click around to see what you are up to. If they are interested in your posts, they are likely to follow

FIG 14-2

Focus on the right followers, not just more followers.

you without you needing to ask for their attention. If you are looking to become sponsored on your website, blog, or social media account, then your number of followers matters. If, however, you are looking to build your brand, then you don't want to get obsessed with the number of followers. Instead, focus on getting not a million random people to follow you but followers who know and support your work.

Remind yourself that the right followers are always better than the many. If you want specific people to follow you, frequent their posts and leave comments. They will see you showing up and eventually check you out.

ANOTHER DATING ANALOGY

Just like in dating, when you are desperate nobody wants to meet you or hire you, but when you're confident, everybody wants in on that. When you know someone who is confident, you want to be near that person; the same thing goes in business. You have to remember to project "Here's who I am, here's how I'm showing up, here's what matters to me, here's what I'm passionate about." Often one of the most significant faltering moments when creatives are looking for employment or gigs, or are trying to make connections or get exhibitions—or whatever it is they're trying to do—they get nervous and forget all the things that matter to them. Don't build a social media presence where you hide all the bits and pieces of things you love. It's a waste of your time and energy. Instead, celebrate all the parts and pieces you are. Social media is a way to tell your story before people even meet you. You might have followers you never meet in person. Tell the whole story, not just the work life and perfectly finished things; share all of you and your practice. Offer images of work in progress, other creatives whose work you admire, inspirations, and ideas. Think about what you would talk about on a first date. Do you have those elements covered in your social media posts? They are the same thing you can talk about in an interview or at a networking event.

BE GENEROUS

People help nice people. Every time you are generous in helping others, you have deposited a coin into a bank account that you can use later. Most creative fields are generous, offering advice, loaning tools, sharing leads, and mentoring each other. Generosity with each other is possible because we are often the only ones who understand each other. Any time you hear of another creative who could use support, pull out your Rolodex, wallet, or work gloves and chip in. You can do the same thing online when one of your followers asks for a recommendation or information. Taking the time to direct message someone on social media is like bringing a cup of sugar over to your neighbor in need. Be careful not to overdo it or continue to do it for the same people who ask over and over, but when you can help, offer it.

*"It takes generosity to discover the whole through others.
If you realize you are only a violin, you can open yourself
up to the world by playing your role in the concert."*

—*Jacques Yves Cousteau*

EMBARRASS YOURSELF

Failing at something is an experience all humans share. Find ways to share failure and do things that feel embarrassing. If you're normally aloof, do a little dance on video and post it; capture funny "accidents" and share on social media. It can be one of the best ways to build authentic relationships and uncover new opportunities. If you are afraid of trying something new, ask yourself why. If you are avoiding trying things because you don't want to be embarrassed, then you aren't sharing all of you. Sharing experiments or hacks gone wrong takes away the polished view that social media offers and allows you to be real. As an example, even if you don't have "in action" photos of yourself falling into an almost drained pool, you can post a picture of the green water with the caption, "I just slipped and fell into this sludge while trying to do a photo shoot." Only showing the glossy, perfect image while networking online doesn't benefit you, but being a human who falls, that is offering something real and relatable. It's called failing forward. Fail all the time; consistently fail and embarrass yourself sometimes: Tell people you slipped on your butt, threw the ball in the wrong basket, sang the wrong words to a song, or tell people you love the latest pop star on the radio that everyone is teasing.

IDEAS FOR SOCIAL MEDIA POSTS

You may have a nagging feeling about what to post on your social media profiles. The first thing you must do is get inspired. Go out into the world and find ideas to support you when you are running low on what to post. Where do you find ideas and inspiration? My go-to inspiration places are music shows, nature, bookstores, and travel spots. I take a lot of pictures in those settings and save them to post at various times. I also really enjoy humor, so when I see funny things I will photograph them and prep a caption to post later.

Most importantly, when determining ideas for posts, focus on your authentic self. The things that are of interest to you are interesting to an audience that is following you. Show and share what inspires you, what you are looking at and where you find your ideas. This generosity makes others want to know you more. Post on your social media fun, goofy, inspired things that make you happy. If you're going to build relationships with online followers, offer consistent content. How-tos and tutorials are very popular and if that is something you enjoy doing, share videos or step-by-step instructions. Creatives know how to do all kinds of things that other people don't and have skills that other people would find fascinating. Think about what you could share that might seem simple to you but is interesting for others to see. Another thing that brings people back to your account

FIG 14-3

Build a social media toolbox to pull ideas for posts.

is lists because people love lists. Think about your top ten favorites, such as favorite summer music shows or best books or favorite historical artists. Include your followers by asking their preferences. Offer advice on things you love or are testing. Provide travel tips if that is something you do on a regular basis. If you love your local community, as an example you are a big fan of local breweries, coffee shops, and pizza houses, share the local love in your posts. Go to local places, take photos, and share your experience.

Use social media networking to build your brand and stay in a lane that makes sense for your practice. As an example, don't say you're a food blogger but post all cars in your social feeds; that is confusing. All posts and ideas should be somewhat similar to your other posts. Mix it up and offer variety but maintain consistency within your brand.

Grab your device and comb through your social media right now. Is everything currently posted who you want to portray? If not, make a point to clean it up and delete some posts.

WHERE TO POST

There are many social media sites, and new ones pop up every day. How do you decide which ones to use actively? When you hear about a new site, run right over to it and sign up, even if you are not sure you are going to use it. Do this because if it becomes popular, you will have grabbed your name or handle. You don't want to be a late coming and lose your name or brand to someone else. I always grab my company name for everything and then wait and see where it goes. Many social media sites die early, but some surprise us and you'll be glad you were holding your name when the time comes to use the site. If you never use it, there is no real loss since most sites are free to sign up.

Consistently post to sites that you are interested spending time on. If you enjoy video or photography, choose sites dedicated to that. If you prefer reviews or long-form writing, create your community on those sites. Go where your online tribe lives and build relationships there.

SCHEDULE POSTS

The best thing you can do for your sanity is to sign up for a scheduling app or software program. Build days on your calendar where you prep posts for every platform and then schedule the days and times they will publish live. Always supplement these scheduled posts with on-location or live posts. I use this idea for upcoming events I want to be posted on the day of, or I use a schedule for things that do not need to be posted right away. If you dedicate one day a month to writing and prepping social media posts and then schedule them, you free yourself up to think very little about it the rest of the month.

As a bonus people will say, "You are everywhere online! How do you have time? You are on every social media site all the time." You are not, but to others, it looks like you are. You can achieve this by scheduling posts for different days and times, so it seems spontaneous when it is scheduled, leaving you more time for your practice. Use these tricks of the trade to get your brand out there, everywhere, all the time. You can use services built into social media apps. There are also scheduling services with a monthly membership. Not only do those services allow you to plan days and times, but they also allow you to schedule which platforms you want to push the content to. The selection of sites can be different for every post.

MATCHY MATCHY

Look at your online presence, does every header, color, and font match on each social media site? If not, schedule time to clean it up. All the images, headers, bios, titles, and language should be the same, no matter the site. Some sites allow more images or copy, and in that case it's okay to include more. Make sure the general format matches on all your social media sites so that you offer a consistent brand no matter which site you are using.

NEGATIVITY ONLINE

Don't be a part of the problem. A common mistake is venting about difficulties or annoyances via your social media sites. This will work once, and you will get some sympathetic comments, but once it becomes a regular part of your posts, readers will begin to avoid the negativity they know they will find on your sites, and they will avoid you. If you post negative things often online, you will become known for that energy. On social media sites many people post negative things, but if you are building a business and a brand, avoid doing that. As an example, if I receive an invitation to attend something that a frequently negative person is hosting, I will decline because I don't want to hear more of their negative talk. Even if they don't do this in a professional setting, if I see it all the time on social media, he or she ends up getting known for this. People want to be engaged in exciting, inspiring things; they don't want to act as your therapist, counselor, or mother. That doesn't mean you can't share when something terrible or sad happens; it means save it for your family, friends, or your truth tribe. Posting all the little bummer moment makes you appear like a negative person, even if you are not. Be mindful of how others see you.

TROLLS

As with any networking or person-to-person engagement, you will run in to mean people. They are known online as trolls. It is a part of doing business. There are people who use negativity to make their career, so the best thing to do when negative trolls descend is to control yourself and ignore them. When you do not respond, they will eventually go away and move on to their next victim. You can unfriend and unfollow people, but on some sites, without a total block, they can still follow you. If they continue to leave negative comments, hide their comments. To them, it will look like it is still up, but none of your other followers will see the comments. Search each of your social media platforms to determine how to do this. If you can stand it, troll comments add to the engagement factor, which increases your stats. If trolls appear, learn to live with them, unless they are threatening or harmful, then report them to the platform.

SEVEN CONNECTION

For a stranger, it takes seven separate encounters for that person to fully remember your name. If you're meeting people, unless they're really into you, it takes seven different times for a full recall.

FIG 14-4

Provide special offerings for your followers.

This can be a hard concept for the sensitive creative. Maybe you've said things such as, "I have met her at art openings five different times, but she acts like she's never met me." Don't take it personally and remember it takes at least seven times before they know you. Engaging with a person one, three, or five times still may not yet be enough.

STAY IN TOUCH

Keep connections up with like-minded people. If you want to keep getting invited to the parties, stay in touch in between. You want to be remembered and thought of, so comment on other's posts, and direct message them bravely. You would be surprised to find out many creatives will reply back if you message them over social media. Never be afraid to ask people you admire questions about things they share in their posts. This is another way to build community and relationships.

OFFER YOUR SPECIAL

Think about what you can offer that is special. What do you bring? What's your thing? If you have spent any time on social media, you can easily visualize ads that pop up in between posts. As an example, what if the announcement were inside your post and were an offer to share a gift to your followers? You could announce on social media that you have a pop-up event where you give a sneak peek to followers. Use social media to offer real face-to-face experiences whenever possible. If your gift is a Rolodex, then use your social media platform to give shout-outs to other creatives. Do you make stuff that you can sell in flash sales, in person or online? Find your thing and include it in rotation on your social media calendar. This is a calendar where you create a plan to space out your posts so that you have variety.

TESTIMONIALS

Get testimonials from clients who have praised you or your work. If you get an e-mail, a card, a note, or a letter from someone thanking you for being outstanding, scan them and keep these items in a file. If you are given feedback verbally, be brave enough to ask if you can use their compliment as a client testimonial. Share testimonials on your branding materials and social media. Take pictures with clients and customers and post those; celebrate your supporters. They don't need to be famous, just people who believe in you.

HEADSHOTS

Every creative should have a professional photograph of him- or herself and his or her work or an action shot, depending on the practice. If you are in the performing arts, you already require headshots. Everyone needs a headshot for your social media accounts. Have a professional shot taken and update it every three to five years. Ask the photographer to provide digital files that are high resolution for print (480 DPI) and low resolution (150 to 72 DPI) for online. Request these also in both color and black-and-white versions. You will need an updated headshot every two to three years depending on your field.

NETWORKING

When you attend an event that offers networking, a good rule of thumb once you get your name and what you do out of the way is to not talk business the rest of the time. People would prefer to talk about their families or their hobbies over their work. If you can get people to share their personal stories, they are more likely to remember you and feel connected. Everyone else will talk about work all night, and they will all blend. I obtained some of my best clients by being human with them and getting to know them before we connected on business. If you are attending live networking events, always bring business cards to hand out if requested. Never shove a card in someone's hand who didn't ask. Have stories ready to share in case there is a conversational lull. Have your elevator pitch prepared to share. Make sure it matches your online bios across all your social media platforms because this person is going to look you up and you do not want conflicting messages.

HANDSHAKES AND NAME TAGS

Learn to shake hands well. If you shake with a weak, limp hand you will appear to be weak. If you have a strong handshake, people will notice you and prepare to listen to you. Practice your handshake with your truth tribe to get the perfect grip. Once you have the handshake down, decide where to put your name tag at the next event you attend. Proper etiquette states a name tag should be worn above the pocket on the right side of your shirt or jacket. Networking events have encouraged people to wear nametags on the left side because you shake with your right hand and could cover up your name tag as you shake. Creatives generally push back against the entire concept of name tags, and you might put it on your hip or on your leg. The idea is to have the person you're networking with hear and read your name to better remember it. If you stick the name tag to your hip make a point to show them. They may remember you for that very reason. You can determine the best style for yourself. Help people remember your name for different reasons than just reading it on a name tag alone.

START NETWORKING BEFORE YOU GET THERE

There are many different kinds of networking opportunities that you will encounter over your career. An important thing to remember, whether you are attending a networking session, a conference, or an opening, is to do your homework and find out who might be there.

Will Mitchell of StartupBros said, "A big thing is, we start a Twitter list before we go. We'll add all of the people that we want to meet to a Twitter list, and we even have a secondary list of people that we wouldn't mind meeting. We have those so that any time we have some down time, we can just pull out our phones and see where the people we want to meet and network with are at."

From Mitchell's example, you can see it is not only essential to know who will be there, but to find creative ways to discover where they will be. It ensures a possible encounter. Pure genius!

REFLECTION

Humans are social creatures, and our need to connect will always be present. Social media and online networking are a constant to maintain professional relationships. Join the social party, be authentic even before you arrive, and steer clear of trolls and negativity online. Don't be desperate and don't get caught up in how many followers you have, but notice those with who

take action

Just because you are creative, it doesn't mean you are a designer or are good with tech. If you need a little help dressing your social media pages, jump online and research third parties that sell themes, frames, photographs, and templates. Make a list of sites that offer items you are interested in. Periodically buy something to spruce up your pages. If you are skilled at design tools, create them yourself or barter with a designer.

you build relationships. Stay in touch and share creatively. Take actions to make the process easier for your practice.

HOW WILL THE CREATIVE USE THIS INFORMATION GOING FORWARD?

Directions: Take a few minutes to think about how you will update or alter your current social media based on the information in this chapter. Write down three ideas in the space provided.

1. _____

2. _____

3. _____

BUILDING YOUR CREATIVE NETWORK

Directions: Think of current followers you have engaged with minimally. Write down ways you can connect with them more in the space provided. Write a specific goal for contacting one of them today through direct messaging.

1. _____

2. _____

3. _____

Goal: _____

SECTION V

GO THE DISTANCE

CHAPTER FIFTEEN

Identifying Your Strengths

EXERCISE DEVICES

INTRODUCTION

Your best shot at having a successful career in a creative field is to get to know your strengths. It's easy to get distracted by shiny offerings, but are those opportunities playing to your best strengths? This chapter is about getting honest with yourself about your skills. So many creatives think they must do it all themselves, but there is a better way that will create more time and bring in more money, but you have to do the work in this chapter to find out what you are best at and focus there.

TERMS THE CREATIVE NEEDS

ASSESSMENTS Evaluation or ability of someone

CHAMBER OF COMMERCE A form of business network; for example, a local organization of businesses whose goal is to further the interests of fellow small business owners

SCORE Service Corps of Retired Executives. Note: This is their former name; now they are known as SCORE For the Life of Your Business

NSBA National Small Business Association

SWOT Strengths, weakness's, obstacles and threats

WHAT THE CREATIVE NEEDS TO KNOW

Having clarity on what you are best at will be a personal game changer. Instead of spending your time trying to make clients happy or waiting around for them to show up to ask you to create something, do what you are best at and produce every day. You can get help or hire out the rest. Knowing your strengths leads to a more successful business and practice.

WHAT THE CREATIVE WILL LEARN IN THIS CHAPTER

Through activities in this chapter, you will have a clear sense of where you should be focusing your time and energy. You will also learn strategies for getting all that that you are not good at off your plate. You will learn about assessments that determine your strengths and services that support your practice.

MEASURING YOUR STRENGTHS

Creatives often see themselves as "get it done" types who do everything themselves, but just because you can do so many different things doesn't mean you should. Likely, you have been wearing many hats and playing every role of a small business owner for a long time; this can lead to the illusion that you are holding everything together and that you have skills in all the areas. Do you know your biggest strengths? Are you playing those up?

If you're not sure what your strengths are, how do you find out? Start online and search "professional assessment companies and tools," as many offer this very information. Some of the more well-known are Strength Finders, Kolbe, DISC, Myers-Briggs, Foresight, and Emergenetics. I have taken them all and more that are out there. They offer valuable insight into your personality and what show up as your strengths. The other gift that comes with doing a self-assessment is permission to stop doing the things you do not have an aptitude for and focus only on those that you do. The online assessments have varying price points from $20 to $200.

> *"The most difficult thing is the decision to act. The rest is merely tenacity. The fears are paper tigers. You can do anything you decide to do. You can act to change and control your life and the procedure. The process is its own reward."*
>
> —Amelia Earhart

FIG 15-1

Eliminate your weakest skills by tossing burdensome tasks out and hiring or trading for help.

tip

If you take any of the assessments, read the definitions of the words or numbers identified as matching your personality. If you just read a couple of sentences, instead of a couple of pages, you will miss the wealth of information that can offer insight into how to spend your time.

Once I learned what categories were my strongest, I merely eliminated any areas that were not, and this was freeing. It will allow you to stay in your lane, hire out, trade, barter, or eliminate tasks.

If you enjoy doing these types of things and going more in-depth, start filling them out to discover your results. If you are not interested in sitting down at your computer to fill out online surveys, there are other ways you can discover your greatest strengths. There are free worksheets available online that can walk you through different ways to identify your strengths. One of these is SWOT Analysis (strengths, weaknesses opportunities, threats). Any search engine can find a SWOT worksheet. These online sheets walk you through questions specific to identifying your strengths, weakness, obstacles, and threats. This is a chance to build confidence in what you do well and focus on that. Another free option is to visit a local SCORE office in your city. They have many free resources and a network of former volunteer CEOs and business experts with thousands of volunteers to support your practice. Another great organization is NSBA or the National Small Business Association. In addition to assisting in building strengths, NSBA offers small business owners resources, insurances, and disaster assistance. Start-up organizations, chamber of commerce, and other business organizations in your local community can help with the business end of your practice.

take action

Grab a journal and write at the top of a blank page: Current load. Then, write down all the things you must do or take care of for your creative business. Take as much time as you need and walk through the things you do daily, weekly, monthly, and annually.

Once you have written down everything thing, grab four different color highlighter markers. Next, move through the list with the following criteria:

1. *Choose one color for anything you would do all day long for free, meaning you won the lottery and did not need to make money—which items would you keep doing for free?*

2. *Choose a second color for things you love doing and are good at but you need to be paid to do them. Otherwise, you would feel resentful.*

3. *Use the third color highlighter for anything you know you are capable of but would prefer not to do. Think errands; there are people who enjoy standing in lines and could support you.*

4. *Finally, use another color for all the things you hate to do, and if you never had to do them again, you would be thrilled. Think taxes, writing applications, shopping.*

Once you have everything on your list highlighted, take a minute to study what you felt you would do for free. Are you being honest; if you didn't have to think about an income, would you do everything all day long for free? Anything that remains is your strength because it is your biggest passion. You are best at what you love doing the most.

Next, give a hard look at the things you love doing and are good at but you need to get paid. Are there things on that list you are good at but don't want to be paid for? Let me give you an example. For years, I worked in nonprofit and managed hundreds of grants, I taught grant writing workshops and worked as a freelance grant writer. I know

FIG 15-2

Learn what your passion is and what you would do all day long for free. For everything else, charge well or hire it out.

how to write a grant, however, I wouldn't put that in my'"love it but need to get paid for it" category, because even though I could make money at it, I don't love doing it, not at all. Dump those type of things into the "never want to do it pile." Be mindful of what you put in this category that can make you money because it can pull you away from other things you are stronger at and love more.

The last two categories can be a challenge for creatives to admit to because of the desire to do everything yourself and the desire to save money often overrules logic. For everything you highlighted under "anything you are capable of but would rather not do" and the "hate it, never want to do it' categories, consider hiring out, bartering, or arranging for a trade with someone who loves to do those things. It is essential to have the perspective that for everything you do not enjoy doing, such as databases, spreadsheets, and taxes; there is a person out there who would put these things on their "all day long for free" list.

Repeat this same exercise for your personal life, too. If you live with others, have them do it as well; you might find a change in the division of labor would help everyone get more done.

FIG 15-3

Ask others what your strengths are.

OTHER WAYS TO DISCOVER YOUR STRENGTHS

Ask those who know you well to share what they see you doing best. They will know this because it will cover things that you talk about frequently, that you've shown them you have created, or that you invited them to experience. Your actions speak loudly, and friends and family who spend the most time with you can likely tell you when they see you at your happiest. When you are doing things you love the most and vice versa, it could be because you are doing something you hate. Ask your tribe to give you feedback on your strengths.

Think about the things throughout your life you are most proud of; was it the outcome of what you created? Was it the process you went through? Was it the feeling it created in you? Was it that you delivered on time? Was it something you did a little dance over to celebrate? Looking at past accomplishments and the feelings they gave you can help provide clarity on what you are best at doing and enjoy the most. It is essential to focus on your experience, not that of a client. It does not mean something is your greatest strength just because your customers praise you for it. If it was uncomfortable for you to produce, then even if you have happy customers it is not your strength because it is not your highest passion.

WHO DO YOU ADMIRE?

What is it about people you admire that makes you pay attention to the work they produce? Is it the product, the craftsmanship, their general style, energy, or something else? You can find your strengths and the things you would like to work toward by looking at those you are inspired by. Do you see yourself attracted to things or people you would like to model? Knowing who those people are and the background on how they got to where they are should inspire you. Investigate their stories, and that may aid you in finding yours.

Ask yourself when you are the most confident. Those moments when you feel ultimately in control and in command of your actions, that is confidence. Look back at when you experienced the feeling of confidence; what were you doing? The feeling of confidence is an ongoing process that, when achieved, even in moments, will show you when you are strong. Notice what you are willing to jump at even if it doesn't pay as much as you'd like and what you want to say no to, even if it pays well. Also, notice what you do not hesitate to say yes to even though it will take up a great deal of time. It's likely that you'll do this because it is a project where you will get to use your greatest strengths. Your decisions are not random; they are connected and offer you information when you pay attention.

FIG 15-4

Find your own strengths by looking at the people you admire.

Never take a project that consumes so much of your time that you become resentful. If this occurs, it is a tell-tale sign that you are operating not from your areas of strength but from an area that you hate and therefore have no business working on.

REFLECTION

Remember that just because you worked hard in school and got straight A's doesn't mean your biggest strength is academics. Or, if you do a job well, all day long, it still may not use your greatest strengths. As you are unearthing your greatest strengths, use this as an opportunity to make changes in your personal and professional life. If you discover you are doing things that are on your "I hate it" list, get it off. I often work with creatives who think they don't have the time or the financial resources to hire things out, but ask yourself how much time you are spending on this part of the project that you don't want to do. Could you make more money focusing only on areas inside of your strengths? Could you make enough to pay someone else to do the things you don't want to do? Learning your strengths is about your mental health, wellbeing, overall capacity, and improvement your happiness. Knowing your strengths means improving these other areas of your life so you can devote more time to your practice.

HOW WILL THE CREATIVE USE THIS INFORMATION GOING FORWARD?

Directions: Take a few minutes to think about how you will identify the greatest strengths of your professional and personal life. Write down three things from this chapter you will commit to doing in the space provided.

1. _____

2. _____

3. _____

BUILDING YOUR CREATIVE NETWORK

Directions: Think of people, organizations, or other resources that you can connect with to ask for feedback on your strengths. Write down these creative network connections in the space provided. Write a specific goal for contacting people in your network for this assignment. Follow through with it!

1. _____

2. _____

3. _____

Goal: _____

CHAPTER SIXTEEN

Dreaming Big and Setting Goals

IT'S A DESTINATION *AND* A JOURNEY

INTRODUCTION

Goals are a tool to focus your creative efforts and move you in a targeted direction. Goal setting matters because it is a way for you to visually see where you're headed and where you want to be in the future. As you move forward in your career, setting concrete goals is important for planning your next stage, and you're next after that. Goal setting gives you a reason to get out of bed in the morning and focus on what you want to work toward every day. It's important to know where you're headed next and to do that with focus and intention.

TERMS THE CREATIVE NEEDS

GOAL The object of a person's ambition or effort; an aim or desired result

TO THE TRADE ONLY (TTTO) Buying and selling of goods either on the domestic (wholesale and retail) markets or the international (import and export markets) with no direct sales to the public (manufacturers sell directly to wholesale buyers)

TRADE SHOW An exhibition at which businesses in a particular industry promote their products and services

SHORT-TERM GOALS Goals that you want to achieve in the near future (within one to two years)

LONG-TERM GOALS Goals you want to accomplish in the future that can require time and planning; they are not something you can do within a year

BUCKET-LIST GOALS Goals to achieve before reaching a certain age or dying

WHAT THE CREATIVE NEEDS TO KNOW

Start setting goals by dreaming a little and answering questions. You need to know how goals work and how to set them in motion to create the things in your life that you want the most.

WHAT THE CREATIVE WILL LEARN IN THIS CHAPTER

In this chapter, you will learn about different types of goals for different areas of your life. You will learn how and when to set goals and how to create plans and take steps to achieve goals. Learn to create goals in each area of your life, personal and professional. Learn to create timelines for every goal because when you are committed, you will accomplish them.

> *"Your goal is to be the first thing people do when they start their day. If you're an artist, a leader or someone seeking to make a difference, the first thing you do should be to lay tracks to accomplish your goals, not to hear how others have reacted/responded/insisted to what happened yesterday."*
>
> —*Seth Godin*

FIG 16-1

Keep your list of goals on your fridge so you will see them everyday.

WRITE IT DOWN

You might feel scared to write your big dreams down because that makes them real, and it makes you accountable. This takes bravery. Take the time after this chapter to invest in your future by creating a plan filled with goals. Write down some that are quickly achievable so you can taste success and then write down some that will push you to reach for them. Once you write goals down, post them somewhere you will see them often—in your bathroom or on your refrigerator or use an app with reminders, whatever it takes to stay committed.

WHAT IF I ACHIEVE ALL MY GOALS?

The fear of setting goals and then reaching them can be a scary experience because it means you must dream up new goals. Maybe you are afraid to set goals not because you won't achieve them, but because you know you can. If you're scared you might reach it, or you know you can, that will sometimes grind forward motion to a halt. To get over the fear of doing well, which so many creatives carry with them, you need to be brave enough to believe you deserve to achieve those goals. Fear can paralyze creatives, because if you completed the highest goal you set for yourself, then what? The thought of starting over does not appeal to most creatives. But, let's hope that exact feeling is gifted to you again and again. The act of creatively reinventing your practice is an experience all creatives should have several times over their career.

> *"Decide . . . whether or not the goal is worth the risks involved. If it is, stop worrying. . . ."*
>
> —*Amelia Earhart*

Know that you are not alone in feeling that achievement can sometimes feel more frightening than failure itself. From the time I was a little kid, I had a dream of having a greeting card business. When I was little, I folded construction paper into cards, and with markers on the back, I made a logo and a company name, and the price was always $80. These cards were never for sale, but I thought the $80 price tag would impress my family. Growing up, I thought the highest thing to achieve would be owning a stationery company. It was always in my head, growing up and in college, but I never wrote it down. I made lists of other goals and other ideas of things that I could do for a career, but none of them came true because they weren't real for me. After I graduated from graduate school, I had a government job working for the state arts commission, and while I loved the work, I knew something was missing. One day a friend asked me what I wanted to do and at that moment I said, " I've always had this dream of having a stationery company." I then admitted to him that I didn't know the first thing about starting a manufacturing business. Fast forward a few months later, and he invited my husband and me over for a dinner party at his home. We sat at our assigned table and asked everybody who they were and what they did for a living. We went around the table, one by one, and when I turned to the guy next to me, he told me his name and shared he owned a greeting card company. At that moment, I looked across the table at my friend who invited us, and I gave him the raised eyebrow, excited face; my friend just made the "uh huh, I know'" shoulder shrug, with a smile. I spent all night talking to the guy with the greeting card company, and he told me the National Stationery Show was to be held in two weeks; I didn't even know what that was. He said, "Get a plane ticket and come to New York City to check out the show." I went, and I walked the national stationery show which is a "to-the-trade-only" trade show for wholesale buyers of stationery. Buyers from every store, both brick and mortar and online, attend the show and buy for the next year. I began to walk around the national stationery show, held in a gigantic convention center, and as I was walking around, all booths I saw are giants such as Hallmark and American Greetings. I was thinking, "I'm so out of my league; this is ridiculous," but I knew I had to get back in there and figure it out, take advantage of this opportunity.

While I was roaming the show, looking for a dash of hope, I came across a smaller designer with a medium-sized booth. He asked me how it was going, and I spilled my entire story. I was messy, and he sat and listened, and then when I finished he said: "Oh my goodness honey; you're on the wrong level." Of course. I said, "No kidding! I am so not on this level!" Then he said, "No, literally, take the escalators downstairs, open the doors, and you will find your people." I did and thank goodness I didn't give up. I went down the escalators, opened the double doors, and suddenly the lights were shining on 500 booths of small business artists. They were 8 x 8' booths with stationery and cards on display. I met a lot of people that year who coached me, guided me, and gave me advice. Then, the next year I went myself, and eventually I started a greeting card company for several years, which was successful and enjoyable. I learned so much about manufacturing, buyers, vendors, and, most of all, how to run a business. And then it ran its course when I realized all of the shops I dreamed about carrying my line now had them on their shelves. I felt done and ready to move on to my next big thing. I had to start all over again, dream up what I want to do next and how I was going to do it.

tip

Lack of confidence can make you scared. Scared to try new things, to take risks, and to put yourself out there. Dig deep, all the time, and stay determined to move past the fear. To do this, set small, medium, and large goals, both short and long term. This allows you to have more immediate success while you are working toward the larger goals.

After I closed my stationery business, I was scared and felt rudderless. I hope you have those "what am I going to do now" moments because those are the opportunities that teach us what our next big thing will be. While it can initially be a terrifying feeling, ultimately those are the moments that push us to grow our practice in places we hadn't imagined. I have reinvented my practice every two to three years since. My practice always focuses on creativity and problem solving, but the content and outcomes change. You can learn a lot from the experience of having accomplished your biggest goals. It can force you to consider what else you are capable of and what you are interested in spending time doing.

take action

Use this activity to create goals right now. Grab your journal and pen and write down answers to the following questions:

1. *What would make me feel like a successful creative?*

   Don't just write a single sentence; take your time and ask yourself how that would feel. Would it feel comfortable and natural, never forced? Would it feel relaxed and fun?

2. *What would my life as a successful creative look like?*

   Would it look like a big fancy house or a brand-new car? Would it look like having all kinds of books and publications with your name as the author? Would it look like performing at a venue that is the most prestigious in your industry? What would it look like for you to achieve your success? You can dream whatever you want; ask yourself, "When you think of your future, what do you see?"

3. *What is the highest, most significant, boldest, thing I could achieve as a creative?*

   Go big on this one—make it your ultimate dream. Everyone's final is different, so don't decide based on others' ideas. What is it for you? What is the most significant boldest thing you could accomplish?

STEPS TO GOAL SETTING

Think of a goal as something to visualize, like a map. Imagine you are looking at a map and your goal is your destination; based on where you are currently, where do you want to go? What is your destination? That's your goal.

The steps in goal setting are known as objectives or steps—see them as mile markers on your map. Mile markers are those little green panels on a stick along the highway. As you're driving, they count the numbers up or down, depending on the direction you're driving. As an example, you notice mile marker 200 and the next one is 211, and the next one is 220; if you know a goal or a destination is at mile marker 500, then you know you are you going in the right direction. However, if the numbers are going down, 190, 175, then you know you are headed in the wrong direction. Take steps to head toward your goals, not away from them. The purpose is to show you are you on a focused path toward the desired destination.

STEPS

1. Schedule time on your calendar to reflect on where you see your future.

2. Sit in a place you can be alone in this process.

3. Bring along paper and pen or your laptop.

4. Start by writing down everything you are interested in and would love to do in your future. Don't worry about the order or if the goal is based on reality. Just free write for five to 10 minutes.

5. Look at your list and focus on which goals you want to go after first. Use a highlighter to identify the things that light you up the most.

FIG 16-2

Your goals are your destination. The steps are the mile markers letting you know if you are headed in the right direction.

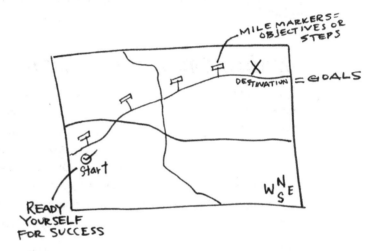

6. Write down five short-term and five long-term goals.

   Short-term goals are achievable in one to three years, and long-term goals take between three and five years.

7. For each goal, write down three to five steps that you can use as your mile markers to ensure you are headed in the right direction. If ever in doubt use the step "research" to better learn about actionable steps.

8. Indicate a clear timeline for each goal. Write down "by when" next to each goal and select a date.

9. Post your goals where you will see them daily, such as in your bathroom, home office, or on the refrigerator.

   Bonus step: Share your goals with someone who will help keep you accountable toward achieving them.

FIG 16-3

Find ways to carry your goals with you to reference often.

GOALS ON THE GO

If you want to get hyper-focused on making your goals happen faster, create a system to remind yourself of them multiple times a day. As an example, carry around a small laminated card with goals written on both sides. Tuck it into your phone case to review current goals often. You don't need to share this with anyone else. Find a system that you can use as a daily reminder to read your goals. This type of goal setting helps you to achieve things at a more rapid pace. Some of the most successful people in history, the most successful people you know of right now, are goal setters; they have a target they're always working toward. Always have a target, personally and professionally, to focus on and carry with you everywhere to achieve it faster.

DISTRACTIONS AND DERAILMENTS

Do you find that you get distracted by shiny objects or juicy opportunities that you just can't pass up? We're all guilty of this because creatives think opportunities could lead to something, but is that the right approach? While it's true that sometimes you do have to ride an opportunity and see where it takes you, if your actions are not connected to a focused purpose, then you're not going to get to your destination. If you are distracted while driving, you could lose control; the same thing happens in your life when you are distracted all the time. You never get anything done. Pause before jumping at every opportunity and ask yourself if the opportunity gets you closer to your goals. If the answer is a resounding no, then let it go so as not to derail yourself.

You should always write down and maintain both professional and personal goals. One will not function without the other. You are a whole person with complicated layers to your life; acknowledge your goals in all areas, not just one.

BUCKET-LIST GOALS

It is ongoing work to dream, build, and work toward your goals and then reinvent once you achieve them. To add fun to this brave new world of goal setting, you might also consider setting "once in a lifetime" goals. Think of something colossal, something crazy, but also something you are going to do in your lifetime. There is no need to include steps on your big bucket list. Write down the big, fun things you would like to do in your life. Post these where you can see them often.

STAY AWAKE

Reaching your goals means a daily practice of reading your goals and working toward them in all your actions. If you find yourself waking up years from now and feeling like nothing is happening in your life, take another look at your life goals and see where you progressed and where you did not and why. Better yet, don't wake up years from now saying that; instead, wake up now and ask yourself what is next for your practice and your personal life. Find the best time of your day to review your goals. Just before bed or first thing in the morning works well for many people.

TYPES OF GOALS

There are many different categories of goals. Set both personal and professional goals, but go even deeper in your goal setting and write goals down for several categories. Here are some examples:

Career: This goal will likely change throughout your life. Continue to dream and reinvent. Consider taking a class, reading about, or talking to someone in the field you are interested in; this will make the dreaming of the goals clearer to see.

Creative: Always have your next big idea for things you can do in your career. The goals connected to your practice should be a high priority, even if they aren't your day job. With confidence, you can achieve anything you set as a goal.

Exploration: Where do you want to go? What do you want to see? Are there places you dream of traveling? Write it down to experience it!

Family: Setting goals around family involves time, so get out a calendar and schedule it. Have a family meeting to discuss goals.

Financial: For financial goals, you will want specific numbers. As an example, if you want to pay off your student loans, don't just leave it at that, create dollar amount steps so you can see your progress. Post a visual chart.

Intellectual: Think about this both professionally and personally: Create challenges to push yourself. Maybe you want to go back to school? Read a book series? Take a class?

Physical: This is often on everyone's list, but what does it mean for you? Get specific. Make charts to track your progress.

Social: This is about time with friends and networking for your career. Set goals to make time for these activities; schedule them on a calendar.

Service: Looking to volunteer more? Studies show* that those who volunteer the most are the happiest. Looking to do more for others? Make it a goal to find volunteer opportunities that would be a good fit for your interests.

FIG 16-4

The years can fly by. Create goals to make your accomplishments.

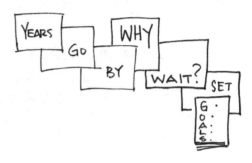

*The first study to examine the effect of motives of volunteers on their subsequent mortality was conducted in 2011 by a team led by Sarah Konrath of the University of Michigan. Respondents who volunteered were found to be at lower risk for death four years later, especially among those who volunteered more regularly and frequently.

BE ACCOUNTABLE

You can keep all your goals to yourself or find an accountability partner to share them with. This might be a trusted friend or family member. If you do choose to share, set a specific time, weekly, monthly, or quarterly, to measure your progress. You could do this in person, by phone, or over a video call. Building relationships with people who are supportive and helpful dramatically increases the likelihood that you will achieve your goals. Rather than surrounding yourself with negative nay sayers, find a tribe that will support your goals.

> *"If you hang out with chickens, you're going to cluck, and if you hang out with eagles, you're going to fly."*
>
> —*Steve Maraboli*

Don't let yourself off the hook. If you're not making progress, figure out what's holding you back. Revise your goals and then commit to yourself all over again. If this goal-setting stuff is new to you, be patient with yourself, and be kind and generous with yourself, but then kick yourself in the butt and get back at it if you have fallen off course.

take action

Make a creative, visual permission slip. On your permission slip write the following:

I have permission to create big goals and share my dreams.

Put this permission slip somewhere where you will see it daily. Remind yourself that you do, in fact, have permission. Design and decorate this permission slip in a way that suits you and is something you will enjoy looking at for weeks, months, or years to come.

> *"We are what and where we are because we first imagined it."*
>
> —*Donald Curtis*

To achieve big things, you must plan and spend time thinking through how you will accomplish your desired outcomes. Don't move through life not knowing what you want to do. Write it down and commit to it.

REFLECTION

Be creative with your goals. Goals work when you write them down and you commit; you don't have to show anyone else. When you write them down, you're committing to yourself that it matters, and that is an essential step in goal setting. It's also important to narrow your focus and get specific, or you could end up with pages and pages of goals for your life; instead, highlight just a few at a time. If you have too many goals at once, you can become scattered, and you won't remember what you're working toward. Look at your goals often, and put them in place where you will see them daily. Think about your goals and tie your tasks to your goals. When you are consistent, actions become things. Create schedules for everything, both personally and professionally. Your schedules are your tools—use them to organize tasks, activities, actions, and your time. Create timelines for every goal set and write down these timelines as reminders. If you do not set deadlines for goals, there is no urgency to accomplish them. Use a calendar as if your life depends on it because a calendar allows you to not only remember events, appointments, meetings, and to-do's, but you can add notes to a calendar as reminders for hitting your goals.

FIG 16-5

Create a permission slip to remind yourself to take action.

PERMISSION SLIP

I HAVE PERMISSION

HOW WILL THE CREATIVE USE THIS INFORMATION GOING FORWARD?

Directions: Take a few minutes to think about how, specifically, you will make time to build goal setting into your personal and professional life. Write down three ideas in the space provided.

1. _____

2. _____

3. _____

BUILDING YOUR CREATIVE NETWORK

Directions: Think of people, organizations, or other resources that can help you realize your goals. Write down those creative connections in the space provided. Write a specific goal for contacting or making use of one of them.

1. _____

2. _____

3. _____

Goal: _____

CHAPTER SEVENTEEN

The Job Hunt

HOT CAREERS AND TEMPORARY GIGS

INTRODUCTION

Every day we get closer to the gig economy being the norm for all professions. Creatives have always lived this way, and we know how to navigate it better than all other professions—out of necessity and choice. The freelance gig economy allows you to work on a variety of projects and have flexibility, which is where creatives thrive. This chapter shows a path for creatives to build their dream job, do something different every day, change things up, challenge their mind, and maintain their muscle memory.

TERMS THE CREATIVE NEEDS

GIG ECONOMY A labor market characterized by short-term contracts and freelance work as opposed to permanent jobs

FREELANCE Working for different companies at different times rather than being permanently employed by one company

MUSCLE MEMORY The ability to reproduce a particular action without conscious thought, acquired as a result of frequent repetition

NEGOTIATION A discussion aimed at reaching an agreement

WHAT THE CREATIVE NEEDS TO KNOW

Creatives do not have the same career pathways as any other industries. The nature of the work you engage in allows for a great deal of invention. Creatives have the privilege of making up the parts and pieces that go into their work. Never forget that looking at the classifieds for a job is just about the worst place you could go. Creatives build their careers not through ladder climbing, but glad handing. If you are looking for a successful job as a creative, it's all about who you know and, even more, it is who knows you. We build our careers as creatives through our tribe and creative community.

WHAT THE CREATIVE WILL LEARN IN THIS CHAPTER

In this chapter, you will learn about careers in the creative fields, interviews, thank-you notes and follow-up, negotiation tips, references and a list of career options for creatives. The ideas shared in this chapter can be used no matter if you're applying for and interviewing for a job, grad school, a residency, representation by an agent or anything else in a creative field.

THE HUNT

Once you decide to choose a creative career, the hunt and the hustle will become a constant part of your work day. Careers that are typical "nine-to-five" day jobs are a bit simpler when applying for the job. Once you get the job, you show up every day from nine in the morning until five in the evening to keep it. Creatives do no such thing. Your nine to five just repeats—at five in the evening you flip over the hourglass sand timer to read 5:00 p.m. to 9:00 p.m., and you do it again because your creative muse doesn't have a concept of time and she shows up when she is ready. Knowing this means finding or creating a job that allows flexibility. This flexibility will come in handy because you will spend a percentage of your work day hustling for work. It takes time to connect and reach out to potential clients or buyers. Even if you have long-term gigs, you are likely never satisfied and are always looking to challenge yourself. This is the hustler at work; the creative craves new and different experiences and will put in the work to hunt them down. The other way to job hunt is to find people you admire and ask if you can work for them. Find organizations or causes you believe in and see if they are hiring or if you could create a job within their organization.

FIG 17-1

Don't wait for things to come to you. Connect to create opportunities.

STAY IN JOB-READY SHAPE

Find energy in defeat and learn from it. If you apply for gigs and don't get them, use that as motivation to get clarity on what you want. Take each rejection as a lesson and see that there is something to be gained from experience. Stay in fighting shape; this means keeping your resume and professional documents current, having updated certifications or training so that you are ready. If there is specific vocabulary connected to your area, have it down, along with any acronyms used in your industry. Know who the major players are and why they are the major players. Study people who have come before you so you can give credit where it is due.

Use your network and your network's network to find out about job opportunities. Connect whenever possible, attend events in your industry, meet people who know people. That is where the creatives job hunt begins.

JOB BOARD

So, you can't find what you are looking for in the newspaper or on a job board? That's because the creative industry uses its community to fill positions. Why is that so prevalent in creative fields? Because we care deeply about the humans who surround us, meaning creatives will ask their colleagues in the field if they know someone who is applying for a job with them. They will also listen to their colleague's either negative or positive recommendation and act accordingly. Creative positions carry some of the best, zany titles—because we can make them up! The downside is it's hard to look for jobs when they have made-up position titles. Throw out the newspaper, get off the job boards, and start talking to your cousin's, dog walker's hairstylist about who he or she knows who could be a lead for you.

> *"Discovering your voice is rarely a linear path, but instead*
> *is the culmination of a lifelong process of observation,*
> *course correction, and risk-taking that eventually leads*
> *to the recognition of a valuable contribution."*
>
> —*Todd Henry*

THE INTERVIEW

Once you find a job that feels like a good fit, prepare yourself to show off all of your assets during the interview. A tricky thing about the creative industry is our lack of formality. That often means your interview might be held at a coffee shop, but that does not mean you can look and act casual. It is still an interview, and even if you don't get the job, remember that an interview is a chance to meet people and build relationships. You won't get every gig for which you interview, but the practice is priceless. If you shine, you will likely be considered for other things in the future. Every person you meet in your field is a potential connection.

Interviews can be unnerving, even if you're a great conversationalist and a social person. The hard thing about the interview is that it feels personal. You need to know what the interviewer looking at is your skills set and what you're bringing to the company and that they know you are nervous; if you weren't a little bit nervous you'd look cocky, and that is never good. Shake off the nerves and allow your honest self to come through. If your personality doesn't fit, it's a good thing for both of you to know up front.

DO YOUR HOMEWORK

Do research ahead of time on the company, the organization, and the person(s) you might work with or be interviewed by so that if you get called, you are prepared. It is beneficial for you to find out everything you can about the organization or person or company and the company culture. These things matter because if they don't fit with your creative practice, your values, or your interest, then do not waste time, both yours and the interviewers. It's impressive if you show up and you're able to talk about the company and demonstrate that you did your homework.

PRACTICE, PRACTICE, PRACTICE

The next thing to do as you prepare for any interview is to practice. Likely you have heard this before, and it makes sense, but the truth is most people don't do it because it's awkward. You may not want to have this sort of experience with family and friends. That means finding someone to practice with pre-interview. If an interview doesn't go well, you need to have your truth tribe on standby to share the questions you fumbled over. Ask your tribe to hit you with more of those type of questions so you can practice and grow. Change and adapt for each interview because they will be with different companies and people. Learn from the previous interview and prepare for the next.

FIG 17-2

Look into the mirror each day and remind yourself to be brave and confident.

SHOW UP EARLY

Always arrive on time, if not early. Park outside or sit outside if you took public transportation. Take a few minutes to calm yourself by taking deep breaths, and meditate to center yourself before you walk into the interview. Being late to an interview says you're going to be late to your job. There is no excuse: flat tire, car ran out of gas, car accident, it doesn't matter. It's unfortunate, and that stuff happens, but that's the end for most people right there. It is because they've heard it before; people in business have a lot going on; their time is incredibly precious and valuable, so show them that you respect it. This is the beauty of car services that you can call on your device; if you get in a bind, have a car pick you up so you can make it to the interview on time.

GO SOLO

Go alone to your interview; don't take your mom, your best friend, your sister, your kids, or anyone else. You need to be strong, brave, and confident all by yourself. If you need to have another person bring you, have him or her drop you off and ask him or her to wait in the car or drive around to wait for you. To bring a companion to an interview could mean not getting the gig at all. Landing a gig is rarely a team effort, so brave it alone.

Tell yourself one last time you are confident. All too often creatives are self-effacing and negative in their description of themselves—break that cycle!

WHAT TO BRING

If you applied online submitting everything electronically, always bring hard copies to an interview. If they have printouts in front of them, they may use them for reference. It can also be helpful for you because sometimes in your nervousness you may forget things such as dates, names, and other things you could find with a quick glance. Bring your list of references, even if they asked for it in advance. Bring a bottle of water as nervousness can cause a dry mouth and you can use the act of sipping water as a pause to think about a question or break eye contact. Bring a pen and a pad of paper in case you think of things you want to say and need to jot them down to wait until the moment is right. No one is ever going to think it odd if you break eye contact to take notes. Mind you, this does not apply if you are taking copious notes and never look up. If you feel the need to take a lot of notes because you are nervous, consider using a recording device and record the interview. This technique may be helpful for you to review questions asked and your answers to those questions. Always get permission to do this first, though. Also, bring your portfolio, deck, demo reel, or whatever item used in your area to showcase your creative practice. Bring a laptop but never rely on wi-fi; always have anything you would want to show an interviewer downloaded to your desktop.

DRESS THE PART

Before you step out to meet people or interview, make sure you have a wardrobe that is professional for the occasion. Creatives miss opportunities because of the desire to dress any way they want. No one is asking you to not be yourself, but for an interview or networking event, you must dress appropriately for the environment. If you are unsure, ask around, visit the workplace, and see how people show up to work. Then, dial it one or two notches up for the interview. It shows that this opportunity matters to you and that you are taking it seriously. Khakis and jeans may be appropriate, but a pair with holes or stains along with a wrinkled t-shirt are not appropriate for an interview.

A GREAT HANDSHAKE

When you enter a room, the next engagement after hello is the handshake. While there are some people who are germ-a-phobic and won't shake your hand, they are rare. Ask your friend who will help you practice the interview to help you practice your handshake. Do you have a wet fish, wimpy handshake? If you shake a hand with a weak grip what you just told the person, with no words at all, is that you lack confidence. If that is you and you are frightened by the handshake, work on it. No one wants to work with someone with a weak handshake because they don't want to deal with your lack confidence. Also, don't get carried away and shake like an aggressive person. It's a fine line. A polite, confident handshake starts the interview off right.

SMILE AND MAKE EYE CONTACT

As you walk into the building, smile and talk with the person at the front desk. Tell him or her who you are and who you are there to see. If he or she seems available to make small talk or answer a few questions, make him or her feel right away like you care. This is important because the person hiring for the gig might just ask the person at the front desk about you, and if they give a glowing review, that is one leg up for you! Properly greet the person you are there to meet with a smile and a hello. Thank him or her for inviting you in and immediately make eye contact. Eye contact can make everyone feel uncomfortable, at times. However, you must do it because it is an important way to communicate; that's the way people know you're hearing them and understand. Look someone in the eye and let him or her know you are confident enough to hold the contact. This doesn't mean you stare longingly until the other person gets uncomfortable and has to look away. It is okay to break eye contact to take notes or take a drink of water. It may seem obvious, but these tools help you look and feel calm and help it look like you have it all under control.

At any company or organization, the person at the front desk, the janitor, the cleaner, and the maintenance person are some of your most important allies. They are the folks who get things done. Always remember their birthdays, bring them holiday treats, say hello, and ask how they are doing. They matter more than you know.

LISTEN AND ANSWER

It is hard to answer a question if your mind is somewhere else. Listen thoughtfully and carefully when you are meeting with people; don't rush, and don't just listen to the beginning of something and already start formulating an answer. When we get nervous, we tend to have selective hearing and start answering without fully listening. Break that habit; listen fully and then answer. It is also perfectly okay to say, "That's a good question; let me think about that" and then calmly begin your answer when you are ready. Answer questions as directly as possible; if you do not know the answer to something, it's better to say, "I need to think about that. Can we come back to that?" or, "I wasn't prepared to answer that question today." Being honest is preferable to you going on and on and trying to get it formulated in your head. When you answer questions, speak up, speak clearly, and don't mumble your responses.

STAY POSITIVE

Everything that comes out of your mouth when you are interviewing should be positive and upbeat. If you just had the worst job because you were fired or you hated the boss, or you're frustrated with the industry, do not ever say negative things in an interview. The creative world is a small community where everyone knows everyone, and it is never worth it to speak poorly about yourself or others you've worked with. Save that conversation for hanging out privately with your tribe.

ASK QUESTIONS

Every time it's possible to ask a question, ask one. Do your homework and be prepared to ask questions before you are in front of a person. The absolute worst thing you can do at the end of the interview when the interviewer asks if you have any questions for them is to not have any. They're testing you; have questions, because you don't want to look like you have not given it any thought. If you think of questions after you leave, follow up and ask the appropriate person.

FIG 17-3

TALK UP YOUR SKILLS

Every chance you get, when meeting people, talk about your skills and your abilities and how they relate to what you do. Showing off your skills adds value; it's not cocky, it's not overdoing it—it's saying you know the things you love and are good at doing. Don't be shy about your skills; don't hold back because it could be the deal sealer. If you mention the extras you would bring to the position, you are more likely to give yourself a leg up. There is nothing worse than finding out someone got a gig you wanted simply because they revealed a hidden skill, and it is worse if you have that same skill and failed to mention it.

FOLLOW UP

After meeting with anyone offering you a gig, there are a couple of follow-up things you need to do. The very first follow up is a thank you. I'm a big believer in the thank you. Whether you want the gig or not, you still thank the person because they are connected to the larger creative community. You don't know what he or she may have thought of you; you don't know how he or she is connected to the community, so immediately following the interview, stand up, shake his or her hand firmly, and with direct eye contact you thank him or her for his or her time. On your way out, request the mailing address to send him or her a thank-you note. Immediately after you leave the building, send an e-mail from your device, thanking him or her for his or her time and stating that you look forward to hearing from him or her. Then, follow up, if appropriate, two weeks after the interview by asking if he or she needs anything additional from you and then leave it at that. Do not bug; if he or she wants to hire you, he or she will. That said, if you have a potential client who needs more hand-holding, follow up often to remind him or her you are there, but do not ask for anything; just check in.

THANK YOU

Walk away from meeting someone or out of an interview and sit somewhere immediately. Calmly send an e-mail, the subject header saying "thank you," and when he or she opens it, a simple sentence that says thank you again. For the next step, write a thank-you note and send it via post office mail. For the thank-you note, take three minutes only to write three sentences, ending with a thank you and your name. Then, get it into the mail within three days. This promptness is unheard of in almost any industry, and if you do it, you will stand out. When you mail a thank-you note, make sure to both write and sign your name and include your business card; this helps the recipient remember you.

take action

Purchase thank-you notes, envelopes, a pen you like to write with, and stamps to create a thank-you kit. Carry this with you if you are meeting with a lot of people so you can get the notes mailed immediately and get it off your plate.

FIG 17-4

Build a follow-up thank-you kit with envelopes, pens, return address labels, note cards, and stamps.

THANK-YOU NOTE MAGIC

I once shared an assistant with a colleague, and we had to interview for a new person. We had several great candidates. We conducted our interviews, and it came down to two people who we liked equally, and we could not decide between them. It was a Friday afternoon, and we both agreed to think about it over the weekend and come back Monday morning with a decision. Monday morning we both looked at each other and admitted that we still couldn't decide. We always had a staff meeting on Monday morning, and when we came out, the mail had been delivered. One of the two candidates immediately sent a thank-you note. To receive it in the mail on Monday meant she dropped it off at the main post office immediately following her interview. We looked at each other and acknowledged that if she's going to be that responsive in sending us a thank-you note, she's going to do that on behalf of us, and she would be fantastic. She was a great hire; we chose her over the other candidate because she sent a thank-you note.

Sometimes that's the only way to stand out; there are so many people applying for the same jobs that if you are the one who does a little bit extra, that's how to get noticed. There's no other way to do it because everyone has a degree, everyone is qualified, and the competition is stiff. Write thank-you notes for everything. After you finish a project, every vendor you work with, every person you meet, could be a potential client.

Have thank-you notes printed with your designs or of photography from your events. They are fantastic to send post interview. The receiver will flip it over and see your name and contact information again and will likely enjoy the custom note.

NEGOTIATION

Part of the application and hiring process involves negotiation. People with whom you interview are prepared for it. Do not allow your lack of confidence stop you from asking for what you want or need. These might include things such as time off, telecommuting options, vacation time, sick time, travel, benefits, and pay. Always ask if these things are negotiable. Most companies are going to encourage telecommuting because they get bonus points for having more staff who are not driving into work every day. Negotiation is not just about getting things you want, though; it is about standing up for yourself and asking. This takes confidence and bravery to get into the mindset that you deserve these things enough to ask for them.

To begin the negotiation for pay, first know your bottom line when you begin interviewing. Have your budget done; know what you need to earn. Otherwise, there is no point taking a job. If a gig is going to pay you so poorly that you can't pay your rent, car payment, utilities, and whatever else you have budgeted, then it is not for you. If you are applying to a large company, check the salary ranges to ensure they offer equal pay to all. If they don't, ask for the amount equal to all others in the same position. To become a great negotiator, you have to know you're worth, your value, and you have to believe it. If you are confident, it is easier to ask for what you need.

During a negotiation, don't talk too much. The idea of silence when negotiating is very powerful; silence means you don't need to feel pressure to reply to an e-mail or a phone call. Wait and reply the next day, or, if you're in front of somebody and they are asking if you are ready to leap, have the confidence to say that you want to think it over. Talking less during negotiations is powerful because it demonstrates that you are thoughtful and you're filtering the options through your values.

TAKE YOUR TIME

It takes bravery to ask for time if someone is trying to speed the process. You should never feel rushed if someone demands that you make a decision right away; trust your gut. If you need more time, tell them. If you're feeling rushed, you'll make a poor decision where more time allows for you to negotiate. You need the time, and you need to say "I need to sleep on it," and if they don't want to give you that time, that is a reason to walk away. Think about the conversation;

take your time and make decisions only when you are ready. That said, don't take too much time. Waiting two to five days is standard,; any more than that, though, and you look indecisive.

GET IT IN WRITING

Always be brave enough to ask to get anything offered to you in writing. Save every e-mail into organized folders; these exchanges are the proof you need if something was promised and not delivered.

REFERENCES

Throughout your career, you will have to offer a list of references who can speak to who you are. For this reason, it is important to hold on to people who know your work and your personality and stay in touch with them. Always ask before using someone's name, and then if you are in a new round of applying for something, send those people on your reference list an e-mail sharing that they may hear from a specific organization. You do not want anyone getting a cold reference call, and the person does not have a handle on what you are currently up to. That reflects poorly on you for not keeping your references in the loop.

FIG 17-5

Provide references that are either acedemic, character, or community focused.

There are different types of references for different things for which you might apply. You can have a character reference, a professional (career) reference, and an academic reference or a volunteer/community reference. Whichever category you choose, you to need their name, title, place of employment, e-mail address, and phone number. Place their contact information into a list and keep it current in case you are asked for it.

INTERNSHIP

If you are just out of school or are changing careers, consider an internship. They can be both paid and unpaid. Internships get your foot in the door, give you experience, and allow you to

tips for internships

1. *Do your homework and research companies in your field.*
2. *Don't reinvent the wheel; ask others what to expect and what you need to know.*
3. *Treat it like a job search.*
4. *Ask for help, advice, and introductions.*
5. *Start earlier then you think you need to.*
6. *Read the application carefully—make sure you qualify before applying.*
7. *Once you're in, gain trust and prove yourself.*
8. *Pay attention to the culture at the company.*
9. *Focus while you are there; don't get distracted.*
10. *Take your work seriously, no matter what it is.*
11. *Ask for feedback from coworkers and superiors.*
12. *Watch your coworkers and learn from them.*
13. *Participate, engage, and speak up.*
14. *Dress appropriately.*
15. *Say thank you.*

meet people in the industry. As with job hunting, research before applying for an internship. Treat your search for an internship just as you would a job because it is just like one. Get ahead of the game by applying early because waiting until you graduate or quit your job is too late. If there is an application, read it completely to make sure you qualify and the work you would be doing fits where you're headed in your career.

The following is a fun list of potential careers for the creative. While this list is expansive, it is not finite. New career paths and titles pop up constantly in the gig economy. This list is meant to be an inspiration and a place to begin your research. Not familiar with all the titles listed? Take this opportunity to look up what they are; you might just find something for yourself that you never knew existed. There is also space on the table for you to add things.

LIST OF CREATIVE CAREERS

TABLE 17-1 JOBS TABLE

A	B	C	D
Art historian accessory designer	Baker	Ceramicist	Dancer
Advertising	Butcher	Chief creative officer	Design director
Artistic director	Bartender	Colorist	Design strategist
Art administrator	Barista	Color mixer	Digital archivist
Archivist	Brew master (Master brewer)	Color developer	Docent
Art sales	Blogger	Color expert	Design thinker
Actor	Book illustrator	Creative director	Designer
Agent/Representative	Balloon artist	City planner	Dress maker
Animator	Buyer	Curator	Developmental editor
Art appraiser	Board member	Columnist	Disc jockey (DJ)
Art authenticator	Brand designer	Conservator	Drafter
Art consultant	Bridge designer	Cartoonist	Decorator
Auctioneer	Broadcaster	Coin designer	Digital illustrator
Art fraud investigator	Barber	Comic book artist	Documentary film maker
Art handler	Bee keeper	Children's book writer and illustrator	Dean
Art project manager	Biographer	Collector	Draper
Art supply store owner	Blacksmith	Copy editor	Dubbing machine operator
Art therapist	Bookbinder	Camera operator	
Art teacher	Book seller	Concept artist	
Art instructor	Box office attendant	Cabinet maker	
Arts administration		Costume designer	
Archeologist		Cicerone	
Anthropologist		Crafter	
Assistant to the director		Calligrapher	
Author		Culinary	
Architect		Clown	
Animal groomer		Critic	
Architectural technician		Cartographer	
App designer		Character artist	
Agent		Cheesemaker	
Advocate		Candle maker	
Auto designer		Carver	
Audio engineer		Cobbler	
Acrobat		Chef	
Aerialist		Caterer	
Aquatic performer		Cosplay character	
Accessories designer		Comedian	
Audio/Video specialist		Casting	
Art dealer		Cinematographer	
Arranger		Composer	
		Chorographer	
		Conductor	
		Creative writer	
		Cultural liaison	
		Candy maker	
		Cake maker	
		Cake designer	
		Commercial designer	
		Contractor	
		Caricature artist	
		Courtroom sketch artist	
		Curriculum writer	
		Cultural planner	
		Crocheter	
		Coach	

E	F	G	H
Essayist	\Fabricator fundraising	Graphic recorder	Hairstylist
Event planner	Forensic sketch artist	Graphic facilitator	Historian
Editor	Framer	Game designer	Host
Editor, projects and digital	Freelancer	Graphic designer	Handbag designer
Archiving assistant	Floral designer	Gallerist	Hacker
Education	Florist	Game designer	Hand sewer
Evangelist	Fashion designer	Graffiti artist	Hatter
Event planning and marketing	Fiber artist	Graphic novelist	Hosiery designer
Ergo specialist	Fabric designer	Grant writer	Hot air balloon designer
Embosser	Farmer	Grip	
Engraver	Funeral directors	Grapher	
Etcher	Furniture designer	Glass blower	
Experience designer	Fashion merchandiser	Garment fitter	
Entrepreneur	Fun house operator	Golf course designer	
Exhibit designer	Fire works designer	Gift wrapper	
Exhibit artist	Foley artist		
Exhibit builder	Flavor creator		
Eye glass frame designer	Food stylist		
Esthetician	Foxing painter		
	Fretted instrument Makers		
	Film maker		
	Film/TV:		
	Developer		
	Loader		
	Spooler		
	Costumer		
	Writer		
	Editor		
	Director		
	Producer		
	Set designer		

I	J	K	L
Illustrator	Jeweler	Knife designer	Lacer
Medial illustrator	Journalist	Knitter	Layout designer
Scientific illustrator	Juggler	Kiln operator	Leather cutter
Imagineers		Kite designer	Lyricist
Inker			Lecturer
Industrial designer			Luthier
Interior designer			Landscape
Ice sculptor			Architect
Image consultant			Landscape designer
Interpreter			Landscaper
Impersonator			Lighting designer
			Lithographer
			Loom operator
			Lapidarian
			Librarian

(Continued)

M	N	O	P
Make-up artist	Novelist	Outdoor guide	Party planner
Marine designer	Narrator	Offset press operator	Prop designer
Media designer	Neck tie designer		Professor
Musician	Neon sign designer		Podcaster
Mixologist	Nail tech		Packaging designer
Marketing	Novelty designer		Pattern maker
Makeup artist			Penciller
Medical illustrator			Projectionist
Medical sculptor			Perfumer
Model maker			Pastry chef
Mask maker			Photographer
Media specialist			Photo retoucher
Memorial designer			Photojournalist
Mortuary beautician			Public speaker
Museum attendant			Pastor
Music copyist			Poet
Music engraver			Potter
Mosaicist			Production designer
Mock-up artist			Producer
Muralist			Preparator
Musician			Printer
Mannequin maker			Printmaker
Mime			Performer
Manga artist			Presenter
Minister			Playground designer
Model			Product designer
Mascot			Print designer
Milliner			Production manager
Multi-media designer			Promoter
Magazine designer			Public art administrator
Magician			Public artist
Malt roaster			Puppeteer
Manicurist			Parachute designer
Maple syrup maker			Personal shopper
Museum:			Personal trainer
administration			Plastic surgeon
docent			Painter
membership			Photographer
development			Political cartoonist
tour guide			Public relations
education			Play writer
			Piano tuner
			Pie maker
			Piercer
			Pin ball game designer
			Police artist
			Publisher
			Philosopher
			Panelist

Q	R	S	T
Quilter	Registrar	Sculptor	Tattoo artist
Quick sketch artist	Researcher	Sand sculptor	T-shirt designer
Quiller	Renderer	Set decorator	Theorist
	Record producer	Set designer	Teaching artist
	Refinisher	Stage designer	Theatre assistant
	Restorer	Screen writer	Tailor
	Reader	Sign designer	Talent agent
	Reviewer	Soapier	Translator
	Ring master	Spicer miller	Travel guide
	Remodeler	Stenciler	Theme park designer
	Rug designer	Story editor	Textile designer
	Reporter	Sales	Technical writer
		Stationary designer	Technical illustrator
		Sports arena designer	Taste taster
		Special effects makeup	3D modeler
		Silversmith	Taxidermist
		Sound technician	Ticket agent
		Sous chef	Transportation designer
		Shoe designer	Toy designer
		Seamstress	Typographer
		Sound designer	Town planner
		Sound effects designer	Terrazzo-tile maker
		Sign painter	Teacher
		School director	
		Silhouette artist	
		Singer	
		Songwriter	
		Small business owner	
		Show room	
		Social media platform engineer	
		Spokesperson	
		Story boarder	
		Studio assistant	
		Studio manager	
		Studio director	
		Screen play writer	
		Swimming pool designer	
		Stylist	
		Screen printer	
		Stager	
		Sustainability specialist	
		Sommelier	
		Scientist	
		Scout:	
		location, products,	
		talent	

U	V	W	X
User interface designer	Vintner	Web designer	X-Ray reader
Urban designer	Video game designer	Wedding planner	
Urban planner	Videographer	Wardrobe stylist	
Upholsterer	Video editor	Web designer	
Umbrella designer	Voice- over actor	World builder	
Usher	Vocalist	weaver	
	Visual merchandiser	Woodworker	
	Visual designer	Welder	
	Video jockey (VJ)	Wig designer	
	Ventriloquist	Writer: print, online,	
	Video artist	content	

Y Yarn maker	Z Zoo designer		

REFLECTION

Finding and landing a creative gig is often as hard as the work you will do once you have the job. Knowing that will serve you well and help to eliminate the feeling of frustration. You cannot give up on your creative career because finding the gig is a hard thing. If you want to thrive in this industry, you cannot give up. Build time to hustle into your schedule; it takes effort and this very effort will be on repeat your entire career. If you wanted a nine-to-five day job, you should not have chosen this career. Not that it is hard and you shouldn't do it, just know it is on ongoing process that requires constant upkeep.

HOW WILL THE CREATIVE USE THIS INFORMATION GOING FORWARD?

Directions: Take a few minutes to think about how, specifically, you will prepare for your creative, professional career. Write down three ways you can prep yourself in the space provided.

1. _____

2. _____

3. _____

BUILDING YOUR CREATIVE NETWORK

Directions: Think of people, organizations, or other resources that can help you prepare for the job hunt. Write down these creative network connections in the space provided. Write a specific goal for contacting or making use of one of them.

1. _____

2. _____

3. _____

Goal: _____

SECTION VI

PROCLAIM YOUR PRESENCE

CHAPTER EIGHTEEN

Press Push

TELL THE WHOLE STORY

INTRODUCTION

There is a template that can assist with getting attention from the press. There is also a bit of unknown, randomness, and whim when it comes to catching the eye of the media. This chapter lays out a template for a press release, offers what to include in a press kit, and includes tips for pitching to print media, online sites, TV, and radio.

TERMS THE CREATIVE NEEDS

EDITORIAL CALENDAR The process of creating content, from idea through writing and publication

EDITORIAL MEETING Where editorial staff members, editors, and sometimes publishers convene regarding content in the publication

PRESS OR MEDIA KIT A pre-packaged set of promotional materials that provide information about a person, company, organization or cause and which is distributed to members of the media for promotional use

PRESS RELEASE An official statement issued to media giving information on specific content

WHAT THE CREATIVE NEEDS TO KNOW

Working with press requires a level of preparedness. They move fast and need information immediately, so be ready before sending out your press release. Step into bravery when writing your press release and making an appearance pitch—share an honest story. Being bold in telling the story of your practice takes courage, and that is just the sort of human interest story the press loves.

WHAT THE CREATIVE WILL LEARN IN THIS CHAPTER

In this chapter, you will learn relationship-building skills so that you can attract the attention of the media. You will learn steps for writing an appealing press release. You will also learn about building a press kit and editorial calendars and pitching to TV and radio. Finally, the chapter will close with a cheater's tip.

TELLING YOUR STORY

If you're sending out a press release or pitching to the media, you're hoping that they will pick up your story. Ask yourself if you are offering a story. Is there news? Is something new happening? Do you have a new product coming out? You can't just say, "This little shop continues to sell the same stuff." Have something newsworthy, something timely, something date specific—not ongoing details or an event. Offer a story that is compelling, helpful, informative, and creative. Give the reader of your press release the joy of reading something fun and smart.

> *"It's an artist's duty to reflect the times in which we live."*
>
> —Nina Simone

PRESS KIT

A press kit, also known as a media kit, is a packet of information about your business or product. Think of a press kit as a resume for your practice. It is where you pull all the information on your practice or product together in one place. Include images, articles, a frequently asked questions sheet, along with audio, video or other materials. Target a press kit at the media, possible investors, and future clients. The goal of your press kit is to grab the attention of the reader. You want him or her to reach out and contact you for more information about your event or product.

The items in your press kit will vary depending on the audience. Include the most up-to-date and current pieces of information from your practice. You can include a paragraph or one-pager about the history of your practice if appropriate, but nothing historical beyond that.

The following is a list of items that you may want to include in your press kit. This list is a suggestion for all areas of focus.

1. COVER LETTER

Is where you make your introduction; make sure to include your contact information. In the opening sentence, grab your reader's attention. Make him or her care in sentence two by inserting your passion. Let the reader know what else is included in the press kit. Offer to follow up if there are any questions. Let the reader know you are available for an interview.

2. COMPANY PROFILE

Share the history of your practice, a profile of your business, your bio, and the bios of any other employees.

3. PRODUCT/SERVICE SHEET

A fact sheet about your practice, products or services can be used to share specific and unique attributes of your product or service.

4. OTHER COVERAGE

Include copies of recent press coverage by media outlets different than the one you are pitching. If it is online coverage, take screenshots to include in your kit.

5. PRESS RELEASE

Include your current press release for the product or event you are pitching.

6. TESTIMONIALS AND REVIEWS

If you have testimonials or product reviews, include them in your press kit. Having voices other than your own is helpful for the press to see.

7. FAQS

Include a list of frequently asked questions. If you find yourself explaining a great deal about your practice, products, or services, collect those questions and answer them up front before you are asked.

8. AUDIO/VIDEO/STILL

If you have audio or visual clips, you can share the examples of your work or previous press coverage in your press kit. Have them edited and cued for the viewer. Images such as headshots should also be included in your press kit when appropriate.

FIG 18-1

Build a kit for the press that is always ready and only requires slight updating.

GET CREATIVE

Get creative with your press kit. Play around with different ways to present your materials in a way that is unique to your practice. Don't go too far, though; make sure it is still professional but unique to you.

"Creativity is nothing but the way to solve new problems."

—*Diana Santos*

take action

Grab your journal and pen and write down at least 10 different ways to create a press kit that is uniquely yours. Does it come in a mailed box? Does it open digitally with a fun animation? Is it filled with bright colors and glitter? Write down how you can put your signature on it.

PRESS RELEASE

The following are steps for writing a press release. Please note, if you work for an organization and it uses a different format, you should always use their format. There are many ways to write a press release.

LAYOUT LOGISTICS

Write your press release on your letterhead. It is an excellent way to include your contact information with the statement. A press release is written left justified, using a 12-point easy-to-read font in black ink. If you print it, use only white paper. If you design it digitally, still use black ink color and a clean layout that is easy to read. Research examples of press releases to see different styles of layouts.

ORDER OF PRESS RELEASE

FOR IMMEDIATE RELEASE

1. At the top of the page write "For Immediate Release." Write this so the press knows they can publish it today. If you put a different date for release, then the press understands you may not want to publish anything about it until the launch date.

DATE

2. Next is the date. It is important each time you send out a press release to update to the exact date. You don't want to have someone in the media receive your press release with a date from two weeks prior. They will think it is old news, so always update with today's date.

MEDIA CONTACT

3. After the date include "Media Contact." It lets the media outlet know that the next few lines of contact information are not publishable. Putting your name, phone number, and e-mail in this section is safe because it will not get published under media contact. Once the press release is sent to the media, prepare to field questions.

TITLE

4. Do not bore with your title for your press release. It is your opening to peak the interest of your reader. Us this to capture them so they'll want to read on. Be brave and bold and creative with your title. Do not be afraid to write a title that is provocative, engaging, and interesting—one that grabs people's attention. Write something that is a little edgy, heartwarming, or funny.

NOTE: Everything on your press release is left justified except for your title; center the title in the middle of the page.

"Get rid of everything that is not essential to making a point."

—*Christoph Niemann*

THE BODY

Who

5. The first paragraph of the press release is "the who" of the story. Explain in this opening paragraph: Who is doing this project? Talk about your company or practice, pull from bios, and give impactful information about who you are and what you do. Use this opportunity to talk about why the press should be interested. The media is about human interest stories, both negative and positive. Build your story to share why the who of your practice is exciting and unique.

What

6. The second paragraph is the "what." In this paragraph, you'll tell the story of the event, performance, exhibition, launch, reading, or whatever your activity is. Describe what someone who is attending will see, experience, hear, and so on. People in the press have a lot coming at them, so everything you can do to give robust descriptions helps them to pitch your event to their editor. Making the lives of the press easier should always be a goal.

Where

7. The third paragraph is the "where" in your story. It is less of a paragraph and more of a few sentences or bullets.

    A. The location of where the event is it taking place

    B. The address. NOTE: Take the time to list the physical address. If the address is complicated, include cross streets and significant landmarks

    C. Website listing information relevant to getting there, such as directions, hours, parking, and entrance locations

When

8. After the location is listed, the next thing is the date and time.

    A. Day of the week and the month; the year is optional

    B. Time of day, noting a.m. or p.m. If it's over the course of multiple days, write the date and the times for each day

How much

9. Cost, if there are different prices; as an example, $5 for students and seniors, $10 general admission. If it is a complicated ticketing structure, offer a range of prices and encourage the attendees to visit the website for additional information and details. If there is not a cost, state FREE

Public Contact

10. The public contact information will be published, so determine if you want to include your name. You will need to include the following:

   A. Your phone number

   B. Your e-mail address. If you don't want your personal e-mail published, consider getting an e-mail just for press relationships and events

   C. Your website and social media links for the public to get more information

Closing

11. To close the press release, one inch up from the bottom of the pag, e type three hashtags in a row ###

It lets the person reading the press release know that is the end. It gives him or her confidence that nothing fell off the page, nothing is missing; that's the intended end.

WHO'S INVITED?

If your event is open to the public, promote that. It is a lot easier for the media to cover something that isn't invitation only. If it is family friendly, list that, and if the event offered is for ages 21 and older, share those specific details.

SENDING YOUR PRESS RELEASE

After writing your press release, save it as a PDF with your name or the event title as the file name. Attach the PDF to an e-mail with the sentence "Attached please find a press release for _____." Add your contact information so the recipients can get in touch quickly. When you send out a press release, have images, video or audio ready to send in case they are requested. Have both high- and low-resolution image quality. High resolution allows for print or high-quality video or audio streaming. Low resolution, 72 dpi, works if featured in a post on a blog or social media. If a higher resolution file is needed, you will be contacted. Wait to send big data files so as not to jam recipients' e-mail. If you need more ideas for your press release, search online and ask others in your creative community for examples.

"Whenever you are asked if you can do a job, tell 'em,
'Certainly I can!' Then get busy and find out how to do it."

—*Theodore Roosevelt*

If you are job hunting and you come through the door knowing how to write a press release, that's something you can offer. Every organization writes press releases, and if they do not, they have to hire this type of work out. If they can instead can utilize the staff they have, that saves money, so be the person who shows up with that skill.

EDITORIAL MEETINGS

All editorial publishing, whether print, TV, radio, news outlets, or magazines have editorial meetings weekly or daily, depending on the frequency of publication. The entire editorial team comes together to discuss and pitch ideas. Press releases are submitted to the editor who offers the stories to their writers. If you offer a compelling story, people will fight for it; everybody wants those first. Editorial meetings at most media outlets have a team that is mostly freelancers. This means they are only paid when they write a piece, so giving them interesting projects to write about is a win for all. Have everything ready so you can respond quickly if a pitch about your event is accepted by a media outlet.

FIG 18-2

Editorial meetings are used to pitch story ideas.

EDITORIAL CALENDARS

During certain times of the year, if you go online, turn on the TV, or open newspapers or magazines, you'll see categories of things that are thematically related. As an example, in August and September, you will see a lot of back-to-school stories. So, if you want that type of coverage, make your pitch work for back to school. Every media outlet maintains an editorial calendar filled with themes, holidays, angles, and ideas. Everyone working there is following the calendar because the reporting needs to look cohesive. If you would like to be featured in any specific media, request their editorial calendar so you can fall in line with their schedule. Seeing their lists can help you align with them instead of feeling frustrated that they aren't covering you.

Every day there is a celebration of "national day" of something. As an example, if you are starting a beard wax company, look up national beard day. Find out when it is, write your press release for the launch of your new beard waxing product, and pitch it to the media outlet for national beard day, which, by the way, is always the first Saturday of September. If you give them a hook they can easily connect with, your story will probably get picked up because it makes sense and it fits. Be the one to put that pitch together for the press—get creative!

APPEARANCE PITCH

When it comes to TV or radio, present more of a pitch than just your press release. Think about what your angle is; if you're trying to get media coverage on television, imagine what would happen during your three minutes on TV. Watch or listen to the show you will be on to study the format. Follow how others present and similarly prepare your segment. Some media outlets host on location, which means that there is an activity where they're doing something; it's not just standing there being interviewed. If you know in advance that you'll need an action, create a plan and offer something fresh to viewers. Most TV coverage is about three minutes, so offer to demo something step by step, making sure it is visually appealing. With radio, be verbally descriptive, as it is often live. Prepare your thoughts, stories, and jokes and practice before you go on. With all radio or TV spots, you cannot show up cold. You need to prepare, practice, and think about what you want to say and show. Practicing will help calm your nerves and prevent accidental bloomers.

When you're making the pitch, know your audience; each time it will be little different because each show is different and radio is different from TV. Do your homework and review what they do on their show. Know what would be most appropriate for you to offer and what you can use as a hook. A hook is that one nugget that will get attention.

IT TAKES TIME

Build relationships with people in the press. You can't simply send out a press release and expect to hear from them. You must connect often. People can get frustrated that they can't get press coverage but know that it takes seven times of contact for somebody to remember you. Seven different engagements or interactions before people remember you, so don't get frustrated if you reach out and you don't hear back, just keep doing it. If you keep pitching, promoting, and sending out press releases, eventually, your stuff will rise to the top. If you have the personality to go on live TV or radio, that's something else you could offer to your organization. You could become a spokesperson. If you have the character to build relationships, you'll get asked all the time to come on TV or radio. If that isn't you, let someone else stand in front of the camera, but you can still help write the pitch. Another excellent relationship builder is to pre-write the story. Make it easy for the media: Spell it out so they barely have anything left to do; this is helpful and will help you build relationships. If you're vague, they're probably not going to cover your event. People constantly pitch to the press, so the more you support them in their work, the more likely you are to get coverage.

*"One important key to success is self-confidence. An
important key to self-confidence is preparation."*

—Arthur Ashe

CARRY REMINDER NOTES

Once you send out your press release and make an appearance pitch, prepare for a potential
follow-up phone call. When someone from the media calls to ask questions, have your information handy. You cannot say, "It's in the press release" because he or she may not have a copy
of it handy and want information from you. Never rely on wi-fi; instead carry a printed or hand-writ-
ten reminder note with you instead. If you have a phone case, tuck your reminder note into your
case. You need that little piece of paper so that if the phone rings, you can unfold it and offer
the pertinent information. Never be the person who says, "Let me get back to you." Instead,
say, "Yes, I have that right here."

FIG 18-3

REFLECTION

When you are ready to get attention from the media for your practice or products, revisit this
chapter to prepare your media kit, press release, or appearance pitch. Be bold in your title for
your press release, share generously in your media kit, and practice before you jump in front

of a live TV camera. Build your audience through media spotlights, and build your relationships with members of the press so that they will call on you again and again.

HOW WILL THE CREATIVE USE THIS INFORMATION GOING FORWARD?

Directions: Take a few minutes to think about how, precisely, you will create a plan for working with the press. Looking at the items in this chapter, write down three ideas in the space provided.

1. _____

2. _____

3. _____

BUILDING YOUR CREATIVE NETWORK

Directions: Think of a way to build relationships with the press including specific people and organizations. Write down connection ideas that fit your personality in the space provided. Write a particular goal for making contact.

1. _____

2. _____

3. _____

Goal: _____

CHAPTER NINETEEN

Knowing Where to Show, Sell, Produce, and Perform

KNOW YOUR AUDIENCE

INTRODUCTION

This chapter offers ideas for where the creatives might consider showing, selling, producing, and performing. As a creative, you think differently and function differently than the rest of society. Read this chapter with your lens; look for nuggets that you can apply to your practice. Not every section is for every creative type, but these sections offer a glimpse into options. This chapter is broken into places, people, and ideas for showing, selling, producing, and performing.

TERMS THE CREATIVE NEEDS

AGENT Any professional who works on behalf of a creative to represent, promote, and sell their work. The agent represents the business interests of the creative

BOOKING AGENT Agent who books live performances such as concerts, radio, and TV performances for artists, bands, and DJs. They are responsible for developing the creative's career of a live performance

PLACEMENT DESIGNER Places art, furniture, and décor into homes and businesses, both temporarily (for staging) or permanently (sales)

REPRESENTATIVE Also known as a rep, they sell manufactured products to wholesale and retail customers on the client's behalf

RESIDENCIES A residential post held by a writer, designer, musician, artist, or creative

STAGING Making a home or business more appealing to the highest number of potential buyers, using art, furniture, and décor arrangements, thereby selling a property more swiftly and for more money

TALENT ACQUISITION Process of finding skilled creatives for individual, institutional, or organizational needs

WHAT THE CREATIVE NEEDS TO KNOW

Your specific area of creative practice may not be outlined in the chapte,r as careers are always changing, but read through it to pull ideas from the many different examples throughout this chapter. The idea is to think differently about options for presenting what you do. Some of the best ideas happen when challenges arise. If you don't have the perfect venue for your launch, get creative. Rent out an old oil-changing station or serve canned grape soda and embrace the weirdness. Create an experience by working with what you have; don't focus on what you don't have.

WHAT THE CREATIVE WILL LEARN IN THIS CHAPTER

Throughout this chapter, you will learn new tips and ideas, along with a spin on old methods. This chapter has three major sections: places, people, and ideas to show, sell, produce, and perform. The first section lists a few examples of places you may have thought of before but didn't know the details of. The second offers people who could help in your career as you look for opportunities. The final section offers ideas to show, sell, produce, and perform.

PLACES TO SHOW, SELL, PRODUCE, AND PERFORM

RESIDENCIES

Residencies are designed to give the creative a break from his or her regular work life (day job) and focus on his or her practice. Many creatives use the time while in residence to create new bodies of work. Residencies exist for nearly all areas of creative practices including writers, designers, curators, culinary workers, musicians, performers, and all visual artists. A typical residency is between one month to one year. Some residencies offer a small stipend during the months of your stay; some offer to house; all offer a place to work. Space could be a studio, a room in a house, or a tool shed, but that is included. A residency is not a money-making venture but an opportunity for personal and creative growth. Residencies are great if you are in an

FIG 19-1

There are many places to show your practice off. Find non-traditional outlets.

academic, personal, professional, or creative transition. You can use the time to sort your practice out and find your passion again. Residencies are located all over the world, and many operate year-round. They are located in a variety of places such as old mansions, historic buildings, national parks, shopping malls, farms, seaside cabins, and abandoned grain silos.

take action

Jump online and search residencies in your area of practice. Bookmark sites you are interested in applying to. Review their application dates and make a note of the time of year on your calendar.

GALLERIES

The gallery system has shifted entirely since the boom of the 1950s and again in the 1980s. This is due to several factors including online sales, art fairs, and the current atmosphere for collecting art. We lack cultural institutions where collectors meet and create relationships with creatives. This is due to budget and travel constraints placed on the institutions. Many of the galleries still operational are struggling. Blue-chip galleries are still making profits. Blue-chip galleries focus on reselling art of well-established artists who reliably bring higher prices at auction. That type of gallery does not help the just-starting-out artist nor the mid-career artist. Representation by a single gallery will not be enough to make a living. You can consider selling through multiple galleries in different regions, but it is hard to create a large-enough body of work to sell at several galleries. Representation by galleries is good for your resume and your confidence and is still a worthwhile pursuit, but don't rely on it for all your income. Very few artists can do this. If you are interested in gallery representation to do your homework, get to know the gallery. Learn what they currently sell and what their aesthetic is; learn as much as you can about the gallerist and sales team. Don't waste your time applying to a gallery that only sells watercolors if you are a sculptor. If your goal is to sell occasionally through a gallery, consider joining a co-op. Creative co-ops offer things such as gallery space, rehearsal spaces, co-working spaces, and recording booths, to name a few examples. Co-ops are a membership system where each member pays a monthly fee to use the shared space on a schedule.

Galleries show your artwork on consignment. This means they do not pay you up front when you deliver; you must wait until the work sells to receive payment. This could be months or years, so budget accordingly to keep your practice up and running.

POP-UPS AND TRUNK SHOWS

Pop-up shops and boutique trunk shows are a great way to get the word out about new products or projects. They cost very little to host for makers, performers, and musicians to connect and collaborate with local community shops. Just like galleries, the shops hosting these events are not going to buy anything outright from you; sales are consignment. You can use pop-ups to explore new things to see how buyers respond to them. They are also an opportunity to offer one-of-a-kind items as buyers expect that at these types of events. Partner with a local coffee shop or popsicle cart, and create it into a community event.

OPEN STUDIOS AND BACKSTAGE EXPERIENCES

Opening a studio, workspace, or backstage for the public to tour has a long tradition. Build stronger relationships with your audience, allowing an occasional behind-the-scene peek. Your audience builds a connection to your practice when they are allowed to see you in process. It is useful to host and participate in these types of events to connect personally in your natural habitat. Attendees are more likely to stay in touch with you and follow up on future work. These events are often more casual and allow for relaxed networking. If you are part of an open studio without your gallery rep, never sell at your wholesale prices. Your pieces still need to be priced at retail, and if you are represented, you will still give the agreed-on percentage to your gallery. The agreement states exactly that, and they are building your career and need to be compensated, even if you made that particular sale without them present.

FAIRS

Contemporary art fairs are in many countries around in the world. They take place in all seasons, and creatives from visual artists, performance artists, writers, musicians, and DJs are represented during the run of the fair. Most fairs take place over a long weekend up to a couple of weeks. They are short runs because all the booths showing at the fairs are from galleries and museums around the world and the staff needs to return to their home locations. Fairs offer sales of visual art, DJ appearances, performance art, lectures, and readings, to name a few examples. They are active places that are great for networking. They do cost to attend, in addition to travel and accommodation costs. If a gallery represents you and shows your work on your behalf, you can often attend as a represented artist. Better-known fairs include Art Basil, Miami, SOFA (Sculpture, Objects, Functional Art), Frieze Art Fair, London and the Armory Show, New York, to name a few. There are sites online dedicated to featuring lists of art fairs around the world. Some of them offer information for free, and others charge a small fee.

FESTIVALS

All genres can show, sell, produce, and perform at local, regional, or national festivals. There is one every weekend in every major city and once a month in small towns. Many creatives make a living by touring with festivals. There are art and music festivals, poetry festivals, and comedy and film festivals, and all of them need creatives to have something to show and sell. As an example, if you are a musician, find out who the music producers are in your community and see if you can get on a smaller local stage earlier in the day at an upcoming music festival. Invite all your friends, family, and fans. Take pictures and post it on social media. You can then use all your documentation to book future gigs.

LOCAL FACILITIES

Actors, writers, visual artists, dancers, performers, and set, stage and lighting designers can benefit from relationships with local theatres and playhouses. If space is dark, creatives can negotiate time to practice and perform, but don't limit yourself to a perfect space with all the bells and whistles; check out local high school stages, churches, libraries, senior centers, and unrented buildings. Talk to local business owners, cities, and communities about temporarily using spaces not currently leased. This is becoming a common practice as brick and mortar stores are closing and spaces are left empty. Many municipalities are opening spaces for creatives to bring new energy into dying areas of towns. If you see an empty building, find out who owns it and give them a call. You might be able to rent a space for an affordable price. NOTE: This will be easier if you already have an LLC and business insurance.

TRADE SHOWS

Trade shows are for to-the-trade-only (TTTO) wholesale buyers. This means manufacturers sell directly to buyers. Trade shows exist in many areas of production. If you make furniture, design greeting cards, or are an illustrator or a car designer, to name a few examples, you will find a lot of options for trade shows. A trade show space is a booth that is sold in 8 x 8' increments. The booths can take over large amounts of square footage and feel like a store or be small, intimate spaces. Shows are not set up for sales at the show. Instead, orders are taken and shipped at a later date. This is easier for the maker because it only needs samples to have orders placed. Creatives can have more work at the show and then receive orders, and for those who do not get orders, they do not have to spend time or money manufacturing them. Trade shows are one of the best places to meet buyers and members of the press. Do your homework to determine which show you should attend, and find out where the most buyers, in your category, attend. Learn what the costs are, not just the booth cost but travel, accommodations, set up, contracts, décor, product samples, and booth needs.

PEOPLE WHO CAN HELP YOU SHOW, SELL, PRODUCE, AND PERFORM

BROKERS AND DESIGNERS

Do you know who buys artwork? Very few buyers are collectors, and most buyers are interior designers or placement designers. The only way you to get in front of the people who make the buying decisions is to have a designer as your broker. The end buyer hires the designers to make decisions for him or her. You need these brokers because you don't have access to the buyers. There are exceptions, and some collectors and art lovers remain, but to make a living selling art, you need an agent or broker, and often a designer plays this role.

FIG 19-2

Learn who can help you show, sell, produce and perform.

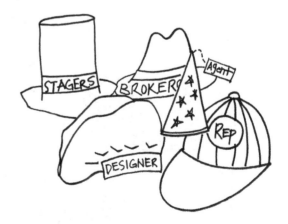

AGENTS AND REPS

In many creative fields, the only way to find gigs or clients is to work with a representative or an agent. An agent is someone who works on behalf of a creative to represent, promote, and sell the creative's product, process, or service. The agent represents the business interests of the creative. This is especially true in the performing and literary arts. A booking agent books live performances for the creative and is responsible for developing his or her live performance career. A representative, also known as a rep, sells your products to wholesale on your behalf. These professional agents are of great benefit to the creative because he or she can stay focused on your practice while agents pound the pavement. It is their job to find leads for you and set up opportunities. Reps and agents take a percentage of your payments to cover their costs. This percentage is well worth it because you do not know the clients and you do not have a Rolodex like your agents. You need them to do the work for you so that you can stay focused. You can seek out agents attending public events, as talent acquisition is a part of their job descriptions.

STAGERS

Stagers temporarily design interior spaces for real estate sales, furnished rentals, and business launches. People with a great understanding of aesthetics can pull together everything, from art on the walls to furniture, to sheets on the bed. If you create objects or products that could be included in temporary projects by a stager, consider researching firms in your area. Find networking events where you can meet stagers, get to know them, and pitch your work as a part of their rotation of goods. Your work is rented by the project, with a fixed set of prices determined by the industry and region.

Before you begin working with a broker, a placement designer, agent, rep, or gallerist, have a frank discussion about expectations, schedules, and fees. Know what their percentage cut per product or project is, and never begin any partnership without a written agreement, signed and dated by both parties.

FIG 19-3

Act like a DJ and bring in a little of this and that to build ideas for your practice.

IDEAS THAT CAN HELP YOU SHOW, SELL, PRODUCE, AND PERFORM

GETTING THINGS PRODUCED

MANUFACTURED

1. The first step to getting your product mass produced is to create a sample or prototype. The sample should look visually like the final product. It can be made from a different material than the final product, but it should look like the final.

2. The second step is to find a manufacturer. This requires homework for your area since different materials mean different locations. To start a search online, you will need to know the keywords specific to your area. Look at industry directories as a source for lists of manufacturers used by other makers. You will also need to determine if you want a domestic or international manufacturer.

3. Once you find the manufacturer, begin the process of quoting the product. This means asking the manufacturer a series of questions including the following:

   A. Do you offer sample pricing (the cost of manufacturing a small run to see what the products will look like when manufactured?

   B. What are your minimums? This is the smallest amount you can order and still take the job.

   C. What is your price per piece and are their breaks at specific numbers? Some manufacturers offer a discount if you order 250 or 1,000 or 10,000, as an example, and if you sell that many, it can be worth it to invest for better savings.

   D. What is your turnaround time? This is the amount of time it takes from the day the order is placed with the manufacturer until the day it is delivered to you.

   E. What are your payment terms? Most companies are Net 30 (pay within 30 days) when you are a new customer, but they will sometimes extend the terms out to Net 60 or Net 90.

4. The next step is the production process. There are many steps in the production process, and they are determined based on the product you are manufacturing. Have a clear conversation with the manufacturer you select and ask for a production flowchart. This chart allows you to see the steps in the process and allows you to ask questions at each step before they happen.

5. The final step is to place your final order and await delivery of your product.

PRODUCED

How do you get in front of a producer? It is all about who you know and who you network with. Get out there and get in front of the right people. Tell everyone you meet who you want to connect with; people will support your bravery.

If you are shopping your script, play, story, album, or event, know your story inside and out so that you are prepared for every question that might come your way.

Do your homework and know the previous work of the producer you are pitching to. If possible, comment on details of his or her film or album that you liked.

Ask the person you are pitching to if he or she is reviewing new material. If he or she tells you he or she is open, share your project.

Share your passion for the project and that you are committed to the project. Offer any partners or collaborators that you may already have on the project.

Keep your heart in it. It can take years to get something picked up by a producer. Don't give up! There will be rejections. J.K. Rowling was rejected from 12 different publishers before finally getting a contract for the Harry Potter series. You'll learn a lot about yourself and your practice with each attempt, both the failures and successs.

> *"Test knowledge through experience, be prepared to make mistakes, and be persistent about it."*
>
> —*Leonardo Da Vinci*

OUTDOORS OPPORTUNITIES

The great outdoors are often overlooked as an option for performing, displaying, or sharing creativity. It is easy to get a permit from a city or town to host an outdoor event. If you find collaborative partners, you could split up the work and up-front costs. Figure out first, in written detail, what you would like to do and present that to the permit office. It is often cheaper to rent an outdoor space than it would be to rent space inside a building. You may have to rent additional equipment depending on the city requirements; make sure you read the contract and know your responsibilities. Hosting your show outdoors could offer a special opportunity to your audience. Don't just think about parks; find out about using alleyways, parking structures, or side streets that could be closed for a day.

> *"Collaboration is the essence of life. The wind, bees and flowers work together, to spread the pollen."*
>
> —*Amit Ray*

COLLABORATIONS

If you are looking for funding for a project, look to other people who could help you realize the completion of the project. Connect with creatives and individuals in other fields to collaborate.

You might co-create from beginning to end or work together on just a few areas of your overall project. There is often more funding offered for team projects. It can also be an incredible learning experience. Collaboration allows you to expand your skill set and scale the work you alone would normally be capable of. Collaborate outside of traditional art mediums. What if you pair a robot and a group of dancers? Try it; both you and the robotics could learn from wild collaborations. Collaborations are a great way to build your contacts list and fill it with interesting thinkers.

REFLECTION

This chapter offers just a glimpse into ideas for where to show, sell, produce, and perform. An entire book could be written just on this topic. It is an important one in our ever-changing gig economy because, as a creative, you will have to continually reinvent yourself, your practice, and who you partner with. Keep your eyes open for unique places where you could host your next event. A dusty field in the middle of a downtown construction zone can serve as a great pop-up for a futuristic comic book launch.

HOW WILL THE CREATIVE USE THIS INFORMATION GOING FORWARD?

Directions: Take a few minutes to think about the places section (part 1) of this chapter. Write down three of the ideas you will consider investigating further in the space provided.

1. _____
2. _____
3. _____

BUILDING YOUR CREATIVE NETWORK

Directions: Think of the people section (part 2) of this chapter. Write down three creative network connections in the space provided. Write a specific goal for contacting one of them.

1. _____
2. _____
3. _____
Goal: _____

FIG 19-4

FRESH IDEAS

Directions: Think of the Ideas section (part 3) of this chapter. Write down one "out there" idea you would like to pursue in the space provided.

1. _____

CHAPTER TWENTY

Thinking Differently

BLAZE YOUR OWN TRAIL

INTRODUCTION

Creatives have filled many different roles for hundreds of years. That has all changed. We do not wait around for patrons to find us. It is possible to insert your creative skills into every industry you can name. Now more than ever, the way you think is highly sought after. The creative mind is the way the future is designed, built, and explored. Problem solving requires creativity, and there are a lot of problems to be solved.

TERMS THE CREATIVE NEEDS

CHAMPION A type of mentor who has something to gain from your career achievements; their reputation is enhanced by recommending you

CHIEF CREATIVE THINKER A person who leads thought change, innovation, and creativity throughout an organization through thoughtful, creative disruption

COMMONALITIES The state of sharing features or attributes

COLLABORATION The action of working with someone to produce or create something

SCALE To increase something (or be increased) in size or number

THINK TANK Experts providing advice and ideas on specific cultural issues

TERRAZO FLOOR Chips of marble, quartz, granite, glass, or other suitable material, poured with a binder to create designs on floors

WHAT THE CREATIVE NEEDS TO KNOW

You have something great to offer. Your creative mind is a hot commodity. You think differently. In this chapter, you'll explore ideas for offering your different way of thinking. You need to know that if you want to make a go of this creative life, you can't wait around for a magical someone to show up and finally make your career. Make it yourself; find ways to do cool, creative stuff your way. This chapter will offer ideas for just that.

WHAT THE CREATIVE WILL LEARN IN THIS CHAPTER

You will learn more about ways to think differently. You'll learn new ways to see the offerings you have and the ideas for collaborations outside of your industry. You'll discover ways to find commonalities across industries. The chapter closes with why you need to speak up, use your creative vision, and stay open.

WHY YOUR CREATIVITY MATTERS

Your creativity is a gift. You posses a special way of seeing the world. To you, it not only looks different, but it also sounds different, tastes different, and feels different; your mind also processes the world different from everyone else. Your creative mind can help alter industries, changing the shape of processes and production. Through bravery, you can offer your unique way of thinking to more than just your band mates.

FIG 20-1

Creativity breaks down silos as ideas emerge.

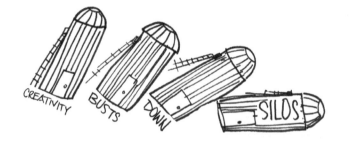

THINKING DIFFERENTLY

Finding commonalities in different professional fields can be exciting. An example of this is if a dancer and cancer researcher partner together because they are both studying flow in their practice. Once the commonality is discovered, the two could make co-applications to funders and collaborate on their work. As a creative, you can connect through your ideas in many different industries. Creativity is needed everywhere, and if you are interested in busting down silos and stepping into new territories, then you are wanted.

take action

Take out your journal and write down any and all fields you would be interested in exploring. What type of collaborations could you imagine? Have you thought about what it would be like to partner with a certain maker or thinker? Write it down and turn your ideas into goals.

CREATIVE COMMONALITIES

To find professional commonalities and links with other industries, first explore where you might be interested in investigating. You are going to shine when you partner with others with like passion. Pay attention to all sorts of opportunities and possibilities because what makes a creative professional: seeing differently and finding links.

Throughout this book, you have been offered exercises for creating a dossier for your professional practice. While doing the work of putting your professional documents together, you'll get to know yourself better. Getting to know what your values are, what you dream of doing, who you want to work with, where you want to work, and how allows you to explore differently. There are many possibilities when creating a career—likely more than you were told to explore while in school.

To offer an example of how to think differently, allow me to share a story. I am trained as a fine artist; my undergraduate degree is in fine art sculpture and my master's degree in what is now called social practice. My career has spanned nonprofit, for-profit, corporate, all levels of government and education, K–12, higher education, and beyond. I have always used my understanding of confidence to insert myself where an artist would normally not have been invited. My clients are mostly higher education and government agencies. I work for think tanks and the nation's largest university. I also have numerous clients who seek my brain because I think radically different than most and I am proud of it. Instead of feeling like a weirdo or an outsider, I step into bravery and wave my creative flag. Even if I fail or am wrong, I will express my ideas because I have learned it might not solve that problem but it might help with one down the road. The work I do intentionally disrupts current thought and uses my creative abilities to see situations in a new light. I spend my days proposing wild, "out there" ideas to push my clients to see differently. I use creativity to help clients look at problems they are facing and explore solutions. I work in weird and wonderful spaces, and I am often asked, "How did you end up getting into the work you do?" I realized if I wanted to experience something, I would have to invite myself in instead of waiting for an invitation. Inviting myself built confidence, and I became braver. Now when I see a project I am interested in, I find out who I know affiliated with the project and I reach out to that person. So, my answer is always the same, "I completely invented up the career I wanted. I didn't wait for the phone to ring or for a knock on the door."

ASK YOUR WAY IN

Do you want a dream career working with a variety of people from different industries? Propose something, reach out to those industries, and share your desire for collaboration. The idea is not to change what a collaborator is doing or steer him or her down a different path; it is to enhance what he or she is doing by encouraging a creative approach. If you can build within yourself the bravery to start asking to participate in projects, you will achieve great things. Try first to connect with people that your network can introduce you to rather than cold calling. It is easier to get your foot in the door if you have a mutual connection. This also helps you build industry trust and a portfolio of such projects.

take action

Grab your journal and make a list of people who have connections to industries you would be interested in connecting with. If you don't know anyone in your immediate circle, ask teachers, local leaders, or your politicians or contact offices directly.

SPEAK UP

Many creatives prefer to work alone, and for your private practice that is fine and completely understandable. However, what if your day job could be exploring the depths of your creative mind to help others think differently? What if you were brave enough to say what you thought about all sorts of issues and pressing problems in the world? If you have thoughts about how to do something differently or you think a solution would work because you've tested it and it did, speak up! Share your knowledge; you have just as much right to be at any table as any other field. Creatives' vision of the world is so vastly different than other industries, no one may ever see the problem from the angle you do.

Most creative miss out on opportunities because they stay quiet. Take out your journal and write down a commitment to use your voice and speak up. Inserting yourself into situations you are interested in isn't bossy; its smart. Make a commitment slip and post it somewhere you will see it often.

FIG 20-2

Commit to using your voice to speak up and to insert your practice into other industries.

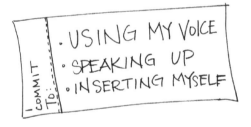

SHOW THEM

Show them what you can offer and don't give up if one door slams in your face. Being a creative and wanting to play with folks in other fields is a brave thing to tackle, but you must go gently. Many industries do not get to fail and explore as much as the creative fields. You are used to things not working on the first, fifth, or tenth try. This means you are a perfect balance to work with other industries where failure is not as encouraged. Respecting each other's processes and sharing what each of you does and how you think opens new doors. Have a clear sense of who you are before stepping into this arena because you want to make sure you are true to your convictions and not saying or doing what you think the client wants. That is not helpful to them; they need to see your vision and hear your ideas, even if they are counter to their own.

CHAMPIONS

Sometimes the idea to think differently comes not from ourselves but the voice of others. If you make connections with people inside and outside of your industry who offer opportunities to you, don't shut them down; listen. Say yes if you have something to learn from the opportunity. As you work with people, maintain those relationships because they will think of you as new projects emerge. As you show up to opportunities offering fresh and creative ideas, these same people will become your champions. They are the people who throw your name into the hat before you even knew you were being considered. They are the people who follow your career and see opportunities for your advancement before you knew you were ready. I have many stories of champions I have had over my career. One example is a friend and colleague in the field who knew my 2D work and thought of me when a public art opportunity came up to create a terrazzo floor for an airport. She called and shared the opportunity, but I had not done a public art project before and didn't feel qualified. She assured me the translation from my paintings to a terrazzo floor would not be hard. She was familiar with my work enough, knew me personally, and was willing to take the time to work with me through the process. I applied for the opportunity and was a finalist. While I was not awarded the project, I learned so much, and it was an incredible opportunity. Without having a champion who knew I could think differently, I wouldn't have considered applying.

SCALE

If there is one thing most creatives do well, it is imagining going big. Even if you create small things, you can see not just one of them, but volumes. Other industries that are trained to think differently may have struggled when it comes to going from small to large or one to many. You do not need to fully grasp the content of the other industry to offer your imagined vision of how they could scale. It is a brainstorming process where you offer crazy ideas to get people to think differently. Someone must create the next big SXSW, TED or music festival scene. It will take grand imagination to build the next human-connected event.

FIG 20-3

Use your creativity to create projects of large scale.

Pay attention when you attend events where a lot of creativity is present. Notice the elements that are on a grander scale. Take note of when you have the sensation you would do something differently. It isn't a competition; don't focus on what you would do better, just different. That is your creative mind processing.

> *"A creative man is motivated by the desire to achieve, not by the desire to beat others."*
>
> —Ayn Rand

STAY OPEN

Creative thinkers are historically open to welcoming all, experimenting, and exploring new things. If you continue to stay open to new things throughout your career, you will be gifted with many opportunities. Stay open to new, different, and contrary ways of thinking to fuel your practice. You will build a fascinating Rolodex. An open mind means you will learn a great deal, see many perspectives, and receive offers you never imagined. Model this for clients, encouraging them to stay open, too.

SEE WHAT OTHERS MISS

Most individuals trained in other industries see only what they know they are working on. They are laser focused on specific and individual tasks. They are unable to see other options because they are suffering from inattentional blindness. It is when people are unable to see something right in front of their eyes because they are so focused that they miss the obvious.

"Vision is the art of seeing what is invisible to others."

—*Jonathan Swift*

Creatives are needed and should be embedded into every company in America. Bringing in wild imaginations of creatives and disruptors supports new thinking company wide.

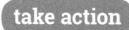

Rework this posting to fit the career you will create for yourself.

Posting

Position: Chief Creative Thinker

Job description: Wild thinker who dares to be brave enough to share his or her imagination and vulnerability in front of entire company

Responsibilities: Toss in wild thoughts to all discussions to assist greater team in shaking up traditional thinking

FIG 20-4

Create a posting that describes your ideal dream job.

"Sane is boring."

—*R.A. Salvatore*

REFLECTION

Your creative mind is your ticket to the future you are designing, as long as you don't close up and stay narrowly focused. Look for new opportunities at every turn. When someone in another industry expresses interest in your ideas, ask to meet with him or her to discuss future projects and possibilities. Keep your eyes and ears open to see and hear what others do not. That is an incredible service of the creative mind. If you want to work on something, knock on every door until someone lets you play across industries.

HOW WILL THE CREATIVE USE THIS INFORMATION GOING FORWARD?

Directions: Take a few minutes to reflect on times you have experienced your different thinking. From that, write down three ideas in the space provided for ways you could share your way of thinking.

1. _____

2. _____

3. _____

BUILDING YOUR CREATIVE NETWORK

Directions: Think of people, organizations, or other resources that can help you step into working with other industries. Write down these creative network connections in the space provided. Write a specific goal for contacting or making use of one of them.

1. _____

2. _____

3. _____

Goal: _____

CHAPTER TWENTY ONE

Have a Plan

FOLLOW YOUR MAP BUT CONSIDER THE DETOURS

INTRODUCTION

As you head out into the wilderness that is your creative life, go with confidence and have a plan in hand. This program will shift and change, but you need bullet points to check in with yourself. You will need to do this frequently to make sure you are facing the right direction. In this chapter, you will receive a final lesson on the essential ingredients to having a successful life as a creative. Guides, ideas, and inspiration will be sprinkled throughout the chapter to support you in creating a plan to begin your creative career or to take it to the next level.

TERMS THE CREATIVE NEEDS

BRAVERY Acts of courageous behavior

BURNING THE CANDLE AT BOTH ENDS Go to bed late and get up early, mainly to get work done

COMPARISON The representing of one thing or person as similar to or like another

CONFIDENCE A feeling of self-assurance arising from one's appreciation of one's abilities

ROLODEX A person's list of business contacts

WHEELHOUSE Within an area of expertise or interest

WHAT THE CREATIVE NEEDS TO KNOW

The number one thing you must possess to be creative is bravery, even if only for moments. Courage will get you everywhere. When you can push through fear and show up brave, not concerning yourself with what others might think, is when you find success. It is a hard thing to do, but it has the most payoff. Design a plan for your life as a successful, professional creative—don't just wing it.

WHAT THE CREATIVE WILL LEARN IN THIS CHAPTER

This chapter offers the opportunity to think about the things to consider when developing a plan for one's professional practice. There are tools, techniques, and ideas to include in a working, living plan that motivates and inspires the creative to develop a sustainable method, balanced with personal life.

"It is not the critic who counts. Not the man who points out how the strong man stumbles. Or where the doer of deeds could have done them better. The credit belongs to the man who is actually in the arena whose face is marred by dust, sweat, and blood, who strives valiantly, who errs, who comes up short again and again. Because there is no effort without error and shortcoming. But who does actually strive to do the deeds. Who knows great enthusiasm, with great devotion? Who spends himself in a worthy cause, who at best knows in the end the triumph of high achievement and who at worst, if he fails at least fails while daring greatly so that his place shall never be with those cold, timid souls who neither know victory nor defeat."

—*Theodore Roosevelt*

FIG 21-1

Pay attention only to those working as hard as you. Those who complain from the sidelines can be ignored.

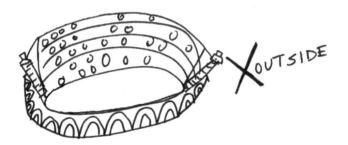

Credit goes to Brenè Brown for sharing this quote in her book *Daring Greatly*. The quote and her book elevated my understanding of bravery.

That is being brave. Knowing you are going to get your butt kicked, a lot, but you do it anyway. You'll do this because when you are brave, you'll hear the critic yelling "You will fail" and realize you are stronger. The critics or trolls are standing on the outside looking in at you putting in the effort. If you step into every room, every time with full bravery and you come out a little beat up and bruised, immediately focus on what you learned. That's bravery.

take action

This chapter focuses on tools for building a plan. Have your journal and favorite pen ready as nearly every paragraph offers opportunities to workshop ideas for developing a plan.

STAND UP/SPEAK UP

If you feel like you have made attempts at bravery in the past but nobody listened, then speak louder. Because if no one hears you, you must stand up and speak up even louder. Most creatives do not like using their voices; find the courage to ask questions and to express what you want as outcomes. This is much easier when you have a plan, so your ideas and thoughts are clear.

As a creative, you can't let your work or your practice do the talking for you. Learning to communicate with others will ensure avoiding misunderstandings and drama. As you are building your plan, factor in your best modes of communication and always ask your clients how they best communicate. Are you better at e-mail or text, in person or over the phone? Know this preference about yourself and build your practice around it. Be willing to bend when the client requests, but for the most part if you find it distracting to have to leave your working space to go to face-to-face meetings, ask what your preferences for communication are and make that part of your plan. Work toward being in your creative space when your muse is; this means scheduling meetings at odd hours sometimes. Communicate your needs to avoid frustration and distraction.

EMBRACE FAILURE

Failing forward is a fantastic thing; if you never fail, you are not learning enough. When building your plan, schedule in time for mourning the things that didn't work out. Look at the process and investigate why it didn't work out. Learn from that and ask yourself, "What else is coming? What else should I learn from this?" Then, stay open and allow for other opportunities to show up. Creatives have great stamina and endurance, yet when a defeat appears, the first instinct is to give up. If you are willing to fail over and over, you will know more than others, and once your wounds heal you will know better than others that you can get up and do it all over again.

HEALING THE CREATIVE WOUNDS

Write down your plan for how you will move through failures so that they do not stop you from growing and moving on. If you'll need more than ice cream, write down steps you can reference to remind yourself how to move past the disappointment to lessons learned.

PRACTICE BEING AN OPTIMIST

Practice being an optimist every day. When you practice being an optimist, you see all the glasses as half full. As you are launching your plan for your creative life, lead with confidence that you are capable of achieving your goals. If you begin this journey a pessimist, it is going to be hard to get off the ground. Don't fake a sunny attitude, though; learn what about your creative life makes you happy and carry that with you. Be mindful that you can be lured into the darkness because of the general sensitivities that wrap around the DNA of creatives. If you dwell in negativity, you are wasting time; as creatives, we need to see the darkness to be creative sometimes, but see it, recognize it, get mad about it, use it, and work with it to make something new. It's just a tool, like anything else in your tool belt.

It takes practice to have an optimistic outlook. Take time to write or say aloud a positive affirmation as you enter your creative space. As you end each day, think about a challenge you faced and write down or say aloud one positive thing that you learned from the experience. Doing this reminds you of the good parts and balances out the hardships that come with creativity.

DON'T TAKE THINGS PERSONALLY

If you can master being a creative who can separate him- or herself from his or her practice and therefore not take things personally, you'll have a long successful career. When things happen that are uncomfortable or confrontational, and they will happen, what will your plan be for handling those experiences? Ask yourself if you are capable of letting go. If you feel like someone's doing something with you and you're taking it personally, that's a problem.

FIG 21-2

Don't take things personally. It is a waste of time.

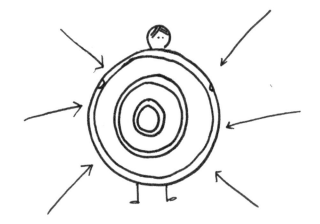

"Nothing others do is because of you. What others say and do is a projection of their reality. Their dream. When you are immune to the opinions and actions of others, you won't be a victim to needless suffering."

—Miguel Ángel Ruiz

MANAGE YOUR EXPECTATIONS

A part of your plan must include what to do when you get disappointed so as not to dwell in defeat. Manage your expectations by acknowledging that every offering could have 50/50 chance of success or failure. Creatives' greatest skill is their imagination, and that means they can use it to imagine a positive or negative outcome. It is your imagination to use. Allow for dreaming but leave room to check in with yourself. When disappointments happen, and they will, how does your plan allow you to flip them into opportunities? Note that the faster you get back on track after a setback, the more successful you will be. The management of your emotions has to be built into your plan.

CREATIVE HAPPINESS

Create a page in your plan to remind yourself of things that make you happy and are fun; use those to push away things that feel like an attack. If you can see things on the bright side, you are less likely to take them personally. How can you quickly flip from defeat to lesson learned? Build this into your plan.

"Comparison is the thief of joy."

—*Theodore Roosevelt*

COMPARISON IS NOT A MOTIVATOR

Comparison steals the joy out of your work, from you and your practice. Creatives like to tell themselves that comparison is akin to competition: They see it as a motivator. A competitive spirit can be useful, but comparing your practice to that of others is useless. Stay in your lane; do your own thing, the thing that guides you in your practice. It can be useful when we look at other people's work in our industry; we can look, learn from them, and be energized by them. But comparing for the sake of comparing means making yourself unhappy for motivation. That is useless, and it steals joy from your life. Instead, build into your plan what you will do when the desire to compare your practice with another creeps in. Have a plan to experience it and then something that will encourage you to move on quickly, because you do not need to linger there for long. Learn to fall in love with and enjoy what you make.

YOUR PLAN—COMPARISON PAGE

Build into your plan what you will do when the desire to compare your practice with another arrives. What will you have in place to remind yourself of your talents?

CONFIDENCE IS A MOTIVATOR

If you showed up at work every day and your coworkers said things like, "You look amazing today," or, "I love your new project," you would beam and feel confident. That is what creatives want the world to tell them about their practice. Step one in receiving that kind of feedback, though, is to believe in yourself. If you love what you make and know it is the very best you are capable of at this time, put it out there so you can grow and make new work from what you learn. Don't wait until it's perfect. If you've poured your heart into it, you will find the right audience. On the other hand, if you lead your practice with uncertainty, your clients will feel that from you and be less inclined to engage. Believe in what you create so that your clients can too.

YOUR PLAN—UNSHAKABLE CONFIDENCE PAGE

If you are not confident and this is something you work on, get a plan together to work on building it up. Often, this can mean learning to be comfortable in your skin. Create a page in your plan that is focused on building confidence.

ALWAYS BEHAVE LIKE SOMEONE IS WATCHING

No matter where you are in the world, keep in mind that the person near you could be your next client. This means mind your manners, don't gossip, don't talk about other people except with the closest people in your life behind closed doors. If you are sitting in a coffee shop and know you could be overheard and your words could even be taken out of context, stay silent. It doesn't mean you don't get to vent; just don't do it in public. Practice that, and you'll always be in good standing. Plan to ask the people you are closest to how they feel receiving your venting sessions. Then, respect the answer and use those folks accordingly. As an example, if you have a close friend who is willing to hold a space for you to vent and she mentions that she's always happy to be there for you but please text her first and schedule after 9:00 p.m. when the family is in bed, then do that.

VENTING THE RIGHT WAY

Knowing the rules ahead of time and having a plan of action for venting helps you to wait until you are behind closed doors. Ask your truth tribe if it is okay to vent and take note of the schedules for those who say yes. When you need someone, check this page as a reminder. Sometimes cooling off and waiting to call can help, too.

SLOW DOWN. PAUSE. TAKE CARE OF YOURSELF.

If you are going fast and furious, you are going to burn out; it's not sustainable, it's not efficient, and it's not productive. Take time for yourself. As a part of your plan for yourself, build in rejuvenation experiences. It is tough to ask your creative muse to show up when you are burning the candle at both ends. Slow down and let creativity take over. Taking care of yourself means being mindful of your needs. When you are most relaxed, that is the place to go when you see yourself running on a metaphoric treadmill. For me, a bubble bath is where I can close the bathroom door, sip a cup of tea, read a book, and enjoy the lavender-scented bubbles. Where is your space to steal away? Know this and build it into your plan. Next, learn how to pause, not just to gift yourself time to think, but to use as a delay tactic. Always allow yourself time to think through requests, for your work, your time, and your talent. An example might include if a potential client asked to meet you in person to discuss an idea; do not immediately move your schedule around to accommodate. Ask to get back to him or her and make sure a face-to-face meeting is what you want to do, and then make sure the time and date offered works in your schedule and for your

FIG 21-3

Slow down, take a breath, and allow yourself to pause.

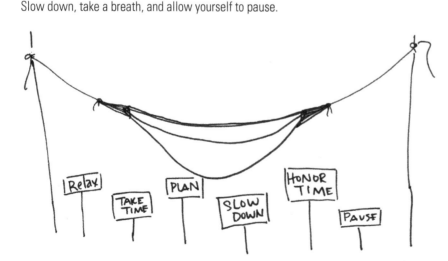

practice. It may very well be fine, but don't jump every time a request comes in. This goes back to managing your expectations, and it is about honoring the time you commit to your practice; don't interrupt that.

YOUR ME TIME PLAN

Include your regrouping time into your plan. Do you know how you best reboot? Start by asking yourself when you are most relaxed. Use that as your place to reboot.

INSPIRATION

There is so much to be inspired by. As you build your plan, prepare for what to do when you find your creative practice in a funk. Maybe you've got writer's block or a creative block; whatever it is, what will you do when it shows up? When I am blocked, I know I have to get out and go somewhere outside; as an example, I find new inspiration at a music festival. This works for me because I am not a musician, so I can enjoy the music. I have created more products and outcomes at music festivals than any other place because my mind is free to wander. Where is your place of inspiration? Knowing where it is can mean all the difference when you need inspiration that will shake the block so you can get back to your practice.

KNOCK THE CREATIVE BLOCK

Figure out where your place of inspiration is. Know this ahead of a creative block and build it into your plan to be a frequent visitor to the place that inspires you.

> *"We delight in the beauty of a butterfly but rarely admit the changes it has gone through to achieve that beauty."*
>
> —*Maya Angelou*

THE GIFT

My midwestern manners say that you never show up at someone's home without something in your hand: flowers, a bottle of wine, or a freshly baked loaf of bread. That's good, but what is even better is you showing up as the gift. You do this by showing up a giver, as somebody who has something to offer—people will remember. Your offering as a giver can be useful, humorous, high energy, or thoughtful. Whatever you bring, do it every time for consistancy.

YOUR GIFT

As a part of your plan, think about your most significant contribution. Is it kindness, humor, excellent listening skills? Whatever you can consistently bring, make that your thing; be known for it.

DON'T BE A SEAGULL

When you show up, be a part of the scene. Never show up as a seagull, which means you fly in, you lurk a little bit, you're listening, say nothing, and then you fly back up and poop on the party. Instead, be ready to engage and leave behind a feeling that you brought a gift.

SHOW UP CURIOUS

Curiosity is an amazing feature of human capacity. When you show up curious, you will learn so much. The opposite of being curious is being a know-it-all. No one enjoys spending time with a person who seems to know it all and has experienced it all because it closes the door for conversation and engagement. As an example, if someone just returned from traveling to a place you would like to go and you share your curiosity, you are creating a relationship and learning new things. If you are open and willing to learn new things all the time, you are more likely to be invited into experiences. A curious creative gets to play the most and has access to more opportunities.

> *"If you don't know how it works, find out. If you're not sure if it will work, try it. If it doesn't make sense, play it out until it does. If it's not broken, break it. If it might not be true, find out. That's curiosity."*
>
> —*Seth Godin*

FIG 21-4

Hold on to the people you find interesting.

USE YOUR CURIOSITY

Build into your plan opportunities to learn many new things as often as possible. Take some time to think about how you like to learn. Is it by observing, taking a class, reading, traveling? Know that about yourself and plan accordingly.

BUILD YOUR ROLODEX

As a part of your plan, build a way for you to hold on to interesting people, even if you don't know why. By hold on to people, I mean keep in touch and stay authentically connected. Stay in contact with people you find interesting. If you maintain a somewhat active relationship when you have a project that would be perfect for someone, it will be easier to connect. Have a Rolodex filled with names of interesting people you can call. As a creative, you will be asked to do all kinds of things outside of your wheelhouse, but don't do it. Instead, explain that you don't do that work, but you know someone who does and provide the contact information; this is a helpful way to let clients down. They will remember you even if you didn't offer the service this time.

YOUR PLAN—ROLODEX PAGE

Build a plan to create a functional Rolodex for your practice, so you have a name at your figure tips. Continue to build it throughout your career.

HAVE AN AMAZING NETWORK

Throughout your career, you will have to network; this is how you will build your community. Try out all different ways of networking such as meetups, art openings, and industry events. This will allow you to explore your comfort zone, and once you know your preferences you can plan to attend only those offerings that suit your style of networking. Growing a network in your area of focus means you'll be considered for projects because you have relationships with people offering them. If you hide out and don't network, people will not know your capacity and will not know to provide opportunities your way.

YOUR PLAN—NETWORKING PAGE

Have a plan for how often and where you are willing to show up within your comfort level. The people within the network you are building need to see you often and be reminded of the projects you are working on.

STAYING ON TOP OF PROFESSIONAL DOCUMENTS

It's important that part of the plan you build for your creative life includes a schedule to develop and maintain your professional documents. These are living documents that need attention at least three to four times per year. You don't want to fall behind on updating these essential pieces of your career growth, because if asked for your resume, as an example, you should be able to send it out immediately without having to take time to do a year or two worth of updates. Instead, update your resume, bio, and references regularly. This is where the early bird does get the worm. If you are the first to reply to a request because you have a maintenance plan for your documents and you are always ready, you will be the one snatching up opportunities.

YOUR PLAN—DOCS PAGE

Part of your plan is to build a schedule to maintain your professional documents. Use this page to commit to updating your records. Will you update monthly? Quarterly? Annually? Mark it on your calendar.

FIG 21-5

Create systems that work for you to keep track of your to-do lists.

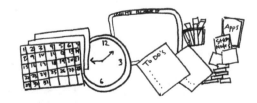

USE A CALENDAR

If you own a portable electronic device, you have virtual and constant access to a calendar. Or, you can go old school and write things down using a paper calendar. Creatives hate being slaves to schedules, but if you want to make a living at this thing, you

FIG 21-6

Into the wilderness that is a creative life you must GO WITH CONFIdENCE AND HAVE A PLAN Don't wing this thing that matters so much to you

must act like a professional and show up on time. This means making and keeping appointments. The calendar can also be useful to block out time for your creative practice. Make to-do lists and write things down on a whiteboard, a chalkboard, or sticky notes. If you prefer to use technology, there are many different apps to make to-do lists. Practice this now before you get overwhelmed by your business. It only works if it works for you. Part of your daily plan must include checking in on your schedule to see where you are supposed to be and when. It may also be helpful, if you are using an electronic calendar, to have it notify you before you are supposed to be somewhere, giving you enough time to exit your creative space and clear your head.

YOUR PLAN—CALENDAR PAGE

It's hard to run a business if you don't know what day it is. Escape into your creative space but create a plan to wind down and attend to the other part of your business.

REFLECTION

Create and recreate plans for your practice throughout your career. If you are ever stuck, revisit your current plan and rework it. You get to direct your practice and to do that you have to give it some direction.

HOW WILL THE CREATIVE USE THIS INFORMATION GOING FORWARD?

Directions: Take a few minutes to think about other parts of your practice where you could create plans. Write down three ideas in the space provided.

1. _____
2. _____
3. _____

BUILDING YOUR CREATIVE NETWORK

Directions: Think of people, organizations, or other resources that can help you build a network and a Rolodex. Write down three places you can start to develop your creative network connections in the space provided. Write a specific goal for contacting or making use of one of them.

1. _____
2. _____
3. _____
Goal: _____

CONCLUSION

A PROFESSION OF REFLECTION

Creatives are reflective by nature; you have to produce work that interprets the world around you. Reflection means taking things in and processing them into something only you would imagine; without reflection, the process couldn't happen, and the product would never be produced.

Know that your creativity is a huge gift in the world. It's amazing. It may be that not enough people have told you that. Instead, they likely said you that you're silly for choosing a profession in creativity. Your creative mind is highly sought after across all industries. The creative mind will solve the problems of the world. Don't shy away from sharing what you have.

HONOR YOUR CREATIVITY

Donate time to your gift. Do this by allowing yourself to learn new things, to fail, to read more, and to keep your eyes and ears open for inspiration everywhere. Carry a journal and write down quotes, questions, and ideas. Note on your calendar to go back to your journal on a regular basis to revisit your notes. Look for ways to grow your creative life. Stay curious and explore every part of your world. As a creative, you can delve more in depth than most and be a reporter to the world through your unique lens. Listen to your muse when she visits. If you can't act immediately, write everything down.

FIG 22-1

Honor your creativity and find inspiration.

LEAD WITH BRAVERY

Learning how to grow in bravery as a creative is a lifelong, ongoing lesson. Listen to yourself. Do you find that you frequently offer up excuses? You may need to check in with yourself and ask why you are doing that. What if all the excuses were gone? What if you believed in everything you did and were proud of it? What if you could be that brave?

To set up your creative practice, you must be brave and let nothing stop you. When I left my day job in government to start

FIG 22-2

a company, I had a plan, I had goals, and I was on a mission; then something happened: I had success. Once I realized there was nowhere else to go with my business, I knew I was done with that type of creative activity. I was ready to do other things—significant projects, working with exciting people. But, at the beginning of forming a new company, I was not brave; I was hiding. When I presented myself or worked on projects, I never used the words "creative," "artistic" or "artist." I did this because I had such personal fear that the clients would think, "Artists are so disorganized," or the worst, "Oh you are an artist, so you don't cost much." I realized I had invented what I imagined clients saying about me because I didn't know my value. Now I am brave, and I'm proud to say I'm a practicing creative, and what I do for my clients is bring creativity. Why did it take me so much courage to get there? Because you don't dip into courage; once you feel it, you stay there. I think I knew that and was afraid. Lead new and ongoing decisions with a brave face; the rest of your body will follow—trust that.

"Scared is what you're feeling. Brave is what you're doing."

—*Emma Donoghue*

CARRY YOURSELF IN CONFIDENCE

FIG 22-3

Creatives are deeply sensitive and when someone comes along and bullies or is mean, it's tough to recover. You must build this recovery muscle. The work you produce is not you; start there and stop taking things personally. That's confidence. It can feel hard to achieve but practiced daily, like anything else, it becomes a habit.

To be successful in the creative fields, you must be confident about your product even if you don't feel confident on the inside. If you lack confidence, figure out how to find it. It's okay to not know everything; don't be passive, don't apologize—get to work and learn about the things you don't know yet. You can always catch up. Confidence in your abilities is vast; starting there will go a long way. If you are not confident in your abilities, ask yourself, "Why not?" and "What are you going to do to change it?"

Being confident does not mean being cocky. A confident person admits when he or she is wrong and when he or she does not know something. A cocky person never does. Steer clear of the latter; it never sits well with people. Speak up, say what's important to say, use your voice, but never talk just to talk. People can see through show-off behavior and it deeply demonstrates lack of confidence. Be proud of who you are, the things you love, where you live, how you work, and the things you create into the world; that is confidence.

PRACTICE GENEROSITY

Don't be stingy with your gift of creativity. Generously share with your audience. Be transparent and open, letting others in to see your process. People are curious because most of the population doesn't have the creative skills you do. Recognize that offering insight into your creative world will go very far.

ALWAYS HAVE FUN

If you are not having fun, ask yourself how you can you make it more fun. There's no shame in enjoying your work. You may think that work should be hard and serious; you are a creative, though, so you get to have fun. Figure out how to make it fun in your practice and work environment.

ALLOW FOR PROCRASTINATION

Is it always bad? It is if it is causing anxiety or if you are burdening others by making them wait for something. However, procrastination can be useful. It is the art of managing possible change, and it can lead to greater success and happiness, to paraphrase Stephanie Vozza (2014) in "Reasons to Embrace Procrastination," in *Fast Company* magazine.

If you procrastinate because you need help or different skills, then you are wasting time. Unless you ask for help or gain the necessary skills, you will never accomplish the action you are putting off. You might be putting things off due to fear that prevents you from moving forward. Whatever it is, something is blocking you. The block could be there because you're not supposed to be doing the very thing you are avoiding. If you have something that's been on your to-do list for months or a year, it is going to stay on the to-do list because you can't or don't want to do it. Stop putting it off and find somebody to help you. If all the stuff on your to-do list were completed by others, how much time would you have—not only working in your practice but the time back you waste fretting about it not getting done?

"Procrastination is the thief of time, collar him."

—*Charles Dickens*

FIG 22-4

Having fun while working is the reason for a creative career.

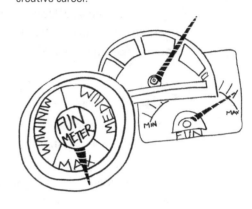

FIG 22-5

Creatives procrastinate until they are under pressure. That's fine in your creative process, and if that is the way the muse shows up, respect her. If you procrastinate on your professional documents, it is a waste of time, much more so than the act of just doing the task. If somebody is waiting for a document or a signature from you and they ask, again and again, that is bad form and leads to a poor reputation. Be the person who prioritizes things for others; there are all kinds of things you can procrastinate on and get away with but not when somebody needs something from you. Don't miss deadlines, and don't make excuses; be the person who can be counted on. If you do this, you will get more gigs because you make people's lives easier and you will build the reputation of someone who doesn't put things off.

FAIL OFTEN

Take big risks; there is no other way to be successful as a creative or as an entrepreneur. Be a risk taker in a way that is comfortable for you, but challenge yourself. The more risks you are willing to take, and the more often you are ready to show up with the face of bravery, the more you will experience failure. It is a simple math problem. There are many sports analogies about taking the shot. If you take the chance, you will miss the basket more times than not. Does that mean you should stop throwing it toward the net? No; it means accepting a percentage of failure and getting over it quickly when it happens. This is easier if you know it will happen.

"Discovering your voice is rarely a linear path, but instead is the culmination of a lifelong process of observation, course correction, and risk-taking that eventually leads to the recognition of a valuable contribution."

—Todd Henry

COMPARISON IS A WASTE

Admiring someone else work is a wonderful thing, you can learn from it and discover new questions. Celebrate and support the work of other creatives. Don't waste time comparing your work to theirs. They are on a different path. Comparing your work and process to others kills your creativity. If you imagine everyone better than you, every day, then eventually you will believe it. Enjoy other people's work and their processes, celebrate their outcomes, and then work hard to carve your path. Giving up is easy; sticking it out, even as the field crowds in, is hard.

"The most difficult thing is the decision to act. The rest is merely tenacity. The fears are paper tigers. You can do anything you decide to do. You can act to change and control your life and the procedure. The process is its own reward."

—Amelia Earhart

GIVE CREDIT

Don't spend too much time worrying about if you get credit for an idea. If someone took something from you, get out in front of it and claim the credit; but if you need credit just for the sake of it, let it go. It can be hard to imagine; you may think that the way to get up the ladder is to have your name on everything, but it's actually in relationships you build along the way. Creative fields aren't like other areas. Our collaborations matter as much as our solo work. Be supportive; even when you get to the top, be supportive of everyone. Get to know the people who matter in your organization. The real VIPs are the front office staff, the janitors, and security. They are the people who know everything, and if you are kind to them, your life is easier. Say thank you often, give them chocolates or baked goods, let them know you appreciate them. When they help you out, give them credit: Tell their boss what a great job they did. Your entire career, the people behind the scenes are the ones who make the magic come to life; credit their actions and thank them.

STAY PASSIONATE

Look around your life at what you are creating; do you love it so much you would do it all day long for free? If not, why not? What do you need to focus your passion for the work you do and the life you lead? Eliminate all the excuses, listen to yourself, and ask what would be the most fantastic thing you could create in your life. Get to doing that.

"Nothing is as important as passion. No matter what you want to do with your life, be passionate."

—Jon Bon Jovi

IT'S ALL IN WHO YOU KNOW

It is who you know and who knows you, and if your reputation precedes you, what will that say about you? Be kind, courteous, and thoughtful toward people because you never know if they might be your next future client. Never gossip in public. Gossip has its place and can be useful, but keep it behind closed doors so no one gets hurt, in case the facts are not right. That's what your family and friends are for. We all need to vent, but to be overheard when you just had a brief hot-headed minute can be harmful to your career. Burning bridges in the creative industry will significantly affect your career. The creative community is a big, small nation. Everybody knows someone one step away from your next contact. If you are applying for a grant, public project, residency, or gig, as examples, the panelists will ask his or her friends and community if they know you. People will offer honest opinions, even if negative, to spare their colleagues. Always behave like someone is watching; be mindful of all that you are doing and be thoughtful.

ALWAYS CARRY A BUSINESS CARD

That's it. Always carry a couple of business cards with you wherever you go.

BUILD TRIBES AND CHAMPIONS

You can't go this journey alone. Creatives want to believe they can operate solo, but the truth is we need each other; we are a community by the sheer nature of understanding each other. Show up and support each other. When you promote someone else, he or she is more likely to promote you back. Have a fantastic network of friends, people in the community, and people you are willing to promote. Create relationships with people who want to work with you and are eager to help you or invest in you. Build these relationships over time, growing them into a tribe of people you can count on. Hold on to champions when they come along. A champion is someone who is beyond the mentor: A mentor gives you advice; a champion closes the deal for you. When you make a connection with someone who has more experience than you and he or she is willing to work with you, let him or her support you.

ALWAYS SAY THANK YOU

It is a big deal. Saying thank you goes a long way and is meaningful to people. People remember thoughtfulness, and making an effort to say thank you takes extra thought. Say thank you in person, when possible, and send a follow-up e-mail. Don't send a text thank you except to your close friends, never professionally. If you want to be a real rock star, send a handwritten, delivered by postal service, thank-you note. Very few people do that, so you can stand out by a simple gesture.

FIG 22-6

TELL YOUR AWESOME STORY

This business of being a creative is a way for you to share what is going on inside your mind. Tell the story you to want be told. You know it best; why wait for others to speculate? Get in front of it and offer the details you want people to know. If you give them no information, they'll continue to seek more. If you share, they will stay satiated. No one can tell your story the way you would. Make sure your creative practice captures the stories that matter most and then you give those freely and frequently to the world.

Index

A

accountability, and goals, 153–154
accounts, social networking, 128
admiration, 144–145
agents, 71, 189–190
agreements
    electronic, 83
    essential elements of, 83
app, 117
appearance pitch, 181–182
applicant pool, 89
app support, 120
assessments, 141
assistants
    and business organization, 119
    virtual, 120
audiences, and biographies, 55
authentic voice, 9
author story, 6–7
avatar, 9
awards, resume, 48

B

backstage experiences, 188
barter system, 121
bid, 81
biographies (bio), 51
    audiences, 55
    building, 52–53
    building your nugget, 53
    closing, 55
    don't date yourself, 53–54
    examples, 55
    highlights and hits are the rule, 54
    longer format, 54
    several needed, 55
    short and long, 54
bookkeepers, 123
brand engagement, and creative personal branding, 13–14
bravery
    and creativity, 211–212
    defined, 201
brick and mortar store, 71
brokers, 81, 189
    contracts and coverage, 85
bucket-list goals, 147, 152
"burning the candle at both ends", 201
business (capital) pitch, 107–108, 111–114
    asking audience, 113–114
    competition, 112
    follow up, 114

pain point, 111–112
    solution, 112
    target market, 112
business cards, 29, 216
    bonus round, 40
    card-carrying member, 33
    clean, clear connections, 31
    color your identity, 30
    creative needs to know, 29–30
    e-mail signature, 35–36
    handmade identity, 33
    identity type, 30
    identity your way, 31–32
    jumping off point, 31
    just like dating, 39–40
    letterhead logistics, 35
    letter writing, 36
    mailing address, 34
    metal business cards, 33–34
    one hundred at a time, 34–35
    print quality, 34
    rectangle, circles, squares, 32–33
    sending it off, 40–41
    standard business card size, 32–33
    steps, 36–39
business insurance, 84–85
business organization
    and bookkeeper, 123
    and ethics, 125
    and payroll, 123
    and taxes, 123
    and wholesale trading, 123–124
    app support, 120
    asking for help, 118
    barter system, 121
    documents storage, 124–125
    grammatical error check, 124
    hiring assistants, 119
    hiring help, 119
    legal side of, 121–122
    Pareto Principle, 118–119
    trading, 121
    virtual assistants, 120
business trading, 121

C

card-carrying member, 33
category-specific bio, 51
C corporation, 117
chamber of commerce, 141
champion, 195, 198, 216
character development, and story telling, 21
cheat sheet, and press release, 183

chief creative thinker, 195
collaboration, 192, 195
color story, 29
commissions, 43, 81
 contracts and, 82
 resume, 48
commonalities, 195–197
companion list, portfolio, 66
comparison
 and creativity, 214–215
 defined, 201
confidence, 201
 and creativity, 212–213
conflict, and story telling, 22
consignment, 81
constituents, 89
contingency, 89
contracts, 81
 before you begin, 82
 brokers, 85
 business insurance, 84–85
 commission, 82
 deposits, 82–83
 electronic agreements, 83
 essential elements of, 83
 health insurance, 85
 hiring a lawyer, 84
 incorporating, 84
 other insurance types to consider, 85–86
costs
 retail, 73
 wholesale, 73
craftsmanship, 9
creative personal branding, 9–18
 brand engagement, 13–14
 designed client, 15–16
 multiple brands, 16
 reading the room, 16
 target audience, 14–15
 watered-down brands, 11–12
 words matter, 16–17
creative playdates, 105–106
creative time, 101
creative tools
 and stress-relief tactics, 104–105
 and time, 99–102
 creative playdates, 105–106
 procrastination, 102
creativity kit, 102–103
credit for idea, 215
curriculum vitae (CV), 43. *See also* resume
 defined, 43
 difference between resume and, 44
 taking time to maintain, 44–45

D
dating analogy, 132
deck (presentation tool), 63

demo reels, 66–67
deposits, and contracts, 82–83
designed client, 15–16
designers, 189
discount requests, 76
dossier, 63

E
editorial calendars, 175, 181
editorial meetings, 175, 181
electronic agreements, 83
electronic signature, 81
elevator pitch, 107–110
e-mail signature, 35–36
estimate, 81
ethics and business organization, 125
expendable materials, 71
eye contact, 161

F
failures, and creativity, 214
fairs, 188
Fast Company magazine, 213
festivals, 188
flash sales, 127
followers, online, 127, 131
for-profit organization, 89
 vs. not-for-profit, 90–91
foundations, 89
freelance, 157

G
galleries, 187
generosity, and creativity, 213
generous statements, 56
gig economy, 29, 43, 157
goals
 and accountability, 153–154
 bucket-list, 147, 152
 defined, 147
 long-term, 147
 on the go, 151
 short-term, 147
 types of, 152–153
goal setting, 147
 fear of, 148–150
 steps to, 150–151
 writing down goals, 148
going viral, 130
grammatical error check, and business organization, 124

H
handles, 127
handmade identity, 33
hashtags, 127, 130–131
headshots, and social networking, 136
health insurance, 85

I

ideas (show, sell, produce, and perform), 190–192
 collaborations, 192
 getting things produced, 191–192
 outdoors opportunities, 192
identity package, 29
initial public offering (IPO), 89
internship, 166–170
interview, 159
investors, 107
invoices, 71
 pricing and sales, 76–77

J

job board, 158–159
job hunt
 adding skills, 162–163
 and dressing appropriately, 161
 and handshake, 161
 and making eye contact, 161
 following up, 163
 internship, 166–170
 interview, 159
 listen and answer, 162
 negotiation, 165
 overview, 158
 references, 165–166
 showing up early, 160
 staying positive, 162
 thank-you note, 163–164

K

keystone, 71

L

lawyer, hiring, 84
layout logistics, of press release, 178
letterhead, 29
letterhead logistics, 35
letter writing, 36
limited liability company (LLC), 117
listening carefully, 162
live networking, 136
live storytelling, 23
local facilities, 188–189
long-term goals, 147

M

mailing address, and business cards, 34
mashup storytelling, 23
materials
 expendable, 71
 reusable, 71
media kit, 175–177
meditation, 99, 105
memberships, and resume, 49
merchant services, 71
metal business cards, 33–34

micro-moments, 99, 104
mid-career professional, 9
minimum order, 71
minimums, 78
multiple brands, 16
muscle memory, 157

N

name tags, and social networking, 137
National Small Business Association (NSBA), 141, 143
negotiation, 157, 165
not-for-profit organization, 89
 completing the application, 92–93
 cost, 95
 feedback, 95
 final reports, 94
 for-profit vs., 90–91
 funding, finding, 91
 panelists and timelines, 94
 pixie dust, 93

O

online followers, 127, 131
online negativity, 134–135
open studios, 188
outdoors opportunities, for selling, 192

P

Pareto Principle, 118–119
passion
 and creativity, 215
 defined, 9
payment types, 78
payroll and business organization, 123
PDF (portable document format), 29
people (show, sell, produce, and perform)
 agents and reps, 189–190
 brokers, 189
 designers, 189
 stagers, 190
philanthropy, 89
philosophy statement, 51, 59–60
photograph slide format, 63
places (show, sell, produce, and perform)
 backstage experiences, 188
 fairs, 188
 festivals, 188
 galleries, 187
 local facilities, 188–189
 open studios, 188
 pop-up shops, 187
 residencies, 186–187
 trade shows, 189
 trunk shows, 187
plan/planning
 and time, 104

building rolodex, 208
calendar, using, 209–210
comparison not a motivator, 204–205
confidence as motivator, 205
curiosity, 207–208
don't take things personally, 203–204
embracing failure, 203
inspiration, 207
managing expectations, 204
network, 209
practice being an optimist, 203
professional documents, 209
stand up/speak up, 202–203
platform, 127
playbook, 63
plot, and story telling, 21
pop-up shops, 187
portfolio, 63
    becoming feedback friendly, 68–69
    call for artists/creatives, 67
    companion list, 66
    demo reels, 66–67
    good looking/sounding, 65–66
    look of, 66
    pieces to include in, 65
    pulling together, 64
    review panels, 64–65, 67
    twenty images strong, 65
    weighing the odds, 64–65
positioning statement, 107
presentations, 69
press kit, 175–177
    audio or visual clips, 177
    company profile, 176
    cover letter, 176
    FAQs, 177
    getting creative with, 177
    goal of, 176
    other media coverage, 177
    press release, 177
    product/service sheet, 177
    targeting, 176
    testimonials and reviews, 177
press release, 175
    and appearance pitch, 181–182
    and building relationship, 182
    and cheat sheet, 183
    and editorial calendars, 181
    and editorial meetings, 181
    importance of story in, 176
    invitations for, 180
    layout logistics, 178
    sending out, 180
    steps, 178–180
    templates, 175
    writing, 178
pricing and sales
    basic formula for service pricing, 74–75

basic pricing formula, 73–74
    discount requests, 76
    homework, 72–73
    invoices, 76–77
    math on shipping, 75–76
    minimums, 78
    payment types, 78
    representation, 78–79
    steps for selling objects, 74
    wholesale vs. retail costs, 73
print quality, of business cards, 34
procrastination, 102
    and creativity, 115–116
product plan, 107
professional bio, 51
professional commonalities. See commonalities
public art, 63

Q
quote, 81

R
references, 165–166
    resume, 49
reps, 71, 189–190
request for proposal (RFP), 63
request for quote and qualification (RFQ), 63
residencies, 186–187
resolution, and story telling, 22
resume. See also curriculum vitae (CV)
    apply some design, 49
    awards, 48
    building, 45
    building categories, 48
    commissions, 48
    curriculum vitae (CV) vs., 44
    dates, 45
    defined, 43
    don't fill up space, 46
    including links, 49
    landing a gig is like dating, 46
    memberships, 49
    name and location, 48
    references, 49
    things to include on, 47
    tough love, 45–46
    volunteer, 48
retail costs, 73
retail pricing, 71
reusable materials, 71
review panels, 64–65
    portfolio, 67
rolodex, 201, 208

S
scale, 195, 198–199
schedule posts, 134
scope of work (SOW), 81
S corporation, 117
Service Corps of Retired Executives (SCORE), 141

service pricing, basic formula for, 74–75
shareholders, 89
short-term goals, 147
skillset, 9
social media
    calendar, 127
    posts, 129, 133–134
social media bio, 51
social networking, 127–137
    dating analogy, 132
    followers, 131
    going viral, 130
    hastags, 130–131
    headshots, 136
    live networking, 136
    multiple accounts, 128
    name tags, 137
    negativity online, 134–135
    relationship building, 129–130
    social media posts, 129, 133–134
    testimonials, 136
    trolls, 135
sole proprietor, 117, 121–122
stagers, 190
standard business card size, 32–33
statements, 51, 56
    building, 57
    generous, 56
    philosophy statement, 59–60
    reflection, 60
    stand-alone document, 57
    steps to writing, 58–59
501(c)(3) status, 90
story, 3–7
    author, 6–7
    examples, 6
storytelling, 216
    building truth tribe, 24
    character development, 21
    conflict, 22
    live, 23
    mashup, 23
    plot, 21
    process over product, 25
    resolution, 22
    serve up sample sizes, 24
    setting, 21
    sharing, 20–21
    styles of, 22
    taking a breath, 24–25

visual, 23
written, 23
strengths, weakness's, obstacles and threats (SWOT) analysis, 141, 143–144
stress-relief tactics, 104–105

T
target audience, 9
    creative personal branding, 14–15
taxes and business organization, 123
terrazo floor, 195
testimonials, and social networking, 127, 136
thank-you note, 163–164, 216
thinking differently
    and champions, 198
    and commonalities, 195–197
    and professional commonalities, 196–197
    and speaking up, 197
    and vision, 199
    creative approach, encouragement for, 197
    introduction, 195
    overview, 196
    scale, 195, 198–199
think tank, 195
time
    and creative tools, 99–102
    and planning, 104
to-the-trade-only (TTTO) trade shows, 147, 149
trade shows, 147, 189
trolls, and social networking, 127, 135
trunk shows, 187

V
values, 9
venture capitalist, 107
viral posts, 127, 130
virtual assistants (VAs), 120
visualization, 99
visual storytelling, 23
volunteer work, and resume, 48
Vozza, Stephanie, 213

W
watered-down brands, 11–12
wheelhouse, 201
wholesale buying, 123–124
wholesale costs, 73
wholesale pricing, 71
written storytelling, 23

CPSIA information can be obtained
at www.ICGtesting.com
Printed in the USA
BVHW011141250121
598681BV00014B/138